JOURNAL FOR THE STUDY OF THE OLD TESTAMENT SUPPLEMENT SERIES
249

Sheffield Academic Press

The God of the Prophets

An Analysis of Divine Action

William Paul Griffin

Journal for the Study of the Old Testament
Supplement Series 249

Copyright © 1997 Sheffield Academic Press

Published by Sheffield Academic Press Ltd
Mansion House
19 Kingfield Road
Sheffield S11 9AS
England

Printed on acid-free paper in Great Britain
by Bookcraft Ltd
Midsomer Norton, Bath

British Library Cataloguing in Publication Data

A catalogue record for this book is available
from the British Library

ISBN 1 85075 677 5

CONTENTS

Part I
BACKGROUND

Chapter 1
WHAT IS CONTENT ANALYSIS?

Chapter 2
QUESTIONS AND HYPOTHESES

Chapter 3
THE THEORY OF CODING AND CATEGORIES

PREFACE

I have long been interested in questions relating to God's activities as recorded in the Bible. These activities not only include what are commonly termed miracles, but also God's blessing and judgment. It is not just God's activities in general, though, which are of interest to me, but more specifically divine interaction with humanity, especially nations. Further, I have been concerned with similarities between divine and human activity.

The following inquiry carries out this interest in a disciplined manner by focusing specifically on a few prophetic texts. My hope is that it will help to illuminate God's personality as it is presented in the Bible.

I would like to thank all those who have participated in this project: Dr Martin Buss, Dr John Fenton, Dr John Hayes, Dr Nancy Ammerman, Dr Jim Miller, Dr Gene Tucker, and the late Dr Gene Bianchi for their criticism and feedback; Dr Mark McLean, for encouraging the study of God's activity; Jim Siman, for computer and programming assistance, especially early in the process; Karen Gleason, for her input regarding statistics; Dr Nancy Eiesland, for suggesting the use of SPSSPC+; God; my parents, Jim and Betty Griffin, for their dedicated support; and especially my wife, Terry, for all her help.

ABBREVIATIONS

BZAW	Beihefte zur *ZAW*
HTR	*Harvard Theological Review.*
IDBSup	G.A. Buttrick (ed.), *Interpreter's Dictionary of the Bible*, Supplementary Volume.
JBL	*Journal of Biblical Literature.*
JETS	*Journal of the Evangelical Theological Society.*
JR	*Journal of Religion*
JSS	*Journal of Semitic Studies.*
TynBul	*Tyndale Bulletin.*
SEÅ	*Svensk exegetisk årsbok.*
ZAW	*Zeitschrift für die alttestamentliche Wissenschaft.*

INTRODUCTION

The purpose of the present study is to describe the image of God as an acting agent as presented in prophetic literature. The study is particularly interested in the conception of God as a thinking, valuing being who acts in ways which affect the physical and mental well-being of others. God will also be examined in terms of one who is the recipient of mental and physical activities by others. The results will help illuminate the personality of God in the prophets.

The following texts will be used to explore divine activity: Isaiah 1.1–4.1; Hosea 4–8; Joel; Nahum; Malachi; and Zechariah 12–14. The book of Joel will be highlighted, comparing and contrasting it with the other five texts. These other five texts are grouped together into what will be called the Selected Prophetic Passages (SPP).

The methodology which will be employed in this study has come to be known as 'content analysis'. *Webster's Ninth New Collegiate Dictionary* defines content analysis as the

> analysis of the manifest and latent content of a body of communicated material (as a book or film) through a classification, tabulation, and evaluation of its key symbols and themes in order to ascertain its meaning and probable effect.

Content analysis, as implemented in this study, includes elements of some other approaches to the Bible. Assertions are often made about biblical passages on the basis of the kinds of terms employed and the relative density of those terms. Another common procedure involves comparing different blocks of literature or scenarios. These tasks are also performed in the present study.

The main difference from other approaches is the *type* of systematic procedure which is employed to determine emphases, characteristics, and comparisons. This approach quantifies and uses statistics to help determine the significance of comparisons, providing data for expected correlations, as well as unearthing unexpected ones, leading to new reflections.

In each step of the process, intuition and experience with the biblical text are essential. These must guide the initial formulation of questions, the construction of categories, the coding of the texts, and the interpretation of results. Nevertheless, quantification and statistical procedures are invaluable tools in the research process, greatly aiding in the determination of the practical significance of the findings.

A subsidiary aim is to present a pilot study for the use of established procedures of content analysis for an examination of biblical texts. An increasing use of computers will most likely make such studies easier and more common in the future than they have been. There is a hope that the process developed in this study will eventually be expanded, within the discipline, to the whole Bible.

Part I

BACKGROUND

Chapter 1

WHAT IS CONTENT ANALYSIS?

1. *Introduction to Content Analysis*

Content analysis is a research technique that 'aims at a quantitative classification of a given body of content, in terms of a system of categories devised to yield data relevant to specific hypotheses concerning that content.'[1] Content analysis includes the determination of linguistic and conceptual patterns, relationships, and associations.[2] The chief values are that it can make explicit what is implicit in a text and can produce results which are not necessarily or easily obtainable by other means.[3]

Content analysis[4] is an established method in the social sciences and humanities, with its modern version beginning about 1890.[5] Early studies tended to concern 'straight subject matter' in newspapers, and 'stylistic features in English poetry and prose' in literature. In the late 1930s and 1940s propaganda, radio, and public opinion were

---

1. A. Kaplan and J. Goldsen, *Reliability of Certain Categories for Classifying Newspaper Headlines* (Document no. 40, Library of Congress, Experimental Division for the Study of War-Time Communications, 1943), p. 1, as quoted in B. Berelson and P. Lazarsfeld, *The Analysis of Communication Content* (preliminary draft; University of Chicago and Columbia University, 1948), p. 2.

2. K. Krippendorff, *Content Analysis: An Introduction to its Methodology* (Beverly Hills: Sage Publications, 1980), pp. 55, 107, 113-14.

3. Krippendorff, *Content Analysis*, p. 11.

4. *Content analysis* is the term which has been used to describe the field only since about 1930 (Krippendorff, *Content Analysis*, p. 9). However, content analysts consider their procedure to date from the late 1800s.

5. It has antecedents in the 1640s in Sweden, using word counts to determine the religious value of hymns (J.A. Baird, 'Content Analysis and the Computer: A Case-Study in the Application of the Scientific Method to Biblical Research,' *JBL* 95 [1976], pp. 256-57; Krippendorff, *Content Analysis*, p. 13).

analyzed.[6] While its primary use continued where it began—the analysis of various types of mass communication[7] (including newspapers, broadcasting [radio and television], and advertising)— content analysis has been used by many different fields (e.g. psychology, history, literature, medicine) for a variety of purposes (e.g. evidence in court, analysis of political messages and reactions to them, and determination of the authorship and authenticity of texts).[8]

a. *Content Analysis and the Computer*

Content analysts were at the forefront in recognizing the value of computers for performing textual analysis;[9] indeed, the method entered a new era. From the outset analysts saw and enthusiastically welcomed the computer's usefulness in the tedious tasks of coding, organizing, and quantifying the massive amount of data. The first 'computer-aided content analysis' was conducted on Cheremis folktales in 1958.[10]

In the early 1960s the interest in computers and content analysis resulted in the development of *The General Inquirer*. P. Stone describes *The General Inquirer* as

> a set of computer programs to (a) identify systematically, within text, instances of words and phrases that belong to categories specified by the investigator; (b) count occurrences and specified co-occurrences of these categories; (c) print and graph tabulations; (d) perform statistical tests; and

---

6. Berelson and Lazarsfeld, *Analysis*, p. 11. For a history of modern content analysis, see Berelson and Lazarsfeld, *Analysis*, pp. 9-17 (for 1890–1946); and Krippendorff, *Content Analysis*, pp. 13-20.

7. As of the time of Berelson's writing (*Analysis*, p. 15), the majority of analyses involved the content of newspapers, but he also notes that they included 'books including poetry, radio, magazines, letters, speeches and addresses, motion pictures, leaflets, other verbal forms, and non-verbal forms'.

8. Krippendorff, *Content Analysis*, p. 155; and Berelson and Lazarsfeld, *Analysis*, pp. 12-14. A recent perusal of the Research Libraries Information Network indicated over 1000 references to content analysis.

9. The last chapter of O. Holsti, *Content Analysis for the Social Sciences and Humanities* (Reading: Addison-Wesley, 1969), pp. 150-94 is on the use of computers; see also I. Pool, *The Prestige Press: A Comparative Study of Political Symbols* (Cambridge, MA: MIT Press, 1970), p. xvi; R. North, O. Holsti, M. Zaninovich and D. Zinnes, *Content Analysis: A Handbook with Applications for the Study of International Crisis* (Evanston: Northwestern University Press, 1963), pp. 129-30.

10. Krippendorff, *Content Analysis*, p. 19.

(e) sort and regroup sentences according to whether they contain instances
of a particular category or combination of categories.[11]

It was designed so that various types of dictionaries could be loaded into
it, with a 32,768 word storage potential in its dictionary.[12] Once the
dictionary was loaded, a text or set of texts could be processed. As of
1965, seventeen dictionaries had been designed for it,[13] including one
by Ole Holsti[14] based on Osgood's semantic differential scales. The
book, *The General Inquirer*, describes fifteen different studies which
were performed on the system. These studies were from a number of
different fields: political science, personality, the study of small groups,
clinical psychology, social psychology, cross-cultural studies, and prod-
uct image.[15] Further, the system could be used to generate 'key word
in context' concordances (cf. some editions of *The Computer Bible* are
based on this concept).

In sum, computers are now being used extensively in content analysis,
and numerous works up to the present consider the various theoretical
and practical aspects of computer usage.[16]

11. P. Stone, D. Dunphy, M. Smith, and D. Ogilvie, *The General Inquirer: A
Computer Approach to Content Analysis* (Cambridge, MA: MIT Press, 1966),
p. 68.

12. North *et al.*, *Content Analysis*, pp. 129-30.

13. For a list see Stone *et al.*, *The General Inquirer*, pp. 140-41.

14. *The Stanford Political Dictionary* is described in Stone *et al.*, *The General
Inquirer*, pp. 186-91.

15. Baird ('Content Analysis', p. 266) recommends use of *The General Inquirer*,
but it is unclear how much he used it.

16. Pool (*The Prestige Press*, p. xvi) lauds the computer for the purpose of per-
forming content analysis. '[In 1953] the prospect of a solution [to the "laborious
business"] . . . was just appearing over the horizon, namely, the computer.' Holsti
(*Content Analysis*, p. 135) discusses what he calls 'the objective and problematic
aspects' of using computers for coding. G. Gerbner, O.R. Holsti, K. Krippendorff,
W.J. Paisley and P.J. Stone (eds.), *The Analysis of Communication Content:
Developments in Scientific Theories and Computer Techniques* (New York: John
Wiley & Sons, 1969) contains a number of computer-related articles which describe
ideas and attempts concerning the use of computers for content analysis of literature,
in addition to mentioning then current content analysis computer programs. Cf.
D. Fan, *Predictions of Public Opinion from the Mass Media: Computer Content
Analysis and Mathematical Modeling* (New York: Greenwood Press, 1988), chapter
4; and various essays in *Message Effects in Communication Science* (ed. J. Braddac;
Newbury Park: Sage Publications, 1989).

b. *Categories*

Crucial for content analysis is the development of categories. These depend heavily on one's particular purposes.[17] Several authors, however, have formulated categories or considerations that appear to have widespread applicability.

C. Osgood analyzed the 'semantic differential' of words and proposed numerical values to distinguish and rank them according to a system of categories.[18] These are seen by many to represent 'three basic dimensions of human affective cognition'.[19] There is evidence that these dimensions operate 'irrespective of culture'.[20] The categories are *Potency* (strong-weak), *Activity* (active-passive), and *Evaluation* (good-bad). Each word is rated on a seven-point scale, from +3 to -3, for each classification.

Osgood also proposed a way to translate statements in texts into assertions, called the actor/action/complement form. The idea is to take statements and reduce them into propositions of who the acting agent is, what was done, and to whom the action was done. For instance, 'the boy was chased by the dog' would be reduced to dog/chase/boy.[21]

J. Laffal has produced two editions of a concept dictionary which are the result of work since the 1960s (and has affinities to studies which go further back).[22] The categories are thought 'to reflect cognitive-conceptual sets which are evoked whenever a pertinent word is

17. For a general discussion on categories and samples of a number of category systems, see Holsti, *Content Analysis for the Social Sciences and Humanities*, pp. 94-126.

18. Osgood's system builds upon the work of other psycholinguists from the middle of the century; see C. Osgood, G. Suci, and P. Tannenbaum, *The Measurement of Meaning* (Urbana: University of Illinois Press, 1967), chapter 1 (pp. 1-30).

19. Krippendorff, *Content Analysis*, p.78.

20. Stone *et al.*, *The General Inquirer*, p. 188; C. Osgood, W. May, and M. Miron, *Cross-Cultural Universals of Affective Meaning* (Urbana: University of Illinois Press, 1975), pp. 189-90.

21. C. Osgood, 'The Representational Model and Relevant Research Methods', in I. Pool (ed.), *Trends in Content Analysis* (Urbana: University of Illinois Press, 1959), pp. 45-47. This basic idea will be used in one of my classifications of verbs, focusing on God and humans.

22. J. Laffal, *A Concept Dictionary of English* (Essex: Gallery Press, 1973); and J. Laffal, *A Concept Dictionary of English with Computer Programs for Content Analysis* (Essex: Gallery Press, 1990).

encountered'.[23] For instance, *cupcake* is classified as FOOD (eating and food), and *God* is LEAD HOLY (authority, leading, and controlling; religious figures, activities and objects). The first edition classifies words according to one (or two) of 118 psychologically oriented categories. The most recent edition includes computer programs for its application to texts. The DOS programs classify and tabulate texts according to Laffal's dictionary of 42,895 words and 168 categories. Each word in a text can have up to five categories applied, and up to eight speakers can be distinguished.[24]

The present study employs Evaluation from Osgood's semantic differential and makes extensive use of Osgood's actor/action/complement theory. Laffal's system heavily influenced the theory of coding and the construction of categories.

c. *Content Analysis: Sample Applications*

Content analysis has been used successfully for a variety of applications in a number of fields. The following is a sampling of a few applications.

Content analysis found its way into propaganda analysis in the middle of this century (especially by the US government). During World War II German propaganda and radio broadcasts were analyzed in order 'to understand and predict events within Nazi Germany and its allies and to estimate the effects of military actions on war mood'.[25] Krippendorff tells us that

> The FCC analysts successfully predicted several major military and political campaigns, assessed Nazi-elite perceptions of their situation, political changes within the governing group, and shifts in relations between axis countries. Among the more outstanding predictions actually made by British analysts was the date of deployment of the German V-weapon against Great Britain. Monitoring Goebbels's speeches, the analyst inferred interferences with the production of these weapons and extrapolated the launching date which was accurate within a few weeks.[26]

23. Laffal, *Dictionary of English*, p. 1.

24. I obtained a demonstration version of Laffal's program (which classifies words beginning with 'a') and tried it out on the RSV text of the book of Proverbs. The demo version helps one to see how the program works, but the resulting data were insufficient to obtain significant results. However, initial tests using Laffal's first edition of the dictionary (without his computer program) produced some interesting results in test versions of the database employed in this study.

25. Krippendorff, *Content Analysis*, p. 16.

26. Krippendorff, *Content Analysis*, p. 17.

P. Stone and E. Hunt demonstrated that content analysis can successfully distinguish between genuine and imitation suicide notes. The imitations were written by people of similar socioeconomic situations as the authors of the genuine notes. An initial test was conducted to infer characteristics of real and fake notes. The distinguishing factors were that the genuine notes were more concrete concerning events and persons, less reflective (in the abstract sense), and mentioned the word 'love' more frequently. On the basis of the preliminary test a further test was conducted, in which 17 of 18 notes were accurately identified as genuine or imitations.[27]

A technique which K. Krippendorff calls the 'simulation of interviews' has been used to detect embedded attitudes toward certain topics by scoring items in relation to specific questions asked about the text.[28] This system was used in a study for detecting racism and sexism in American history textbooks. It was found that vocabulary was used to create impressions about people from non-white non-European ethnic backgrounds and countries without using what might be termed overtly racist language.[29] The tendency was for books to present the white upperclass male as the norm for and builder of America, and to view others in terms of their 'contributions... to *us*'. The conclusion was that, in history textbooks, racism and sexism

> are treated as aberrations, as isolated mistakes of the past. Since oppression is rarely examined from the perspective of its victims, these brief inclusions appear as footnotes to a grander, happier story. Yet even these isolated 'mistakes' are treated in a simplistic, casual manner which downplays their significance.[30]

C. Pettinari used content analysis in the field of medicine in order to examine the relationship between operating room talk and operating room reports. Her conclusion was that much of the former is not included in the latter. Pettinari discusses the 'medicolegal implications' of operative reports, and on the basis of the study, suggests changing their structure. She also demonstrates how medical residents' reports

27. Krippendorff, *Content Analysis*, pp. 101-102.

28. Cf. Krippendorff, *Content Analysis*, pp. 79-80.

29. R. Moore (ed.), *Stereotypes, Distortions, and Omissions in US History Textbooks: A Content Analysis Instrument for Detecting Racism and Sexism* (New York: Council on Interracial Books for Children, Inc., 1977). See especially 'Glossary', pp. 131-34.

30. Moore (ed.), *Stereotypes*, p. 129.

move 'from recounting to interpretation' over a five-year period.[31]

Analyses have been conducted which focus on the response to messages by the recipients 'with little discussion of message generation'. D. Fan examined attitudes toward six different topics: defense spending, troops in Lebanon, the Democratic primary, the economic climate, unemployment versus inflation, and Contra aid. His method was to compare public opinion polls to Associated Press dispatches, both covering a few years. The AP dispatches were run through a set of 'filtrations' to reduce them to portions which were more relevant to the topics, and then scored to determine positive or negative attitudes toward the various topics. Public opinion polls which followed the dispatches were then compared to the dispatches to determine trends and their relationship. It is Fan's contention that 'public opinion can be swayed in a predictable fashion by messages acting on the populace'.[32]

S. Hall and R. Van de Castle performed a quantitative analysis of dreams. One thousand dream reports (500 male, 500 female) were classified and scored in terms of physical surroundings, characters, social interactions, activities, achievement outcomes, environmental press, emotions, and descriptive elements. The classifications were derived after obtaining a familiarity with dream reports themselves, emphasizing that which had 'psychological significance'. The various elements of dream types and aspects of dreams were quantified, first considering female and male separately, and then often totalling the figures. Hall and Van de Castle then noted the various trends of dreams.[33]

C. Toolin examined 49 presidential inaugural addresses for the presence of civil religion.[34] She began with themes proposed by others, such

---

31. C. Pettinari, *Task, Talk, and Text in the Operating Room: A Study in Medical Discourse* (Norwood: Ablex, 1988), esp. pp. 121-22.

32. Fan, *Predictions* (quotes are on pp. 5 and 3). The difficulty of applying this approach to biblical studies is that content analysis of reader/listener/viewer response has been based on actual responses (surveys, interviews, etc.); Fan's study compared public opinion polls to actual news releases. However, for biblical studies, a content analysis of reader response is only possible for the history of interpretation; we lack independent records of original responses. Be that as it may, the biblical texts themselves contain some records of responses of hearers, and these could be examined— if nothing else but to determine the author's perceptions of the response of the people.

33. C. Hall and R. Van de Castle, *The Content Analysis of Dreams* (New York: Meredith, 1966).

34. C. Toolin, 'American Civil Religion from 1789 to 1981: A Content Analysis

as R. Bellah (Exodus, Sacrifice) and C. Cherry (Destiny under God, America as an International Example) and included other related religious themes. The vast majority of inaugural addresses (90 percent) had references to God and other religious themes, supporting the notion that civil religion does exist in the United States. Further, Toolin showed that Bellah's themes are actually minor or infrequent aspects of addresses, whereas Cherry's themes are prominent. However, while Cherry considered 'Destiny under God' and 'America as an International Example' to be separate themes, Toolin found them to be intertwined. Toolin concludes, 'The inaugural addresses give us a very particular picture of American civil religion. We see a president addressing his citizens, in much the same way as a priest addresses his parish.'[35]

Here is a brief description of a few other content analyses:

1. Communication genres within a particular culture have been examined. L. Polanyi examined culturally conditioned storytelling, specifically in America, and produced an abstracted 'American Story' on the basis of the study.[36]

2. A recent collection of essays emphasizes the questions *how are messages conveyed, and what do they convey?* Other essays in the collection address the application of content analysis to TV commercials, entertainment, and violent messages.[37]

3. I. Pool examined the change in political symbols 1890–1950, as seen in newspapers of five countries.[38]

4. G. Gordon conducted a 'logical and psychological analysis of communications. . . ,' emphasizing this century.[39]

5. K. Krippendorff noted that content analysis has been used to determine the authorship of the *Federalist Papers*.[40]

---

of Presidential Inaugural Addresses', *Review of Religious Research* 25 (1983), pp. 39-48.

35. Toolin, 'American Civil Religion', p. 47.

36. L. Polanyi, *Telling the American Story: A Structural and Cultural Analysis of Conversational Storytelling* (Cambridge, MA: MIT Press, 1989).

37. Braddac (ed.), *Message Effects*. This is important for biblical studies, which emphasizes and recognizes the persuasive aspects of Scripture.

38. Pool, *The Prestige Press*.

39. G. Gordon, *The Languages of Communication: A Logical and Psychological Examination* (New York: Hastings House, 1969), p. 305.

40. Krippendorff, *Content Analysis*, p. 106.

6. C. Osgood used content analysis for cross-cultural studies
    by comparing attitudes toward similar topics in different
    cultures.[41]

2. *Content Analysis and Biblical Studies*

a. *Potential*

Content analysis has been used to examine texts systematically for a
number of ends which have parallels in biblical studies. In 1948
Berelson formulated a list of types of analyses outside of biblical
studies,[42] many of which could be used in biblical studies. These especially relate to the determination of intentions, characteristics, stylistic
features, and literary techniques in texts. Overall the approach can
probably do much to illuminate the characteristics of various genres
of literature in the Bible.

In addition, the potential exists for the designing of a content analysis
system which could be applied to the entire Bible, and be useful to the
pastor and the scholar alike. First, it could illuminate characteristics of
any given text, providing a list of what is or is not emphasized by a text.
Secondly, it could be accessed by inputting the characteristics in which
one is interested; the system would then provide a text or texts which
approximate these characteristics. Thirdly, this system could be especially useful for comparing different texts, especially in terms of conceptual similarities and differences.

b. *Explicit Applications in Biblical Studies.*

J.A. Baird is among the first (and few) to advocate overtly the use of
content analysis and the computer for biblical studies.[43] Baird applied
the combined methods of content analysis and historical critical studies
to problems in the Synoptic Gospels, focusing on patterns of a few
varieties: words, agreement of one source with another, and theological
patterns. Baird examined the various sources and units (accepting the
basic results of source criticism) in relation to the different kinds of

---

41. Osgood *et al.*, *Cross-Cultural Universals*.

42. Berelson and Lazarsfeld, *Analysis*, pp. 18-77. Krippendorff (*Content Analysis*, pp. 33-35) lists these and other uses.

43. Baird 'Content Analysis'. The article describes content analysis and how it
can be applied to biblical studies. The results were published in J.A. Baird, *Audience
Criticism and the Historical Jesus* (Philadelphia: Westminster Press, 1969).

stated audiences (the 12 disciples, the crowd disciples, the opponent crowd, particular opponents). He then used his information to challenge and illuminate theories about the Synoptic Gospels. Baird found that 91 percent of parallel passages are in general agreement as to the audience, and 67 percent were in exact agreement.[44] He also found Synoptic discontinuity and noted clear distinctions between material which contained the words of Jesus and the surrounding narratives, stating that 'the editorial stratum simply does not look the same as the logia'.[45] Baird sums up his intentions for using content analysis as follows: 'Above all, the thrust of this method of content analysis... is that the basic premises, the methodology, and the raw data of such biblical study be clearly spelled out.'[46]

Krippendorff mentions a study by A. Morton,[47] who analyzed the books of the Pauline corpus and 'concluded that they were written by six different authors and that Paul himself had written only four'. However, Krippendorff calls Morton's work problematic, in that the same criteria, when applied to other works of known authorship, showed multiple authorship of single-author works and collections.[48]

An Emory University dissertation by E. Ogunyemi used content analysis to examine Christian and Roman documents (including some New Testament documents) for attitudes of each group toward each other. Ogunyemi categorized documents as a whole in relation to beliefs and practices, and concluded that 'the persecution of the Christians was a natural outgrowth of their deviance from the dominant society.'[49] As one of his 'suggestions for future study' he proposed using content analysis for the study of Scripture.[50]

---

44. Baird, *Audience*, pp. 62, 66.

45. Baird, *Audience*, p. 89. Baird has also worked on various volumes of *The Computer Bible*.

46. Baird, 'Content Analysis', p. 276.

47. A. Morton, 'A Computer Challenges the Church,' *Observer* (November 1963, p. 3).

48. Krippendorff, *Content Analysis*, p. 42.

49. E. Ogunyemi, *A Content Analysis of Selected Documents dealing with some Relationships between Christians and Romans during the First Three Centuries* (dissertation; Emory University, 1976), p. ii.

50. Ogunyemi, *Christians and Romans*, p. 74. M.J. Buss (*Encounter with the Text: Form and History in the Hebrew Bible* [Philadelphia: Fortress Press; Missoula: Scholars Press, 1979], p. 30) also notes an unpublished paper by D. Verner which

c. *Implicit Applications in Biblical Studies*

Although the explicit use of content analysis in biblical studies is relatively rare, a number of investigations have employed approaches closely resembling content analysis. L. Eslinger used a computer to analyze various aspects in the Deuteronomistic History, focusing on evaluations of situations by persons of the narrative.[51] He noted, for instance, that of the evaluations of the conquest in Joshua 11–Judges 1, 'only Yahweh's is in complete accord with the facts... Joshua vacillates... The narrator's assessments... are especially puzzling.' Eslinger also noted structures, parallels, chiasms, and associations in the narratives. However, there is no overt link with content analysis; one suspects that the similarity of his method to 'content analysis' is due to a general acquaintance with work done in other fields, in which content analysis is largely implicit.

Martin Buss's *The Prophetic Word of Hosea* has many affinities with content analysis, without being a systematic content analysis.[52] Much of the work examines patterns of language (including content) in the book of Hosea. It employs several different categories (divine versus non-divine speech, direct versus indirect address, emotional tenor, attribution of causes, etc.) and examines correlations in terms of probabilities.

In sum, some exegetical, literary, and historical biblical studies border on content analysis, while few make an overt connection with content analysis.

3. *Previous Studies by the Author*

I began employing procedures resembling those of standard content analysis in 1984,[53] primarily to keep track of a large number of details in order to state trends and make comparisons. Some studies were topic-oriented, examining a particular subject as it occurs in various parts of the Bible. Others were passage-oriented, using the individual

---

'has shown that Jacob is described more frequently as the son of Rebekah than as the son of Isaac, while the reverse holds true for Esau'.

51. L. Eslinger, *Into the Hands of the Living God* (Sheffield: Almond Press, 1989).

52. M.J. Buss, *The Prophetic Word of Hosea* (Berlin: Töpelmann, 1969).

53. However, I was unaware of the field of 'content analysis' until 1989.

word as the recording unit.[54] A few of these studies are outlined in an appendix, for they illustrate some of the procedures used in the dissertation. All were performed using the computer as a tool and using all or part of the Bible to obtain their data.

4. *Formal Connection with Content Analysis*

Unlike most of my previous studies, the dissertation makes a formal connection with content analysis and relies upon it for three major aspects of the dissertation. First, procedures suggested by content analysts, especially those of K. Krippendorff, heavily influenced the study. Secondly, content analysis was relied upon for suggestions concerning methods of coding and extracting results. Finally, some of the categories and scales were influenced by other content analysts. (See the chapters on coding and categories for more detailed explanations).[55]

54. Also known as the analysis of the 'syntactical unit' (Krippendorff, *Content Analysis*, p. 63). Krippendorff (*Content Analysis*, p. 61) notes that 'words are the smallest and as far as reliability is concerned the safest recording unit of written documents.'

55. Mechanically speaking, the current study mainly used a statistics program and a programmable word processor in tandem (*SPSSPC+* and *Nota Bene* respectively).

Chapter 2

QUESTIONS AND HYPOTHESES

The activities of any agent give clues about the personality of that agent. This is true for humans and God. The God of the Bible is a God who acts. This God is known, not just by divine decrees, but by what God does and how others affect God. Examining the characteristics of divine activity, especially comparing it with the activity of other entities, gives insight into God's character.

1. *Questions*

The main question which this book addresses is: what are the characteristics of God as an acting agent and a recipient of actions in prophetic literature, especially in Joel? Subquestions are: (1) How does the portrayal of divine activity compare to that of humans and other living beings? and (2) How does the image of God's activity in Joel compare to the image of God's activity in Selected Prophetic Passages (SPP—see chapters 7, 8, and 9 for these)? In other words, how does the book of Joel differ, in its vision of God, from other prophets?

2. *Hypotheses to Be Tested*

Each comparative analysis will be stated in terms of the 'null hypothesis'. The 'null hypothesis' is an artificial starting point from which assertions are tested, and is assumed unless disproven by a statistical analysis. In our case it means to say that 'situation A is not significantly different from situation B', and then to test whether this is actually the case. For example, 'God does the same amount of bad ethics as Israelites do' would be a null hypothesis. A statistical comparison, though, may show this not to be the case, thus disproving the hypothesis.

Statistically, the null hypothesis actually is stated for each category and for Evaluation, rather than the whole. Practically speaking, each analysis is a compilation of null hypotheses. The degree of similarity is based largely on how often the null hypothesis is sustained.

Occasionally comparisons will be examined to determine whether something may be practically significant even though it is not statistically significant. Some comparisons also include a discussion of the types of actions performed, regardless of the frequency of the individual type of action.

3. *Actors and Complements (Recipients) in the Study*

The main actors and complements are as follows:

1. God.
2. Humans (all types).
3. Israelites.
4. Foreigners.
5. Insects (in Joel only).

God as an actor or complement is compared to the following types of scenarios:

1. God's activity and reception of activity is compared to the activity and reception of each of the other agents/complements.[1]
2. Divine activity is considered in terms of what God does to the other agents versus what the other agents do to God.
3. Divine treatment of/reception from Israelites is compared to the same in relation to foreigners.

4. *Particular Null Hypotheses*

a. *Individual Comparisons within SPP and Joel*

1. God's activity is the same as human activity.
2. The activity of Israelites is the same as the activity of foreigners.
3. God's activity is the same as Israelite activity.
4. God's activity is the same as foreigner activity.
5. God's activity is the same as insect activity Joel alone.
6. God treats Israelites and foreigners the same.

---

1. The exception is that divine reception is not compared to insect reception.

   7.   God receives the same kinds of actions as humans receive.
   8.   God receives the same kinds of actions as Israelites receive.
   9.   God receives the same kinds of actions as foreigners receive.
  10.   What God does and what God receives are the same.
  11.   God does the same to humans as humans do to God.
  12.   God does the same to Israel as Israel does to God.
  13.   God does the same to foreigners as foreigners do to God.

b. *Comparing Joel to SPP*

   1.   God's activity is the same.
   2.   What God receives is the same.
   3.   God treats humans the same.
   4.   God treats Israelites the same.
   5.   God treats foreigners the same.
   6.   Humans treat God the same.
   7.   Israelites treat God the same.
   8.   Foreigners treat God the same.

Chapter 3

THE THEORY OF CODING AND CATEGORIES

1. *Introduction*

There are two kinds of procedural issues to be addressed. One relates to the coding of the database, and the other to the use of the database. The coding question is: what are the characteristics of the semantic universe of the texts? The 'use' question is: given the coding applied, what are the characteristics of God as an acting agent in prophetic literature?

The theory behind the coding of the text is extremely important, for it has a strong bearing on the final results. In this chapter I wish to discuss recording units, the debate concerning standardization of categories, and the construction of categories.

2. *Recording Units*

There are different types of recording units which can be coded. These include words, themes, characters, items, phrases, sentences, ideas, paragraphs, columns, articles, and whole books.[1] The present study uses individual words as the recording unit. As noted above, Krippendorff notes that 'words are the smallest and as far as reliability is concerned the safest recording unit of written documents'.[2]

Content analysis is frequently applied to a large body of literature. When approached in this fashion it is possible to ask a few narrowly

---

1. See B. Berelson and P. Lazarsfeld, *The Analysis of Communication Content* (preliminary draft; University of Chicago and Columbia University, 1948), p. 78; I. Pool (ed.), *Trends in Content Analysis* (Urbana: University of Illinois Press, 1959), p. 202; O. Holsti, *Content Analysis for the Social Sciences and Humanities* (Reading: Addison-Wesley, 1969), p. 116-17; K. Krippendorff, *Content Analysis: An Introduction to its Methodology* (Beverly Hills: Sage Publications, 1980), pp. 61-63.
2. Krippendorff, *Content Analysis*, p. 61.

defined questions and do minimal coding on each text while ignoring major aspects of the texts which do not relate specifically to the questions at hand. Such was the case for my studies on *God's Communication with Humanity* and *The Consumption of Alcoholic Beverages in the Old Testament*. For those studies verses or passages were the recording units, and the bodies of literature were the entire Bible and the Old Testament respectively.

The situation is quite different when the word is the recording unit, as it is in this study. In this case the body of literature is relatively small (about 4850 words in Hebrew), and the coding is extremely detailed.

Different recording units require different procedures, involve different types of categories, and obtain different types of results. Different categories would be employed if texts approximately chapter length were the recording unit to be classified as a whole, rather than individual words. For example, if Gunkel's Psalm classification is viewed from the standpoint of a content analyst, the individual Psalm is the recording unit and receives a particular classification according to its overall contents.

To speak analogously: the differences between classifying different types of recording units are like the differences between classifying tells, the strata within the tells, and the individual artifacts within each stratum. The coding of the present study is most like identifying the particular artifacts within six similar strata at different tells, cataloguing the artifacts, and then comparing the strata to each other. Just as it is generally considered legitimate to catalogue the contents of various strata and compare them to one another, it is likewise legitimate to catalogue and compare the contents of the prophetic passages in the study.

3. *Category Standardization*

> Communication content is so rich with human experience, and its causes and effects so varied, that no single system of substantive categories can be devised to describe it.[3]

Standardization of categories has long been a topic of debate within content analysis. Calls for standardization express the desire to be able to perform and judge various studies by the same criteria. Indeed, a

---

3.   Berelson and Lazarsfeld, *Analysis*, p. 1.

number of content analysis dictionaries have been produced.[4]

However, most content analysts recognize that standardization of categories is not possible nor desirable. The main arguments against standardization of categories are: (1) that it is not possible to construct a set of categories which can describe any and every text; and (2) it is not possible to construct a set of categories which matches the interests of all content analysts.[5]

Non-standardization is viewed by many as a positive thing. I. Pool states that '. . . there is a good deal to be said for *ad hoc* categories'.[6] As Hall and Van de Castle put it, 'No set of categories is ever complete, but if the investigator cannot find what he wants among those that have already been devised, he is free to formulate new ones which can be added to the existing ones.'[7] Holsti urges content analysts to individualize for each study.[8]

As with studies in other fields, standardization of categories in biblical studies likewise seems neither practical nor desirable. One need only consider the different Psalm classifications of Gunkel, Mowinckel, and Westermann to see that a classification system depends upon the analyst. Each of their systems can produce useful results, but to demand that all Psalm studies conform to one of these would hinder scholarship.

It is not as though everyone makes up their own categories which are completely divorced from the realm of common human experience. J. Laffal's description of his concept dictionary applies to many category systems, including the one employed in this study:

> A conceptual dictionary is a collection of the words of a language organized to show the kinds of content represented in the words. The categories of content are presumed to reflect cognitive-conceptual sets which are evoked whenever a pertinent word is encountered. . . Like the thesaurus and the synonym dictionary, the concept dictionary has as its major purpose the identification and exploitation of similarities in the meanings of words.
>
> Ordinary speakers are in substantial agreement about the meanings of words, although the words may also carry personal connotations.

4. Various classification systems are mentioned in Pool (ed.), *Trends* (pp. 212-13); Holsti, *Content Analysis*, chapter 5 (pp. 94-126).

5. Pool, *Trends*, pp. 212-13; Holsti, *Content Analysis*, p. 102.

6. Pool, *Trends*, p. 214.

7. C. Hall and R. Van de Castle, *The Content Analysis of Dreams* (New York: Meredith, 1966), p. 9.

8. Holsti, *Content Analysis*, p. 102.

> Commonality of meaning stems from the similarity of our experiences as
> human beings and from the similarity of the processes by which we learn
> our language. It is to the commonality of meaning that a concept dictionary
> addresses itself.[9]

It is not as though category construction is a complete free-for-all
with no concern for the way the rest of humanity thinks. The analyst
assumes and hopes that a set of categories will be meaningful—and
useful—to others. Classification schemes which have been employed in
one place can be used in another; there may be tremendous value in
importing other dictionaries into one's study. (The present study has
certainly been influenced by others, especially Laffal, Osgood, and the
Harvard Third Psycho-Sociological Dictionary.) However, one can
expect to have to modify any particular dictionary to more closely
match their texts, topics, and questions.[10]

To sum up: categorization is a human endeavor, and therefore highly
dependent upon whoever is doing the categorizing, and especially on
the purpose for which it is used.

4. *Construction of Categories*

The basic idea behind the construction of categories is pragmatic: they
must thus fit the material and fit the questions. As Krippendorff has
said, 'Categories have to be justified in terms of what is known about
the data's context. Content analysis research designs have to be *context
sensitive*.'[11] The categories should be representative of the interests of
the analyst as well as the content of the text.[12]

All words must be categorized, but not all possible distinctions will
be made. It is legitimate to have a 'Does not apply' or 'noscore' category, as well as to lump various types of low frequency words (or low
frequency concepts) together into one category.[13]

Content analysts generally urge that a category system be more

9.   J. Laffal, *A Concept Dictionary of English* (Essex: Gallery Press, 1973),
p. 1.

10. The present study has even found it necessary to modify grammatical
classifications of words, for traditional Hebrew grammatical designations inade-
quately convey the sense of many words. (See below, chapter 5 ['Category and Field
Descriptions'], 'Part of Speech.')

11. Krippendorff, *Content Analysis*, p. 49.

12. Berelson and Lazarsfeld, *Analysis*, pp. 88, 96.

13. Krippendorff, *Content Analysis*, p. 75.

specific rather than less.[14] A person may have a particular set of interests and predetermined questions which they bring to the text. Determining ahead of time all of the relevant categories is hermeneutically unsound, for it does not allow the text to inform and correct us about its contents.[15] The coding process will reveal concepts which were not directly addressed by the analyst's initial set of categories. Specificity can be improved by creating new categories from previously uncoded words (also known as the 'leftover list'). There are a few benefits derived from this approach. First, the category system becomes more thorough, leading to a more accurate analysis. Secondly, having too many words in a 'leftover list' opens up a study to the charge that it has ignored large portions of the material. Thirdly, it has been said that a content analysis is never finished. In the future there may be an interest in working with other aspects of the text.

The rationale is to have enough logically distinct categories in any given classification to produce useful results. Usefulness is defined by the study (either the immediate one or derivative ones); what works for one may not for another. Logically distinct does not necessarily mean that a particular word cannot have more than one category applied to it, but that the categories themselves must be distinct.

Krippendorff has said 'That "categories must be exhaustive and mutually exclusive" is an often stated requirement.'[16] The main benefit is that statistical significance is easier to achieve when comparing one category with another.[17] However, mutual exclusivity is not always possible nor desirable—items are often not mutually exclusive in all their characteristics; only some of them. For instance, the term 'animal sacrifice' (one word in Hebrew [זבח]) as it shows up in Malachi (and elsewhere) relates to two institutions: animal husbandry and the cult. The categories animal husbandry (ANHS) and cult (CULT) are exclusive, but not necessarily the objects to which they are attached. Categories, then, can be mutually exclusive without the objects they assign being mutually exclusive.

14. Berelson and Lazarsfeld, *Analysis*, pp. 88, 116-17.

15. For coding and classification suggestions, see Krippendorff, *Content Analysis*, pp. 49-50; and R.P. Weber, *Basic Content Analysis* (Beverly Hills: Sage Publications, 1985), pp. 15-40.

16. Krippendorff, *Content Analysis*, p. 75.

17. Weber, *Basic Content Analysis*, p. 23.

Category construction, then, is one example of the hermeneutical circle. The analyst has an idea of what categories would be useful, while the text corrects and informs the analyst.

Chapter 4

THE CODING/CATEGORY SYSTEM

1. *Introduction*

What is the conceptual universe of a text? It is the world created by the author. This world includes the physical, emotional, psychological, institutional, spiritual, ethical, and valuing aspects contained therein. It includes who does what kind of action (or has what kind of attitude) toward whom. It includes the means by which the message was given (speaker, grammar). This world contains people, places, actions, and how they relate, physically, socially, and mentally. The theory behind the category system employed in this study is to describe the conceptual universe of the texts.

There are two main means being used in this study to describe this conceptual universe.[1] The first is a system of categories which is analogous to the popular question, 'animal, vegetable, or mineral?' The database, though, has a far more specific and complex set of categories. The second means of describing the conceptual universe of the texts is a numerical scale which considers the effect of objects or actions on those encountering the object or receiving the action.

2. *The Category System Illustrated*

A few examples should illustrate the category theory employed in this study. The words 'priest, farmer, barn', and 'temple' will be considered with some help from Webster's Dictionary.

Priest: Webster defines 'priest' as 'one authorized to perform the sacred rites of a religion esp. as a mediatory agent between [a human being]

---

1. See K. Krippendorff, *Content Analysis: An Introduction to its Methodology* (Beverly Hills: Sage Publications, 1980), p. 78 for a chart describing one way to break down the universe according to categories.

and God; *specif:* an Anglican, Eastern Orthodox, or Roman Catholic clergyman ranking below a bishop and above a deacon.' 'One' in this context refers to a human being (coded as HUMAN). The description to the actions performed refers to a societal role, specifically cultic (CULT). Further specification describes the rank of the cultic human in particular denominational settings. A 'Roman Catholic Priest' could be specified as HUMAN, CULT, ROMAN CATHOLIC. An ancient Israelite priest would be coded in the database as HUMAN, CULT, ISRAELITE.

Farmer: 'A person who cultivates land or crops... ' 'Person' refers to a human, 'cultivates land or crops' describes the role of the human as related to agriculture and food. A farmer, then, is HUMAN, AGRICULTURE, FOOD.

Barn: (*storehouse* in the database). 'A usu. large building for the storage of farm products, for feed, and usu. for the housing of farm animals or farm equipment.' In ancient Israel it most likely would have been for the storage of produce (e.g. grain). Its most obvious physical characteristic is that it is a building, and its function has to do with agriculture and food. A barn, then, is BUILDING, AGRICULTURE, FOOD.

Temple: 'An edifice for religious exercises... ' Following the above reasoning, a temple is a cultic building, coded BUILDING, CULT.

The above examples consider physical objects. Actions and other types of words often involve different kinds of codes, although there is often overlap. Consider the words 'lament' and 'murder'.

Lament: 'To express sorrow or mourning often demonstratively.' To express is to send communication, and sorrow or mourning concern the emotion of sadness. It would be coded SENDING COMMUNICATION, SORROW.

Murder: 'The crime of unlawfully killing a person esp. with malice aforethought.' It is a criminal act involving death. It is inherently unethical and always destructive. The database coding is CRIMINAL, DEATH, ETHICALLY BAD, DESTRUCTION. The word 'murderer' would add the code HUMAN (human).

Categories are grouped into larger sets of categories, called *metacategories*. BARN, FARMER, PRIEST, and TEMPLE all have institutional connotations (AGRICULTURE and CULT) and therefore would also have the metacategory INSTITUTIONS.

In sum, the categories are intended to describe many of the characteristics and roles designated by words in the texts. In the present study, multiple categories are utilized to describe the meanings of words.[2]

In addition to describing the meaning of words themselves (as in the above examples), the present study categorizes action words on the basis of Osgood's actor/action/complement theory. (See above, 'Introduction to Content Analysis'.) Words of action are coded according to the type of acting agent and the type of recipient. Using the above examples, consider 'The foreign farmer murdered the Israelite priest.' The word 'murder' would be coded as follows:

Actor: HUMAN, AGRICULTURE, FOOD, FOREIGN
Action: CRIMINAL, DEATH, ETHICALLY BAD, DESTRUCTION
Complement: HUMAN, CULT, ISRAELITE

Action would be coded according to the meaning of the word itself. *Actor* and *complement* would be derived from the context and then applied to the action word.[3]

It must be emphasized that all words in the passages were coded, not just verbs (or other words of action). However, not all words have actor/complement coding.

3. *The Numeric Scale, Evaluation*

In addition to categories, a numeric tag, Evaluation, has been added to words in order to indicate positive or negative semantic aspects of words. Evaluation is one of the scales used in Osgood's semantic differential.

As noted in the introduction, C. Osgood's semantic differential scales are seen to represent 'three basic dimensions of human affective cognition.'[4] The scales, which are anthropocentric in nature, concern to what degree something is beneficial, powerful, or active in relation to the one encountering something (e.g. encountering a thing or action). As Osgood puts it,

---

2.   See above, 'Construction of Categories', in the previous chapter.

3.   It is not always possible to indicate exactly which word is the actor or complement.

4.   Krippendorff, *Content Analysis*, p. 78.

Consistent with my behavioristic theory of meaning, it is these pervasive affective features which dominate much of our behavior, including language behavior. . . What is important to us now, as it was back in the age of Neanderthal Man, about the sign of a thing is: First, does it refer to something *good* or *bad* for me (is it an antelope or a saber-toothed tiger)? Second, does it refer to something which is *strong* or *weak* with respect to me (is it a saber-toothed tiger or a mosquito)? And third, for behavioral purposes, does it refer to something which is *active* or *passive* (is it a saber-toothed tiger or merely a pool of quicksand, which I can simply walk around)?[5]

This study employs only one of these scales, *Evaluation*.[6]

Evaluation could be described as a 'niceness scale,' indicating the relative benefit/detriment to the one directly encountering a particular person, situation, or attitude. Evaluation coding is somewhat immediate in its scope, rather than looking for a possible 'ultimate' good or harm. For instance, when Yahweh is described as taking revenge on His enemies in Nahum 1.2, 'take revenge' is coded negatively, even though the action might be beneficial for Israelites. It is the more immediate help/harm which is of interest, rather than secondary effects.

5. C. Osgood, *Focus on Meaning* (The Hague: Mouton, 1976), p. 89.

6. It is not the point of this study to defend Osgood's theory of *semantic space*. Dr Jim Miller at Emory University (personal discussion, Fall 1991) noted some difficulties with the theory. The primary problem seems to be that the evaluation scale operates on a different logic than potency or activity. Potency and activity are scales from nothing to all. While the 'I' could be placed in the center, as Osgood suggests, the potency and activity scales do not really go from -3 to +3; it is from 1 to 7 (or 0 to 6). Evaluation is different. It is not a scale of no evaluation to all evaluation. It has a neutral point, and is a real negative to positive scale. Thus, while these three scales can be applied to words, they may not be logically connected.

Be that as it may, the primary reason for including evaluation while excluding potency and activity is pragmatic: evaluation is considerably more useful in this study. Although not quite stated exactly this way, my analysis is not simply 'what is God like in various situations?' but 'how nice is God in various situations?' and 'how does God think in various situations?' Evaluation, in conjunction with the two emphasized category groups (i.e. *Helpful/Harmful States and Processes* and *Psychological States and Processes*; see chapter 6, section 1. h below), seems to best illumine the personality of God, i.e. how God thinks, feels, and operates beneficially or harmfully in the physical and ethical realms. Just as noting that God walks and talks is not nearly as valuable for these questions, it is unclear how potency and activity would illumine these questions.

When used in conjunction with actor/action/complement coding (AAC), a mean Evaluation of activity can be calculated which can help to show the general trend of the types of actions which occur. Mean Evaluations from different AAC scenarios can then be compared. For instance, the mean Evaluation of what God does to Israelites in the average prophet is -0.50, while the mean Evaluation of what God does to foreigners is -1.98. On the surface it appears as though God is considerably harsher to foreigners, but statistics can be used to determine if the -1.48 difference really is significant. In this case the answer is yes (see this particular analysis in Part II.

The specific numbers for Evaluation are based on Osgood *et al.*, *Cross-Cultural Universals of Affective Meaning*.[7] These have been modified on the basis of my knowledge of the Old Testament prophets, Hebrew, and ancient Near Eastern history. In addition, the Evaluation scale was adjusted to make broader distinctions than in *Cross-Cultural Universals* and rounded to the nearest whole number.

The Evaluation scale in this study ranges from +3 (beneficial) to -3 (harmful). Here are examples of some of the general Evaluation trends. Terms which tend to be neutral are coded neutrally: 0. These include many terms of quantification, degree, and generic action words (e.g. 'do'). Other generic words are often no-scored. People in general are mildly positive (+1); it is usually better to be around people than not. Many communication terms also fall in here. Food in general and many positive emotions (e.g. joy) receive a +2, while life and extremely positive emotions (e.g. love) are +3. Weakness is a -1. Negative mental states (e.g. sorrow, fear) are fairly negative (-2), and emotions deemed more harmful (e.g. hate) are -3. Murder, which has more easily demonstrable permanent harm than sorrow, is evaluated -3. Opposite concepts usually receive the opposite Evaluation number. (See the appendix for the *Evaluation of Activity* dictionary designed during this study.)[8]

---

7. C.E. Osgood, W. May and M. Miron, *Cross-Cultural Universals of Affective Meaning* (Urbana: University of Illinois Press, 1975), pp. 422-52.

8. The Evaluation scoring for the person 'God' was removed in order to (a) determine the prophetic view of God on the basis of God's activities; and (b) the common high Evaluation of God seemed to skew Evaluation results on test runs, making passages look more positive than they actually are.

4. *Coding Systems which Informed the Present Category System*

There are three main coding systems which heavily influenced the present study. They are J. Laffal's *Concept Dictionary of English*,[9] the *Harvard Third Psycho-Sociological Dictionary*[10], and C. Osgood's semantic differential, especially as described in *Cross-Cultural Universals of Affective Meaning*.[11]

Laffal's dictionary informed the construction of the present category system.[12] I applied his *cognitive conceptual sets* (from his first edition)[13] to the database. The application of Laffal's system proved to be invaluable practice, informed my own category system, and provided test data for early stages of the project. Words were not simply classified according to their English equivalents in Laffal's dictionary. It was necessary to make some modifications on the basis of ancient Near Eastern history, customs, and Hebrew. Take, for instance, the word *chariot*. Laffal categorized it as VEHC (vehicles). However, since a chariot in the ancient Near East has more the connotation of a modern army tank, it was classified as such (VEHC DAMG [damage]). My category system coded it as VEHC MILI DEST TRAN (a military vehicle which is involved in destruction and transportation).

My original plan was to use Laffal's categories as a control, but this idea was later dropped. His system was useful, but was unable to answer many types of questions which are common in biblical studies, mainly because some necessary distinctions were not maintained.[14]

The *Harvard Third Psycho-Sociological Dictionary*[15] mainly helped in the organization and grouping of categories (called groups and

9. J. Laffal, *A Concept Dictionary of English* (Essex: Gallery Press, 1973); and J. Laffal, *A Concept Dictionary of English with Computer Programs for Content Analysis* (Essex: Gallery Press, 1990).

10. As described in P. Stone, D. Dunphy, M. Smith, and D. Ogilvie, *The General Inquirer: A Computer Approach to Content Analysis* (Cambridge: MIT Press, 1966), pp. 170-86.

11. Osgood *et al.*, *Cross-Cultural Universals*, pp. 422-52.

12. However, my category system is by no means a direct import or even a minor modification of Laffal's.

13. Laffal, *Dictionary of English*.

14. For instance, while both God and priest were classified as 'LEAD HOLY', most who do biblical studies would wish to be able to distinguish these.

15. As described in Stone *et al.*, *The General Inquirer*, pp. 170-86.

metacategories in this study). It also suggested some important sets of categories, for example institutional ones.

As noted above, Osgood's *Cross-Cultural Universals* was used to help apply Evaluation numbers to words. Osgood's scales run from -3 to +3, with 0 being neutral. The particular application of his scales in his dictionary involved a precision which assigned decimals to words, showed the range of variation in different cultures, and rarely went beyond ±2. Since I am not confident that I can make as precise a measurement as Osgood did, especially on ancient Near Eastern literature, I stretched the scales out to ±3 and rounded all numbers. I also had to make some adjustments when it came to particular words, especially when it seemed that the biblical view was somewhat different from a modern one. The database coding originally included potency and activity, but these were not deemed useful in answering my questions, so they were dropped.

5. *Perfect Coding?*

All coding is context oriented. There are instances where, especially when examining the dictionaries (see appendix), it appears as though a category or Evaluation number does not fit the word. The presence of words which do not appear to fit in a category can be justified by context. Take the word 'great' in the following two contexts. 'Great and terrifying is the Day of Yahweh' (Mal. 3.23 [minus 1]) does not receive the same Evaluation as 'My Name is great among the nations' (Mal. 1.11 [+2]).

For example, one particular area which had been questioned during the process of the study involved many of the words which receive the Evaluation of -1. The questioned Evaluation -1 vocabulary accounted for 38 words in the database. This is only 0.78 percent of all words in the database (4857). Thirteen of these words are not classified as actions, and therefore do not have any effect on the comparison of actions. Of these 38 words, I argued that all but five are contextually at least a -1 (and some possibly more negative). Of the other five, all are Evaluation zero at best, and three are not coded as actions and therefore will not affect any analyses in this study.

This is not to say that there are no mistakes in the database; on the contrary. However, it is not necessary for the database to be perfect to obtain significant results. While minor adjustments would probably make the database better, both in coding and in selection of categories, such changes would not make any significant differences, practically or statistically.

6. *Summary*

The coding system employed here is by no means the only one which could be applied, nor is it a 'perfect' representation of the information contained therein. However, it does provide a means of accessing the text which is useful for my current (and future) questions, as well as being a reasonable representation of the conceptual universe of the texts.

Chapter 5

CATEGORY AND FIELD DESCRIPTIONS

The construction of a category dictionary is an important part of the process of doing a content analysis, and a dictionary which includes categories which might not necessarily be used in an immediate study, but applied to future similar ones is of great value. As Weber has said,

> Another approach to content analysis involves the creation and application of general dictionaries. Content analysis dictionaries consist of category names, the definitions or rules for assigning words to categories, and the actual assignment of specific words. This strategy provides the researcher with numerous categories (60 to 150+) into which most words in most texts can be classified. . . It is worth noting here that dictionary construction is commonly misperceived to be merely a preface or preparatory step for quantification. Although researchers commonly use dictionaries to define variables for quantification, they also employ categories to locate and retrieve text based on the occurrence of semantically equivalent symbols.[1]

This chapter lists, organizes, and defines the various fields and categories employed in the study. Some categories and fields are used to help extract information, while others contain the extracted information. Here the main category system is described in detail and presented in a few ways, including a category 'tree', followed by a description of other fields in the database.

1. *Fields Entered into the Database*

The texts were coded according to the following scheme:

---

1. R.P. Weber, *Basic Content Analysis* (Beverly Hills: Sage Publications, 1985), p. 25.

A. *Conceptual classifications* (concept/theme oriented)

1. Category system

    a. Group   — Grouping of major categories.
    b. Metacategory — Major category groupings.
    c. Category   — Individual categories.

2. Actor/action/complement (who does what unto whom; stated in terms of categories)

B. Non-conceptual classifications

    1.   Part of speech
    2.   Evaluation
    3.   Negation or not

C. Text for study

    1.   Hebrew word
    2.   Hebrew root
    3.   English root translation

D. Indices

    1.   Book, chapter, and verse
    2.   Word number

2. *Sample of the Coded Database*

N E English G Transation	Part of Speech	Metacategories		Category				Evaluation	Book Chapter Verse Word No.	Actor/Complement A=Actor R=Recipient
hear	VI	CO GU				COMR	SENS	+1	HO4.01 0558	ANATN AHUMN AHUGP AISRL RGOD RCOMV
word	SB	CO					COMV	+1	HO4.01 0559	
Yahweh	PN	DV		GOD					HO4.01 0560	
descendant	SB	HU	IF	HUGP	HUMN			ISRL	+2	HO4.01 0561	
Israel	PN	HU	IF LO	NATN	HUMN	HUGP		ISRL	+2	HO4.01 0562	
for	PT	OT		NSCR					HO4.01 0563	
lawsuit	SB	IN				LEGL		+2	HO4.01 0564	AGOD RNATN RHUMN RHUGP RISRL RDWEL
Yahweh	PN	DV		GOD					HO4.01 0565	
with	PP	OT		NSCR					HO4.01 0566	
inhabitant	SB	BN HU IF			HUMN		DWEL	ISRL	+2	HO4.01 0567	
land	SB	IF LO		LAND				ISRL	+1	HO4.01 0568	
for	PT	OT		NSCR					HO4.01 0569	
there is not	PT	QL		NEG					HO4.01 0570	

N E G	English Transation	Part of Speech	Metacategories	Category		Evaluation	Book Chapter Verse Word No.	Actor/Complement A=Actor R=Recipient
N	truth	SB	ET PS		KNOW ETHG	+2	HO4.01 0571	ANATN AHUMN AHUGP AISRL RGOD
	there is not	PT	QL	NEG			HO4.01 0574	
N	faithfulness	SB	CP ET PS	COND	KEEP ETHG	+2	HO4.01 0575	ANATN AHUMN AHUGP AISRL RGOD
	there is not	PT	QL	NEG			HO4.01 0574	
N	knowledge	SB	PS		KNOW	+2	HO4.01 0575	ANATN AHUMN
	God	PN	DV	GOD			HO4.01 0576	
	land	SB	HU IF LO	LAND HUMN	HUGP ISRL	+1	HO4.01 0577	

3. *The Category System: Groups, Metacategories, and Categories*

The description which follows presents the overall grouping of categories (GROUP), the major categories (METACATEGORY), and the particular categories (CATEGORY).

a. *Category Groupings* (GROUPS) [7 total]

Groups are a way of organizing categories, but are not actually coded in the database. The purpose of groups is an organization of the universe according to a broad scheme. All groups can represent action/activity except LIVING OBJECTS and NON-LIVING OBJECTS, although not all words in the other five groups refer to activity. The groups are as follows:

1. Living objects.
2. Non-living objects.
3. States and processes: psychological.
4. States and processes: physical and social.
5. States and processes with strong helpful/harmful Connotations.
6. Relationship to society and nature.
7. Other.

b. *Metacategories according to their Groups* [23 total]

Metacategories are designed as mid-level organizers of categories. They can be especially helpful in tracking overall trends when individual categories may not show significant differences.

The two-letter code indicates how metacategories are coded. However, most charts in the analyses will spell these out more fully. Metacategories within their groups are:

1.	*Living objects*	2.	*Non-living objects*
HU	Human beings	EL	Elements
DV	Divine realm	LO	Locations, places
VG	Plant oriented	MD	Things made by people
AN	Animals		
FN	Nondescript food		

3.	*States and processes:* *psychological*	4.	*States and processes:* *physical and social*
EM	Emotions	CO	Communication
PS	Cognitive (non-emotion)	GU	Guide, redirection
		MV	Movement
		CP	Conditions and processes

5.	*States and processes with strong* *helpful/harmful connotations*	6.	*Relationship to society and* *nature*
ET	Ethics	IN	Institution, society
ST	Status	BN	Basic need satisfaction
WL	Weal, good things	IF	Israelite or foreign
WO	Woe, bad things		

7.	*Other*
QL	Qualifiers
OT	Other

c. *Categories according to their Metacategories and Groups [105 total]*
Here is a breakdown of categories according to their metacategories and groups. (It should be remembered that many objects and actions can have more than one category applied to them.) The next section on detailed category descriptions must be consulted for more complete category descriptions.

Living objects

HU	(human beings)
HUMN	(human)
HUPT	(human part or aspect)
HUGP	(human group [city, nation, people, tribe])

DV	(divine realm)
GOD	(Yahweh or Elohim, the God of Israel)
GODP	(God part or aspect)
DVOT	(non-Yahwistic gods, images, cultic persons, and practices)

| ANGL | (angels, spiritual beings) |
| SPIR | (spiritual things, e.g. miracle) |

AN	(animals)
ANMD	(domestic animal)
INSC	(insect)
ANMW	(wild animal, other)
ANMP	(animal part)

VG	(plant oriented)
VEGT	(plants and plant parts)
VEGP	(processed plant products)

| FN | (nondescript food be animal or plant) |
| FDND | (food, nondescript; could |

Non-living objects

EL	(elements)
COSM	(cosmic [heaven, earth, star])
ELMT	(the elements, esp. weather)
MTRL	(materials [dirt, lye])

LO	(locations)
CITY	(city as a location)
NATN	(nation as a location)
LAND	(land, other locations)

MD	(made by people)
BLDG	(building)
CTPT	(city parts other than BLDG)
CLTH	(clothing)
FURN	(furniture)
MONY	(money)
TOOL	(tool, implement)
VHIC	(vehicle)

States and processes: psychological

EM	(emotions)
JOY	(joy)
SORR	(sorrow)

LOVE	(love)
HATE	(hate)
PRID	(pride, confidence)

SHAM (shame, humility)
ANGR (anger)
DESR (desire)
FEAR (fear)

PS   (cognition)
ALRT (alertness)
NLRT (non-alertness)

KNOW (knowledge)
IGNO (ignorance)

KEEP (keep, accept, obey)
RJCT (reject, abandon, rebel)

REAS (reasoning)

States and processes: physical and social

CO   (communication)
COMS (communication sending)
COMV (communication vehicle)
COMR (communication reception)
COMC (communication content)

GU   (guide, redirect)
ASMB (assemble, league)
ESTB (establish)
SEEK (seeking and inquiry)
SENS (sense [see, hear])
UNCV (uncover, reveal)

MV   (movement)
SEND (causing movement)
FLEE (flee, hide)
TRAN (transportation)

STAY (stay, remain)
RELO (relocation, travel)

CP   (conditions and processes, other)
HEAT (heat, fire)
PROC (other physical processes)
COND (conditions)
DO   (very general action)

States and processes with strong
helpful/harmful connotations

ET	(ethics)
ETHB	(ethically bad)[2]
ETHG	(ethically good)
ST	(status)
EXAL	(high status)
DBAS	(low status)
WLTH	(wealth)[3]
POVT	(poverty)
STRO	(strong)
WEAK	(weak)
WL	(weal)
HEAL	(healing; opp. ILL)
LIFE	(life; opp. DEAT)
PEAC	(peace [shalom]; opp. DEST)
REWD	(reward; opp. PUNI)
WO	(woe)
ILL	(illness and injury; opp. HEAL)
DEAT	(death; opp. LIFE)
DEST	(destruction; opp. PEAC)
PUNI	(punishment; opp. REWD)

Relationship to society and nature

IN	(institutions)
AGRI	(agriculture)
ANHS	(animal husbandry)
CRIM	(criminal)

2.   Note on ETHG and ETHB: righteousness and wickedness are prominent themes in the prophets. ETHG and ETHB are used to qualify words with strong moral connotations. They include societal and religious righteousness and wickedness. These classifications work differently than Osgood's Evaluation—a high or low Evaluation is not necessarily an indicator of a good or bad ethical action, for not everything which is helpful or harmful is ethical in nature. (For instance, drought is quite harmful but is not necessarily an ethical concern).

3.   Wealth and poverty always include economics (ECON) as an institutional category.

CULT	(cult)
ECON	(economics)
FAML	(family)
GOVT	(government)
HUNT	(hunting)
LEGL	(legal)
MILI	(military)
MSTR	(master servant)
PROP	(prophecy)
TRAD	(other trades and professions)
WILD	(wild animals and insects)

BN	(basic need, satisfaction)
DWEL	(dwelling oriented)
FOOD	(food oriented)
WEAR	(wearing, clothing oriented)
SEX	(sex)[4]

IF	(Israelite frgn)
ISRL	(Israelite—North or South kingdom)
FRGN	(foreign, non-Israelite)

Other

QL	(qualifiers)
DIRC	(direction)
TIME	(time, temporal)
MSMT	(measurement)
QNTY	(quantification)
NEG	(negation)
QUES	(question)

| OT | (other) |
| NSCR | (noscore) |

d. *Detailed Category Descriptions*

Categories are listed along with a basic definition and related categories. Most categories include people, things, actions, causes, effects, ideas, and states. An appendix provides lists of words which are included in each category.

4. If prostitution, TRAD is also added.

AGRI   *agriculture*, including all plants, where they are grown, parts of plants, the food from plants, tools used in agriculture, farmers, and agricultural disasters (e.g. drought).

ALRT   *alertness* or arousal, including terms of remembering. Opposite of NLRT.

ANGL   *angels* or other spiritual beings that are aligned with Yahweh. References to Yahweh are coded GOD. References to other gods and images are coded DVOT.

ANGR   the emotion of *anger*. ANGR often overlaps with PUNI.

ANHS   *animal husbandry*, including all domestic animals, parts of animals, that which facilitates the care of animals, people who take care of animals, and animal sacrifices (which are also coded CULT).

ANMD   *domestic animals*. Wild animals are coded ANMW. Insects are coded INSC. Animal parts are coded ANMP. No distinction is made as to whether alive or dead.

ANMP   *animal parts* (wild or domestic).

ANMW   *wild animals*, except for insects which are coded INSC. No distinction is made as to whether alive or dead. Also coded WILD.

ASMB   *assembly*, gatherings or being in league with others.

BLDG   *buildings*. City parts are coded CTPT. Cities are coded CITY. Furniture found in buildings is coded FURN.

CITY   *cities*, both the proper name, the people of the city, and generic cities as well. Nations are coded NATN. City parts are coded CTPT. Buildings are coded BLDG. Also frequently has HUMN. (CITY and NATN are often difficult to distinguish.)

CLTH   things worn on the human body. This includes not only *clothing*, but jewelry and cloth as well. The act of wearing is coded WEAR.

COMC   the *content* or message of a piece of *communication*.

COMR   the *reception* of a piece of *communication*: how received, the one receiving, and commands to receive.

COMS   the *sending* of a piece of *communication*.

COMV   the *vehicle* or means of conveying a piece of *communication*, including the human conveyer or nonhuman medium.

COND   *condition* or state of affairs, whether caused by outside or inside forces (e.g. diluted, sufficiency). Quantity or change in quantity is coded QNTY.

COSM   *cosmic*, celestial bodies (including the earth). Words having to do with weather are coded ELMT.

CRIM   *criminal* people, actions, and states (primarily murder and theft). CRIM is also coded ETHB. (All CRIM is ETHB, but not all ETHB is CRIM.)

CTPT   *parts of a city*. Buildings are coded BLDG. Whole cities are coded CITY. Nations are coded NATN.

CULT   *cultic* persons, places, things, and acts. References to Yahweh are coded GOD. References to non-Yahwistic deities, images, practices, and people add the category DVOT.

DBAS   *debasement*, low status, and insignificance. Opposite of EXAL.

DEAT   *death* and killing, including killers and the results of death. Illness and injury are coded ILL. Sacrifices are coded ANHS and CULT. Death of plants is coded AGRI. Murder includes CRIM. Opposite of LIFE.

DESR   *desire*, longing, and that which is pleasing or desirable.

DEST   *destruction* and violence: causes, processes, effects, and places associated with destruction. Destruction that includes death is also coded DEAT. Opposite of PEAC.

DIRC   *direction* that can be pointed toward. Words such as 'after' or 'above' or 'facing' are coded NSCR.

DO   generic *doing* and acting.

DVOT   *divine other (non-Yahwistic gods)*, practices, objects, and cultic people.

DWEL   *dwelling*, including the act of and places or parts of places in which dwelling occurs.

ECON   *economic* actions, possessions, and states. Criminal actions involving economics include CRIM. References to economic status are coded POVT or WLTH.

ELMT   *weather*, its effect on the earth, and movement of natural forces in the earth. References to that above the earth's atmosphere are coded COSM.

ESTB   *establishment*, appointment, or keeping of actions, peoples, or feasts.

ETHB   words with *bad ethical* or moral connotations and wickedness in general, including bad actions and attitudes toward humans and God. Words with crimi nal connotations include CRIM. Opposite of ETHG.

ETHG   words with *good ethical* or moral connotations and righteousness in general, including good actions and attitudes toward humans and God. Opposite of ETHB.

EXAL   *exaltation*, high status, greatness, including people, attitudes, and land forms. Opposite of DBAS. Often related to PRID.

FAML   the *family*, including its relationships and the breach thereof (e.g. widow).

FDND   *food of nondescript form*. Also coded FOOD. Food straight from plants is coded VEGT. Food prepared from plants is coded VEGP. Food from a wild animal is coded ANMW. Food from a domestic animal is coded ANMD. Food from an animal part (such as milk) is coded ANMP. (See FOOD.)

FEAR   *fear*. (An opposite of JOY in Joel). Confidence would be its opposite (which would require the addition of the category CONF [confidence]).

FLEE   *fleeing*, including the results of and actions which accompany flight. Opposite of UNCV.

FOOD   *food and drink*, animal and vegetable, including the plant or animal that the food comes from, that which is used to consume food, eating, production of food, and the humans whose primary role is consumption. There are many overlaps with AGRI and ANHS.

FRGN   *foreign* (i.e. non-Israelite) peoples and places, including individuals and groups. Foreign humans include HUMN. Israelite people are coded ISRL HUMN.

FURN   *furniture* not only for human use but for animal use (such as feed-trough) as well.

GOD   *Yahweh, the Judeo-Christian God*. References to other gods are coded DVOT. References to spiritual beings that are aligned with Yahweh are coded ANGL.

GODP   *parts and aspects of Yahweh*.

GOVT   *government*, including people, places, and actions.

HATE   *hate*: emotions, actions, and people. Destructive words are coded DEST. Opposite of LOVE.

HEAL   *health and healing*. Opposite of ILL.

HEAT   *fire, heat, and light.*

HUGP   *large and medium groups of humans* (e.g. nations, cities, tribes), including
            clans that go by an ancestor's name. Always includes HUMN as a tag.

HUMN   *human beings,* individually or collectively, including names of individuals,
            cities and nations. Parts of humans are coded HUPT. Can include HUGP. City
            references are also coded CITY + HUGP. Nation references are also coded
            NATN + HUGP. All humans, when possible, are also coded ISRL or FRGN.

HUNT   *hunting.*

HUPT   *parts of humans,* internal and external.

IGNO   *ignorance,* lack of knowledge. Opposite of KNOW.

ILL   *illness, injury,* and other types of physical unwholesomeness. Opposite of
            HEAL.
INSC   *insects.*[5]

ISRL   *Israelite* people and places, including individuals and groups, from the North
            or South kingdom. Non-Israelites are coded FRGN. Non-specific humans are
            coded HUMN without ISRL or FRGN.

JOY   *joy* and celebration. Opposite of FEAR or SORR.

KEEP   *obedience, agreement,* and operating according to another's desires, including
            service and repentance. Opposite of RJCT.

KNOW   *knowledge,* reflection: humans, actions, attitudes, and the parts of the human
            body associated with thinking. Opposite of IGNO. Reasoning is coded REAS.

LAND   *land,* locations, territory, natural features of the earth, non-political locations.
            Included are the proper names of land forms, water bodies, and interrogatives
            concerning specific places. Nations are coded NATN.

LEGL   *legal* systems, law, and punishment, including the humans involved and their
            actions. See also GOVT.

LIFE   *living* and surviving. Opposite of DEAT.

LOVE   *love* and compassion. Opposite of HATE.

MILI   *military* people, actions, tools, and places, including attack and defense.

---

5.   The term 'nation' (that has been coded INSC) in Joel 2 is clearly being used
to refer to the locusts attacking the land.

MONY   *money*, wealth, treasure, means of exchange.

MSMT   *measurement and quantification*: of possessions, time, direction, placement, weight, and speed, as well as numbers themselves.

MSTR   *masters and servants*, and their relationship.

MTRL   processed and unprocessed *inorganic materials*.

NATN   *nations*, the proper name of the nation, the people of the nation, the geographical location, and words that rezesent nations. Usually also coded HUGP and HUMN.

NEG   *negation*; included is the idea of lacking.

NLRT   *not being alert*, sleep, confusion; including humans, actions, and causes. Opposite of ALRT.

NSCR   *noscore* words. Included are all pronouns, directions (if does not fit in DIRC), interjections that are not emotions, words that serve Hebrew grammatical use but are not translatable, and any other words that cannot be put into any other category.

PEAC   *peace*, wellbeing, prosperity, and accompaning blessings—the Hebrew idea of *Shalom*. Opposite of DEST.

POVT   *poverty* and those who are in the state of poverty. Wealth is coded WLTH. Economic issues are coded ECON and may also be coded POVT or WLTH. Criminal activities involved in economics are coded CRIM. Opposite of WLTH.

PRID   *pride*, exaltation, beauty, and fame. Connotation may be positive or negative. Usually includes EXAL. References of shame or humility are coded SHAM. Opposite of SHAM.

PROC   *physical processes*, whether from humans, animals, or plants (e.g. drip, smelt). Thought processes are coded according to psychological categories.

PROP   that which is associated with *prophetic* activity. References to other spiritual Yahwistic entities are coded SPIR. References to Yahweh are coded GOD. References to non-Yahwistic entities are coded DVOT.

PUNI   *punishment* and judgment. References to destruction are coded DEST. PUNI often overlaps with ANGR, DEST, or LEGL. Opposite of REWD.

QNTY   *quantity* and number, including the lack of quantity and changing the quantity. Other conditions are coded COND.

QUES   independent *interrogatives*.

REAS   *reason* and decision. Knowledge is coded KNOW.

RELO   *relocation*, whether actions, humans, objects, or vehicles of relocation. Opposite of STAY.

REWD   *reward*. Opposite of PUNI.

RJCT   *rejection, rebellion*, resistance, and rejection of another's desires; includes persons with the attitude and the attitude itself. Opposite of KEEP.

SEEK   *seeking* and inquiry.

SEND   *sending* or causing something to be moved. References to moving on one's own accord are coded RELO.

SENS   *the senses* of sight, hearing, taste, smell, touch.

SEX   *sexual* behavior, including people and actions. References to prostitution include ETHB and TRAD. (While the category could include ETHG sex, the examples in the passages are all ETHB.)

SHAM   *shame* and humility. Opposite of PRID. Usually includes DBAS. As an action it refers to shaming.

SORR   *sorrow*, lamentation, and bitterness, including actions and expressions. An opposite of JOY.

SPIR   *spiritual* Yahwistic non-humans and miracles. Angels include ANGL. References to prophets PROP. References to Yahweh are coded GOD. References to non-Yahwistic entities are coded DVOT.

STAY   to *stay, the cessation of action*, remaining still, or those who stay. References to lack are coded NEG. Opposite of RELO.

STRO   *strength*, including some terms for God, angels, humans, and fortifications. Opposite of WEAK.

TIME   *time*. Included are duration, special times (e.g. feasts), and points in time.

TOOL   *tools* of various sorts used by humans. Types of tools can often be determined by consulting institutional categories (e.g. weapons are MILI TOOL). Furniture is coded FURN.

TRAD   *trades and professions* which do not fit into another category.

TRAN   *transportation*, including feet, vehicles, roads, and animals.

UNCV   *uncovering, opening, and revealing*. References to hiding are coded FLEE.

VEGP   *food processed from plants*. Unprocessed food from plants is coded VEGT.

VEGT *plants*, their parts, and their produce. Processed food from plants is coded VEGP.

VHIC *vehicles*, non-living modes of transportation.

WEAK *weakness* and difficulty. Opposite of STRO.

WEAR *wearing clothing* and that which is worn. See also CLTH.

WILD *wild animals and insects*. Usually includes ANMW or INSC. References to domesticated animals are coded ANHS and ANMD.

WLTH *wealth* and possessions, gained legally or otherwise. References to poverty are coded POVT. Economic issues are coded ECON. Criminal activities involved in economics are coded CRIM. Opposite of POVT.

e. *Suggested Additional Categories for Expanded Studies*

I have experimented with applying the category system to other texts in the English Bible. These tests have shown that additional categories will be necessary when the study is expanded to include other biblical literature. Here are some categories which should be added in the future but are not used in the present study:

CLEN References to *clean, pure* (physically or ritually).

CONF *confidence.*

DIRT *dirty, unclean, impure* (physically or ritually).

EDUC *education* (teach, learn).

FOOL *folly.*

MUSC *music*, including singing, songs, and instruments.

NAME proper *names* of people, peoples, and places.

SCRI *Scripture*, the Bible.

WEPN *weapons.*

WISE *wisdom.*

WRIT *writing*, writing materials, writers.

WRSH *worship.*

4. *Other Field Descriptions*

a. *Actor/Action/Complement* (AAC)

The purpose of this field is to determine agents and recipients of actions (e.g. human to human, human to God, God to human). The actors and complements (recipients) may be stated or implied, and are coded according to the main category system (but not according to metacategories). Practical subjects and objects are the issue, rather than grammatical ones. An intransitive subject is stated as an ACTOR, and a passive subject is stated as a COMPLEMENT. As noted in the introduction, the expression 'the boy was chased by the dog' would be considered as DOG/CHASE/BOY. 'The boy ran' would be BOY/RAN/, without a complement. 'The boy was chased' would be /CHASE/BOY, without an actor (unless one could be determined from the context).

In general a complement is a direct or indirect object. In other words, while most instances would indicate the recipient of an action, the complement could also be a location where one goes. Further, secondary complements are combined with primary complements in the filtration process for this study.

These relationships are stated by coding action (mainly verbs) in ways derived from Osgood's actor/action/complement system (see above, Chapter 1, 'Categories', and Chapter 4, 'The Category System Illustrated').[6] The actual coding is performed on the action. Often a verbal idea is expressed by a verb like 'to be' or 'to do' plus a noun or adjective. In these cases, the modified word is usually categorized as if it were a verb, and the verb is not categorized. For instance, 'will be' from the phrase 'This will be the plague with which Yahweh will strike the nations...' (Zech. 14.18) is not coded. Rather, 'the plague' is coded, with Yahweh being the actor and the nations being the complement. In practical AAC terms it is YAHWEH/PLAGUE/NATIONS.[7] Actions are also often stated using non-verbs without an accompanying verb. The substantive 'stealing' in Hos. 4.2 implies that Israelites steal from Israelites.

---

6. C. Osgood, 'The Representational Model and Relevant Research Methods', in I. Pool (ed.), *Trends in Content Analysis* (Urbana: University of Illinois Press, 1959), pp. 45-47.

7. The actual coding is *ACTOR*: GOD; *ACTION*: DEST ILL Evaluation -3; *COMPLEMENT*: NATN HUMN HUGP FRGN.

The actual grammatical breakdown of *activity* for all six texts combined is as follows:

Part of Speech	Frequency	% of Total Actions
Verbs	986	63
Substantives	358	23
Verbal instructions	148	9
Adjectives	33	2
Prepositions	24	2
Proper names	5	0.3
Prepositional pronoun	3	0.2
Particles	3	0.2
Interjections	2	0.1

b. *Part of Speech*

The orientation of this classification is grammatical. There are multiple purposes for this classification: (1) it is a connection with traditional biblical studies and linguistics; (2) it is an indicator of style and certain types of emphases;[8] and (3) it serves to clarify other classifications.

Since technical grammatical classifications do not always reflect the sense of the word in question (and the present study is interested in the sense of the word), words are categorized by their semantic function, and not necessarily their technical grammatical classification. In particular, participles and adjectives used as substantives are categorized as substantives; other participles are classed as verbs; and words which are verbal instructions (i.e. imperatives, jussives, cohortatives, some imperfects, negated imperfects) are categorized as imperatives (or verbal instructions).

Key to the database

AV	Adverb
AJ	Adjective
CJ	Conjunction
DA	Demonstrative adjective
DO	Direct object marker

8. E.g. imperatives vs. other verbs indicates a difference between a descriptive account and a prescriptive account. This was noted in my earlier study on Joel (see appendix, *My Previous Studies*).

IN	Interjection
PA	Prepositional pronoun
PN	Proper name
PP	Preposition
PR	Pronoun
PT	Particle
RP	Relative pronoun
SB	Nouns and other substantives
VB	Verb (non-instruction)
VI	Verbal instructions (roughly equals imperatives)

c. *Negation*
The negation of words makes them semantically different from their unmodified counterparts. The particle of negation is not flagged, but rather what it modifies is indicated.[9] It should be noted that a negative particle does not necessarily make what follows negated. This occurs mainly in Malachi (e.g. 'is it not evil?' equates to 'it is evil'). Similarly, words which are questioned are coded according to the expected answer (yes or no). Reversible categories, as well as evaluation, are reversed in the filtration process if a word is negated (see below, 'Reverse Negated Categories and Evaluation' in 'Application of the Method').

Key to the database
N   Negated

d. *Evaluation, Based on Osgood's Semantic Differential Scales*
The scale is as follows:

-3 to +3 - negative to positive; 0 is neutral.

e. *Hebrew Word*
Actual consonantal form of the Hebrew word, based on the Masoretic Text.[10]

f. *Hebrew Root*
Listing words in their lexical form is used to promote consistency and to help track the variety of uses of particular roots, for the inflected

9. Particles of negation are indicated with the main category system by 'NEG'.
10. Neither *Hebrew Word* nor *Hebrew Root* are shown in the above database sample.

form of a word relates to its grammatical use in a particular context, but not necessarily to the semantic value of that word in any context.

g. *English Translation*
A contextual root translation of each word into English clarifies the different uses of the Hebrew, indicates common meanings of different roots, and makes the study accessible to those with limited or no knowledge of Hebrew.

h. *Book, Chapter, and Verse Number*
Book and Masoretic Text chapter and verse numbers.

Key

HO	Hosea 4–8
IS	Isaiah 1.1=4.1
JL	Joel
ML	Malachi
NA	Nahum
ZC	Zechariah 12–14

Groups of texts

SPP   all prophets combined except Joel (HO IS ML NA ZC).

i. *Absolute Word Number*
Each word is assigned a four-digit number according to its position in the particular book in the Masoretic Text. The few combined words (e.g. `l kn 'therefore') are indicate by both numbers (e.g. 0587-0588).

Chapter 6

APPLICATION OF THE METHOD

The purpose of this chapter is twofold: (1) to describe the process of moving from the coded database to written analyses; and (2) to discuss the rationale behind much of the information which will be presented in the analyses.

There are many types of questions which could be answered with a database of this kind. These include:

1. Searching for particular types of words (e.g. what institutions are mentioned in Malachi?).

2. Examining the thematic characteristics of a passage (e.g. what are the dominant themes in Isaiah 1?).

3. Producing a list of actions or instructed actions (e.g. what are Israelites instructed to do in Joel 1–2?).

4. Comparing blocks of literature (e.g. is Nahum a more violent book than Joel?).

I have chosen to examine divine activity, comparing and contrasting it with various other actors, as well as comparing divine activity in the prophet Joel to that in other prophetic literature.

1. The Process of Producing an Analysis

As stated previously, the database has many different fields for different purposes. Some are used primarily for the tracking and extraction of data, while others are designed to describe the semantic function of words. As such, some fields find their way into the analysis, while others will not be seen in the analysis. The fields used to describe activity by God and other entities are the category system (groups, metacategories, and categories) and Evaluation. In addition, within the category system certain groups are emphasized (see below).

The following block diagram illustrates the process from start to finish, beginning with the coding of the texts and ending with written analyses:

Process Flowchart

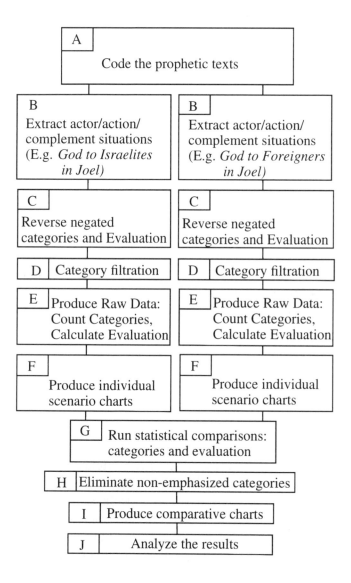

a. *Coding the Texts*
The coding of the texts is the first step in the process. Since this step has already been discussed in detail it will not be repeated here.

b. *Extract Actor/Action/Complement (AAC) Situations*
The next step is to extract all actions in a block of literature which describe a particular actor/action/complement situation. The block diagram describes two situations: *God to Israelites in Joel*, and *God to foreigners in Joel*.

c. *Reverse Negated Categories and Evaluation*
This information is then separated into positively and negatively stated actions. The negatively stated actions are put through a conversion process to make them positively stated (i.e. in a non-negated form). In particular, all Evaluation numbers are multiplied by minus 1, and reversible categories are reversed. This process is necessary to prevent an inaccurate picture of activity. For instance, 'there is no obedience' is the semantic (but not stylistic) equivalent of 'there is rebellion'. If not reversed, it would appear as though obedience existed.

There are a number of categories which have opposites. The following action categories are reversed if negated.[1]

Emotions	*Cognition*	*Processes*
JOY → SORR	ALRT → NLRT	HEAT → PROC
SORR → JOY	NLRT → ALRT	ASMB → FLEE
LOVE → HATE	IGNO → KNOW	UNCV → FLEE
HATE → LOVE	KNOW → IGNO	FLEE → ESTB
PRID → SHAM	KEEP → RJCT	STAY → RELO
SHAM → PRID	REAS → IGNO	RELO → STAY
ANGR → REWD		
DESR → HATE		

Ethics	*Status*	*Weal/Woe*
ETHB → ETHG	EXAL → DBAS	LIFE → DEAT
ETHG → ETHB	DBAS → EXAL	HEAL → ILL

---

1. There are a few opposites whose reversal might be questioned. For example, why do UNCV and ASMB become FLEE, yet FLEE becomes ESTB? This is due to the fact that, in practice, the semantics of some reversals do not go two ways. (So also with ANGR → REWD).

Ethics	Status	Weal/Woe
	WLTH → POVT	PEAC → DEST
	POVT → WLTH	REWD → PUNI
	STRO → WEAK	
	WEAK → STRO	DEAT → LIFE
		ILL → HEAL
		DEST → PEAC
		PUNI → REWD

The reversal of FEAR depends upon the book it is in:

FEAR → JOY   (Joel)
FEAR → RJCT   (Malachi)
FEAR → PEAC (Hos. 4–8; Isa. 1.1–4.1; Nahum; Zech. 12–14)

The metacategories WEAL and WOE, when negated, become WOE and WEAL.

d. *Category Filtration*

A few actor and recipient categories are conflated or filtered out. VEGP is subsumed under VEGT, and CITY and NATN are filtered out.[2] Further, primary and secondary recipients are combined.

The original coding of the database distinguished between non-instructed activity and instructions (i.e. grammatical and practical imperatives). These will be combined in most of the analyses which follow for a few reasons. First, an instructed action generally implies the expectation that an agent could carry out the instruction. Thus it appears as though an author who gives an instruction would consider the instruction a part of the realm of possible actions of any given agent. Since in this study it is the character of what the prophets indicate agents do or could do which is of interest, it means that there is not much practical benefit in distinguishing between the two types of actions. Secondly, in Joel, where the concentration of instructions is the highest, there is not much difference between instructed and non-instructed actions. Thirdly, God is not instructed to do much at all in the six prophetic passages being examined.[3] If the study focused on human actions or considered different literature (e.g. Psalms), then the distinction between non-instructed actions and instructions would be useful.

2.   HUGP (human group) remains for CITY and NATN actors and complements.
3.   Humans are instructed to do many actions in Joel. However, the emphasis of this study is divine activity, not human activity.

e. Produce Raw Data

The next step is the production of raw data. A statistics program counts the various aspects of the actions in terms of frequency and percentage of total actions:

1. Total number of actions.
2. Actors.
3. Actions (in terms of metacategories, categories and Evaluation).
4. Complements.
5. Parts of speech used.
6. The mean and standard deviation of Evaluation.[4]

f. Produce Individual Scenario Charts

This step is an organization of the data produced in the previous step. A variety of individual scenario[5] charts are produced, including a basic description of the frequencies and percentages of actions (in a couple of formats): ranked categories; dominant metacategories, categories, actors, and complements; and missing categories. These charts are mainly used as the basis for the various comparisons which are performed.

g. Run Statistical Comparisons: Categories and Evaluation

At this point two scenarios are juxtaposed. The question then becomes, to what degree are the scenarios different? Statistical comparisons are run for all action metacategories, categories, Evaluation, actors, and complements.[6]

Specifically, a statistics program is used to compare each metacategory, category, and Evaluation, and produce numbers indicating the significance levels for each comparison of two scenarios. If the significance level is small enough (smaller means significantly different) symbols are placed beside the metacategory or category to indicate the degree of difference. Asterisks (*) are used if the category for the one scenario is significantly high, while '§' occurs when a category in

4. Some unused fields are also counted: speaker (divine or human); outline section; potency; activity.

5. A *scenario* is one of the pairs of action relationships, e.g. God to Israelites in Joel.

6. As noted earlier, in practice this null hypothesis is not a statement of all actions together, but each type of action individually. However, the comparison of metacategories helps to determine if a set of categories is significantly different or not.

a scenario is significantly low. One asterisk (*) denotes a 0.05 level of significance (0.05 to 0.015). This means the odds are 1 in 20 that the difference between the actions is purely by chance. The 0.05 level is commonly suggested as a good starting point when considering significant differences. Two asterisks (**) denotes the 0.01 level of significance (0.014 and less), which means the odds are 1 in 100 that the difference is purely by chance. Earlier stages of the production of data use three and four asterisks (0.001 and 0.0001 respectively), but these are combined with the 0.01 level indicator for most of the analysis.

Statistical significance and practical significance are not necessarily the same thing. For instance, when purchasing an automobile, one dealer may be selling the vehicle for $10,000, ten dealers may sell the same car for $10,250, while another may sell it for $10,500. Statistics might not show a significant difference, but the wallet certainly does! So also, there may be instances in this study when a non-statistically significant difference occurs which may be practically significant or noteworthy. Of course, this will be noted. Statistics, though, provide a good pointer.

h. *Eliminate Non-Emphasized Action Categories*
There are many possible types of activities which could be analyzed according to the scheme of the category system. Of the 105 categories which have been applied to words, 72 can be used to denote activity.[7] However, I am not interested in all possible types of activity, but rather I am particularly interested in activity which illuminates the personalities of various actors. Some groups of action categories are emphasized and are listed individually in the charts. Nevertheless, all comparisons are based on total actions, not emphasized actions. Thus all treatments consider the percentage of *all* activity done by an agent, not the percentage of emphasized actions.

Of the five groups of possible action categories, the psychological and helpful/harmful seem to best indicate the personality of thinking beings. The idea that 'God walking and talking' could be used to describe God as an acting agent is obvious, but how these might illuminate God's personality, especially 'How nice is God?' or 'How does God think?' is questionable. The emphasized groups highlight thought processes and how they affect others, especially when combined with the Evaluation scale. These groups, hereafter called 'emphasized' groups, metacategories, and categories, are:

7.   This includes 5 action groups and 14 action metacategories.

1. States and processes, psychological;[8] and
2. States and processes with strong helpful/harmful connotations.[9]

Of the other five groups of categories, only three apply to activity, and little comment will be made in relation to them. These unused (or non-emphasized) activity groups are:

3. States and processes, physical and social;
4. Relationship to society and nature; and
5. Other.

The scope of the study, then, has been reduced to an examination of activity which illuminates the personalities of the various actors, especially God. This includes two emphasized action groups, six emphasized action metacategories, and 32 emphasized action categories.

	Total	Action	Emphasized
Group	7	5	2
Metacategories	23	14	6
Categories	105	72	32

i. *Produce Comparative Charts*
The final step before the actual analysis is the production of comparative charts. Many different kinds of charts are produced which are used to perform the analysis. Various charts include the actors, actions, complements, and Evaluation, with indicators of statistical significance. This information is presented in a number of formats, but only a few types of the aforementioned charts will be displayed in the study.

j. *Analyze the Results*
The purpose of the analyses is to illuminate the prophetic portrayal of God as an acting agent. This is accomplished mainly through the juxtaposition of divine activity with the activity of others, as well as comparisons of how God treats various people groups.

The analysis is a combination of restating the information and interpreting the practical significance of the results. Comparisons will generally include treatments of similarities and differences, making special

---

8. Metacategories EMOTIONS and COGNITION.
9. Metacategories ETHICS, STATUS, WEAL, and WOE.

note of activities which are more frequent (i.e. dominant[10] versus less-prominent[11]). It should be noted, however, that there is no positive significance test for similarity. The term 'similar' in this study should be understood to mean 'not significantly different.'

The discussion will also occasionally mention comparisons which are not part of the main thrust of the study.

2. *Other Particulars Concerning the Analyses and Accompanying Charts*

Because there are many overlaps, the following discussion relates to 'I' (*Produce Comparative Charts*) and 'J' (*Analyze the Results*) above, since the presentation of charts and the written analyses have many issues in common.

a. *Technical Terms*
The following technical terms are assumed in the analyses. The use of these terms will greatly simplify the writing of the comparisons.

High: Significantly high (0.05 or less) compared to the other situation. Indicated by * or **.

Low: Significantly low (0.05 or less) compared to the other situation. Indicated by § or §§.

More: significantly high. This refers to the relative density of the activity, not the actual frequency count.

Less: significantly low (relative density).

Dominant: high frequency, i.e. for metacategories, actors, and complements (recipients): 10 per cent +, and for categories: 5 per cent or greater (percentages less than 5 per cent, if rounded to 5 per cent, are not included).

Less-prominent: less frequent than 'dominant'.

Situation/scenario: One of the pairs of action relationships, for example God to Israelites in Joel.

Comparison: Two situations/scenarios statistically juxtaposed.

Recipient is equivalent to *complement*.

Polar/binary opposites: categories with an opposite (e.g. love/hate, alertness/non-alertness, peace/destruction).

---

10. Metacategories: $\geq 10\%$; Categories: $\geq 5\%$.
11. Metacategories: $<10\%$; Categories: $<5\%$.

Categories, unless otherwise indicated, refers to the 32 'emphasized' activity categories which are included in the following charts (of 72 possible action/activity categories).[12]

Action, *activity*, and sometimes *process* are, in this study, equivalent terms.

b. *The Presentation of Quantities*

The comparative question is not, 'How often do certain types of actions occur?' but rather, 'What is the relative density of certain types of actions for any particular comparison?' In other words, I am not asking, for example, how many times God, compared to humans, does a particular action in a body of literature. Rather, the question is: how much of God's activity is devoted to any particular kind of action in comparison with how much other entities devote to the same action? Comparisons in charts therefore will include percentages and not just frequency counts. It must be emphasized, though, that *all statistical operations are based on real numbers (quantities), not percentages*. Stating percentages provides a better illustration than the raw numbers do when two scenarios are juxtaposed.

For instance, if the only information provided was that God does 93 actions of destruction in the Selected Prophetic Passages while human actors do 86 actions of destruction, it would appear that God is just slightly more destructive than humans are. However, if actions are stated in terms of percentages of the total amount of actions of any given actor, the picture changes: 25 per cent of God's actions are destructive in nature, while only 12 per cent of human activity is destructive. God appears considerably more destructive than humans when presented this way. A problem remains, though: is God significantly more destructive? This is where statistics are helpful. The odds that this difference is purely by chance are less than 1 in 100,000 (0.00000). As noted above, this would be indicated by double asterisks (**). Since a level of 0.05 or less is considered significant, the difference is shown to be significant.

In sum, the listing of percentages with significance indicators gives a clearer picture of the relative density of actions than listing frequency counts. The percentages illustrate the difference, and the statistics confirm the difference.

12. This does not include actors or recipients, who often are designated by other types of categories.

c. *Dominant Activity and the Ranking of Actions*
It is a general assumption by most content analysts that what occurs more frequently is more important. To this point it has been demonstrated that statistics can give an indication as to how different two scenarios are for any particular metacategory, category, or Evaluation. However, an important practical element is missing. If both actors do an activity the same, is it a frequent or infrequent activity? For this reason the actions for each scenario are ranked and more attention is paid to the higher frequency actions.

The type of similarity between any two entities includes the relative proportion of particular elements, not just that they have similar elements, regardless of the proportion. This is true whether one is speaking of physics or behavior.

Let us consider two comparisons, treating them *as if* statistical analyses had been performed. First they will be shown without reference to relative emphasis:

1. Mother Theresa and Ghandi are similar in their emphases on DESTRUCTION and PEACE.
2. Saddam Hussain and Adolph Hitler are similar in their emphases on DESTRUCTION and PEACE.

It is unclear at this point whether either category is indicative of major aspects of their lives. The illustration can be clarified by showing the relative importance of these themes:

3. Mother Theresa and Ghandi both emphasize PEACE.
4. Saddam Hussain and Adolph Hitler emphasize DESTRUCTION.

In the present study, the fact that God and foreigners in all prophetic passages combined do similar amounts of PEACE/SHALOM and DESTRUCTION activities is valuable information. However, without additional information it would not be known how important these activities are.

The juxtaposition of dominant categories (either in paragraph form or chart form) gives a picture of the similarities or differences of the *main* kinds of actions, actors, and recipients. Attention to dominant categories indicates that, for the above example, God and foreigners are both quite destructive, while neither emphasize PEACE/SHALOM.[13]

In sum, the dominant actions by an actor give insight into that actor and provide a clearer picture of the said actor's personality, especially when compared to other actors. Dominance and significant differences are both important.

d. *The Use of Metacategories*

The listing of metacategories can often help to show overall trends, both in terms of similarities and differences. Laffal mentions a similar value in grouping some categories in analyses into metacategories. Metacategories make some conceptual emphases clear which might be missed by looking only at categories, especially when examining smaller bodies of literature.[14] This can be useful in a few circumstances.

The cumulative effect of grouping categories into metacategories can show trends which are not evident by looking at the categories individually. Thus one situation could have high overall EMOTIONS, while no particular emotion is significantly high. Secondly, two situations may have similar amounts of a particular metacategory, but the particular categories are quite different. Situation A and B might have a similar overall emphasis on emotions, but one might emphasize LOVE and SORROW, while the other emphasizes HATE and JOY. In other words, metacategories can provide a view of overall trends which individual categories cannot.

e. *Comparative Evaluations*

Significance can also be determined for comparative Evaluations. This helps to determine the relative 'niceness' of two scenarios.

f. *Action Categories with Positive or Negative Connotations*

There are categories which have inherently positive or negative connotations. The following is a list of all positive/negative categories (all except FLEE are among the 'emphasized' activity categories):

13. Statistical significance indicators are also put beside the metacategories and categories on the dominant list (if they apply) for quick reference. It is possible that although two scenarios could have the same metacategory or category in their respective dominant lists, there could be significant differences. Such is the case when comparing divine and human activity in the Selected Prophetic Passages (SPP). WOE is on the dominant list for both, but God does significantly more.

14. J. Laffal, *A Concept Dictionary of English with Computer Programs for Content Analysis* (Essex: Gallery Press, 1990), pp. 31, 33-47.

1. *Positive*: JOY LOVE ALRT KNOW KEEP REAS ETHG WLTH STRO HEAL LIFE PEAC REWD.

2. *Negative*: SORR HATE SHAM ANGR FEAR NLRT IGNO RJCT FLEE ETHB DBAS POVT WEAK ILL DEAT DEST PUNI CRIM.

3. *Ambiguous*: PRID DESR EXAL.

4. All other action categories are basically *neutral*.

g. *Opposite Categories*

The study occasionally considers opposite high categories. This helps to illustrate extreme contrasts between two situations (see above, 'Reversed Negated Categories and Evaluation' for a list). This also can show the wide range of activity an entity is capable of. There are two possible ways opposites can occur. First, one situation may have a high category, while the other situation has the opposite category as a high one. For instance, situation A might have significantly more LOVE, while situation B might have significantly more HATE. This shows that, at least when it comes to love/hate, the two situations are at opposite ends of the spectrum. Secondly, one situation may have both opposites high in comparison to the other. For instance, God may do more LOVE *and* HATE than humans do. This would indicate a type of emotionality lacking for humans. In both instances noting opposites can help illustrate contrasts between two situations.

Part II

THE ANALYSIS

Chapter 7

SELECTED PROPHETIC PASSAGES (SPP)

The 'Selected Prophetic Passages' (SPP) were chosen to provide a sample of prophetic materials, which could then be grouped together and serve as a standard against which to measure Joel. They include: Isaiah 1.1–4.1; Hosea 4–8; Nahum; Malachi; and Zechariah 12–14. These are five reasonably compact bodies of prophecy that are approximately equal in length. Since they were not chosen in a strictly random fashion from a larger body of prophetic materials, they cannot be seen to represent the whole prophetic corpus of the Hebrew Bible. However, these texts can serve as a beginning point for the description of other prophetic materials, as well as provide a control.

1. *General Description of Activity in SPP*

This section will present some background material for the SPP comparisons. Charts in this section will present frequency counts, but will not include statistical tests; statistical tests will occur in the comparison sections.

Frequencies of Parts of Speech
Designating Activity in SPP

Total actions in SPP: 1278
Parts of speech used to indicate activity (ranked)

	Qty	%
Verbs	820	64
Substantives	315	25
Verbal instructions	85	7
Prepositions	23	2
Adjectives	22	2
Proper names	5	0.4
Prepositional pronoun	3	0.2
Particles	3	0.2
Interjections	2	0.2

Activity in the prophets is indicated by many parts of speech, although primarily by verbs. Unlike what happens in the book of Joel, there are few imperatives (verbal instructions) in SPP.[1]

Actor/Complement Totals[2]

	God		Humans		Israel		Foreign	
	Qty	%	Qty	%	Qty	%	Qty	%
Actions	366	29	734	57	561	44	166	13
Receptions	205	16	576	45	437	34	147	12

Actor/Number of Actions/Complement Totals

Complements/Recipients

	God		Humans		Israel		Foreign	
Actors	Qty	%	Qty	%	Qty	%	Qty	%
God			257	20	204	16	59	5[3]
Humans	188	15	229	18	167	13	63	5
Israelites	172	13	150	12	134	10	25	2
Foreigners	15	1	74	6	46	4	43	3

God is no minor actor in SPP; divine activity accounts for 29 percent of all activity in SPP. God does about half as many actions as humans in general, and about twice as many actions as foreigners. God receives a lower ratio of actions compared to humans in general and Israelites in particular, but more than foreigners do. God receives only a little more than half as much activity as God delivers.[4]

Humans receive three quarters of all divine activity, with Israelites receiving three and a half times as much divine activity as foreigners do. God receives a quarter of all human activity, and humans one third. Israelites direct about a third of their activity to God, while foreigners direct less than one tenth of their activity toward God.[5] Few Israelite

1. 22 per cent of all activity in Joel is instructed activity.

2. Numbers in the chart cannot necessarily be added together, for in a number of instances there are either multiple actors or multiple complements.

3. God does significantly more actions to Israelites than to foreigners in SPP (Significance 0.00000).**

4. All major actors do more than they receive. One reason is the fact that there are more intransitives (208) than passives (74).

5. This is understandable in light of the emphasis of most biblical prophets. The

actions are aimed at foreigners, while over half of foreigners' actions are aimed toward Israelites.

Comparative Frequencies of Activities by the Major Actors in SPP

	God		Humans		Israelite		Foreigner	
Total activity	366		734		561		166	
Action/activity	Qty	%	Qty	%	Qty	%	Qty	%
Emotions	49	13	85	12	66	12	19	11
Joy	1	0.3	9	1	7	1	2	1
Sorrow	5	1	23	3	18	3	5	3
Love	5	1	5	0.7	4	0.7	0	0
Hate	18	5	9	1	6	1	3	2
Pride	1	0.3	5	0.7	4	0.7	0	0
Shaming	16	4	14	2	12	2	2	1
Anger	6	2	2	0.3	2	0.4	0	0
Desire	2	0.6	4	0.5	4	0.7	0	0
Fear	0	0	18	2	11	2	9	5
Cognition	34	9	122	17	105	19	13	8
Alertness	2	0.6	4	0.5	3	0.5	1	0.6
Non-Alertness	3	0.8	20	3	13	2	6	4
Knowledge	6	2	12	2	11	2	1	0.6
Ignorance	5	1	20	3	19	3	2	1
Obey/Agree	3	0.8	22	3	18	3	2	1
Rejection	9	2	40	5	38	7	1	0.6
Reason	10	3	14	2	11	2	2	1
Ethics	18	5	195	27	179	32	13	8
Ethically Good	12	3	44	6	41	7	2	1
Ethically Bad	6	2	151	21	138	25	11	7
Status	26	7	59	8	38	7	19	11
Exaltation	2	0.6	7	1	4	0.7	2	1
Debasement	17	5	14	2	12	2	2	1
Wealth	0	0	10	1	6	1	5	3
Poverty	1	0.3	1	0.1	1	0.2	0	0
Strength	4	1	8	1	4	0.7	4	2
Weakness	3	0.8	19	3	11	2	6	4
Weal	22	6	19	3	12	2	8	5
Healing	4	1	0	0	0	0	0	0
Life	3	0.8	3	0.4	1	0.2	2	1

tendency is to describe God's relationship with Israelites, not foreigners. On the other hand, here is a demonstration of this tendency.

Peace/Shalom	11	3	14	2	8	1	7	4
Reward	6	2	3	0.4	3	0.5	0	0
Woe	127	35	111	15	62	11	47	28
Illness/Injury	21	6	11	2	6	1	4	2
Death	2	0.6	15	2	10	2	5	3
Destruction	93	25	86	12	54	10	31	19
Punishment	54	15	19	3	9	2	10	6

Note: Percentages describe the percentage of an actor's total activity, not the percentage of activity in SPP. See individual comparisons for significant differences.

The two most common actions for God are destruction and punishment. Bad ethics and destruction are the two most prevalent actions for humans in general and Israelites in particular. The activity of foreigners is similar, except that the order is inverted: destruction and bad ethics.

Comparative Frequencies of Activities Directed
Toward the Major Complements (Recipients) in SPP

	God		Humans		Israelite		Foreigner	
Total words	205		576		437		147	
Action/activity	Qty	%	Qty	%	Qty	%	Qty	%
Emotions	30	15	67	12	47	11	18	12
Joy	1	0.5	6	1	5	1	1	0.7
Sorrow	7	3	7	1	6	1	1	0.7
Love	0	0	6	1	5	1	0	0
Hate	3	1	19	35	13	3	6	4
Pride	3	1	4	0.7	3	0.7	0	0
Shaming	2	1	22	4	16	4	8	5
Anger	0	0	6	1	2	0.5	2	1
Desire	1	0.5	2	0.4	2	0.5	0	0
Fear	13	6	0	0	0	0	0	0
Cognition	59	29	49	9	40	9	8	5
Alertness	2	1	3	0.5	2	0.5	1	0.7
Non-alertness	1	0.5	7	1	4	0.9	3	2
Knowledge	4	2	6	1	4	0.9	1	0.7
Ignorance	6	3	8	1	7	2	1	0.7
Obey/agree	11	5	6	1	4	0.9	0	0
Rejection	29	14	11	2	11	3	0	0
Reason	9	4	12	2	11	3	3	2
Ethics	73	36	74	13	70	16	9	6
Ethically good	21	10	25	4	24	5	2	1
Ethically bad	52	25	49	9	46	11	7	5

	God		Humans		Israelite		Foreigner	
Total words	205		576		437		147	
Action/activity	Qty	%	Qty	%	Qty	%	Qty	%
Status	13	6	47	8	33	8	16	11
Exaltation	6	3	4	0.7	3	0.7	0	0
Debasement	2	1	23	4	17	4	8	5
Wealth	0	0	7	1	4	0.9	4	3
Poverty	0	0	1	0.2	1	0.2	0	0
Strength	0	0	5	0.9	3	0.7	2	1
Weakness	5	2	8	1	6	1	2	1
Weal	4	2	37	6	34	8	5	3
Healing	0	0	4	0.7	4	0.9	0	0
Life	1	0.5	5	0.9	4	0.9	1	0.7
Peace/shalom	2	1	24	4	22	5	4	3
Reward	1	0.5	8	1	8	2	0	0
Woe	12	6	221	38	148	34	71	48
Illness/injury	1	0.5	44	8	27	6	17	12
Death	1	0.5	18	3	13	35	6	4
Destruction	10	5	170	30	116	27	54	37
Punishment	1	0.5	61	11	39	9	18	12

Note: Percentages describe the percentage of a recipient's total reception of activity, not the percentage of activity in SPP. See individual comparisons for significant differences.

Bad ethics is a common theme among activities received by the major complements. However, the order varies. The top two types of activity God encounters are bad ethics[6] and rejection. The top activity received by all types of humans is destruction. The second-ranked activity received by humans in general and Israelites in particular is bad ethics. Punishment supplants bad ethics as the second-ranked action encountered by foreigners. Note that neither God nor foreigners are given any love at all. (See analyses which follow for statistical comparisons.)

Evaluation of Activity (Ranked)

Evaluation	Qty	%		
-2	342	27	Mean	-0.69
-3	260	20	Std. Dev.	1.90
+1	212	17	Minimum	- 3.0

6.   God receives significantly more bad ethics** than good ethics (significance 0.00005).

+2	192	15	Maximum	3.0
-1	120	9		
0	101	8		
+3	38	3		
Noscore	13	1		

The top two Evaluations, both negative, account for almost half of all activity. Negative Evaluations account for 56 percent of all activity; neutral (or noscore) make up 9 percent; while only one third (35 percent) of all activity is evaluated positively. This is one indicator of a decidedly negative tone in these prophetic materials.

Metacategories and Categories: All Actions

Action/activity	Qty	%
Emotions	145	11
Joy	10	0.8
Sorrow	30	2
Love	10	0.8
Hate	28	2
Pride	9	0.7
Shaming	34	3
Anger	8	0.6
Desire	7	0.6
Fear	18	1
Cognition	167	13
Alertness	8	0.6
Non-alertness	27	2
Knowledge	20	2
Ignorance	26	2
Obey/agree	25	2
Rejection	50	4
Reason	25	2
Ethics	224	18
Ethically good	60	5
Ethically bad	164	13
Status	100	8
Exaltation	13	1
Debasement	35	3
Wealth	12	0.9
Poverty	2	0.2
Strength	12	0.9
Weakness	28	2

Action/activity	Qty	%
Weal	46	4
Healing	4	0.3
Life	6	0.5
Peace/shalom	30	2
Reward	10	0.8
Woe	306	24
Illness/injury	51	4
Death	22	2
Destruction	241	19
Punishment	76	6

The most common emotions are shaming, sorrow, and hate (all negative). Cognitive actions are fairly evenly distributed, but rejection tops the list. Bad ethics occurs two and a half times as often as activity rated ethically good. The top status activities are negatives: debasement and weakness. The highest-ranked weal action, peace/shalom, accounts for only 2 percent of all activity. The main woe action is destruction, which is about a fifth of all activity.

Ranked Activity[7]

Metacategories

Action/Activity	Qty	%
Woe	306	24
Ethics	224	18
Cognition	167	13
Emotions	145	11
Status	100	8
Weal	46	4

Ranked Categories			Ranked Categories		
Action/Activity	Qty	%	Action/Activity	Qty	%
Destruction	241	19	Death	22	2
Ethically bad	164	13	Knowledge	20	2
Punishment	76	6	Fear	18	1

7.   Since not all categories are mutually exclusive, totals cannot necessarily be obtained by adding metacategories or categories together. It must also be remembered that this study emphasizes 32 types of actions, rather than considering all possible activity (e.g. communication, movement).

Ethically good	60	5	Exaltation	13	1
Illness/injury	51	4	Wealth	12	0.9
Rejection	50	4	Strength	12	0.9
Debasement	35	3	Reward	10	0.8
Shaming	34	3	Joy	10	0.8
Peace/shalom	30	2	Love	10	0.8
Sorrow	30	2	Pride	9	0.7
Weakness	28	2	Anger	8	0.6
Hate	28	2	Alertness	8	0.6
Non-alertness	27	2	Desire	7	0.6
Ignorance	26	2	Life	6	0.5
Obey/agree	25	2	Healing	4	0.3
Reason	25	2	Poverty	2	0.2

Of the top ten types of activity, eight are negative in character, with destructive and ethically bad actions topping the list. Only one positive activity, good ethics, occurs more than 2 percent of the time. These factors further emphasize the negative character of SPP.

2. *Divine versus Human Activity*

Null hypothesis: What GOD does to ALL in SPP is the same as what HUMANS do to ALL in SPP.

Dominant Metacategories, Categories, Actors, Complements
Significance: *= 0.05 **= 0.01 § and §§ = sig. low

	GOD to ALL in SPP		HUMANS to ALL in SPP	
		%		%
Action	Woe	35**	Ethics	27**
Metacategories	Emotions	13	Cognition	17**
10%+			Woe	15§§
			Emotions	12
Action	Destruction	25**	Bad Ethics	21**
Categories	Punishment	15**	Destruction	12§§
5%+	Illness/Injury	6**	Good Ethics	6*
			Rejection	5*
Actors 10%+	God		Humans	
Complements	Humans	73**	Humans	31§§
Recipients	Israel	60**	God	26**
	Human Groups	49**	Israel	25§§
10%+	Foreign	19**	Human Groups	17§§
	Cultic	16*	Cultic	11§

Evaluation

Difference:	-0.13
Significant?	No

Both Evaluations are NEGATIVE

GOD to ALL in SPP		HUMANS to ALL in SPP

	GOD to ALL in SPP	HUMANS to ALL in SPP
Mean	-0.70	-0.57
Std.Dev.	2.01	1.83

GOD to ALL in SPP—HUMANS to ALL in SPP:
Comparative Frequencies
Significance: *= 0.05 **= 0.01 (§ and §§ = sig. low)

	GOD to ALL in SPP		HUMANS to ALL in SPP	
Total activity	366		734	
Action/activity	Qty	%	Qty	%
Emotions	49	13	85	12
Joy	1	0.3	9	1
Sorrow	5	1	23	3
Love	5	1	5	0.7
Hate	18	5**	9	1§§
Pride	1	0.3	5	0.7
Shaming	16	4*	14	2§
Anger	6	2*	2	0.3§
Desire	2	0.6	4	0.5
Fear	0	0§§	18	2**
Cognition	34	9§§	122	17**
Alertness	2	0.6	4	0.5
Non-alertness	3	0.8§	20	3*
Knowledge	6	2	12	2
Ignorance	5	1	20	3
Obey/agree	3	0.8§§	22	3**
Rejection	9	2§	40	5*
Reason	10	3	14	2
Ethics	18	5§§	195	27**
Ethically good	12	3§	44	6*
Ethically bad	6	2§§	151	21**
Status	26	7	59	8
Exaltation	2	0.6	7	1
Debasement	17	5**	14	2§§
Wealth	0	0§§	10	1**

Poverty	1	0.3	1	0.1
Strength	4	1	8	1
Weakness	*3*	*0.8§*	*19*	*3**
Weal	*22*	*6***	*19*	*3§§*
Healing	*4*	*1***	*0*	*0§§*
Life	3	0.8	3	0.4
Peace/shalom	11	3	14	2
Reward	*6*	*2**	*3*	*0.4§*
Woe	*127*	*35***	*111*	*15§§*
Illness/injury	*21*	*6***	*11*	*2§§*
Death	*2*	*0.6§*	*15*	*2**
Destruction	*93*	*25***	*86*	*12§§*
Punishment	*54*	*15***	*19*	*3§§*

In the Selected Prophetic Passages (Isa. 1.1–4.1; Hos. 4–8; Nahum; Malachi; and Zech. 12–14), there are some ways in which God is similar to humans, but more ways in which God is quite different.

Similarities (observable without statistical measurement) include the fact that both God and humans engage in almost all of the 32 possible emphasized actions/activities. They share a dominant[8] emphasis on emotionality and woe (and its category of destruction), and a lack of emphasis on status and weal activities. Both have humans as their top recipients, with Israelites receiving a higher percentage of actions than foreigners.

The following comparisons are measured statistically; in these, 'similar' will mean 'not statistically different.' Similarities between God and humans include Evaluation, with both being somewhat negative; neither God nor humans are very kind in their actions in SPP (God: -0.70; Humans: -0.57). The only dominant activity in which God and humans are similar is overall emotionality, a metacategory. They are also similar in one less-prominent[9] metacategory (status), and fourteen similar less-prominent categories of actions, which appear under all metacategories except ethics. God and humans have a similar lack of emphasis on positive emotions and on many other positive types of actions.

There are, however, quite a few differences between divine and human activity. Four of the six metacategories are significantly different (cognition, ethics, weal, and woe), and so are 18 of the 32

8.   'Dominant' equals 10% + for metacategories, and 5% + for categories.
9.   'Less prominent' or 'nondominant' means less than 10% for metacategories, and less than 5% for categories.

emphasized categories. Divine activity is shown to be higher in nine categories, while human activity is higher in nine other categories. This indicates that God and humans have their own strong characteristics and are not just shadowing one another. A look at dominant activities (those that are most strongly represented for each kind of actor) illustrates the differences well. All dominant metacategories (except overall emotionality) and all dominant categories are significantly different.

All of God's significantly high dominant activities are found in terms of actions which bring about effects—specifically, negative ones. God is more involved in causing destruction, punishment, and illness/injury. God's weal activity, while considerably less frequent than woe, is nevertheless higher than human weal activity. No individual weal categories which occur are dominant ones, but healing and reward are still more common for God than for humans. As far as emotionality is concerned, God is involved more in hate, shaming, and anger. In the realm of status God does significantly more debasing. God does fewer ethical actions of all types, and is involved in cognitive activity.

What makes humans different from God is highlighted by their volitional activities. Human beings are characterized by their dominant and greater involvement in ethics (bad and good) and in cognition. Bad ethical choices occur three and a half times as often as good ethical choices, which is significant.[10] High rejection and obedience also show choices which are binary opposites, and high non-alertness may also show choices of ignorance. Thus when it comes to choices, humans appear to make frequently those which involve poor value judgments.

Humans are also different from God in other ways. Humans show more fear (God does not fear at all!). Even though destructive actions are dominant ones for humans, they still engage in significantly less destruction than God does. Less-prominent human highs are non-alertness, weakness, obedience, fear, killing,[11] and involvement in wealth.

Divine and human activity is also focused differently. Most divine activity is directed toward humans, while only a third of human activity

10. Significance 0.00000 (very strong). This type of comparison within an actor only works when categories are mutually exclusive, e.g. good ethics versus bad ethics, weal versus woe; it does not work on non-exclusive categories, e.g. destruction and punishment.

11. While humans do not do much killing, they do significantly more than God.

is. A quarter of human activity is directed toward God, and a large portion of it is directed toward neither God nor humans, much of this portion being intransitive (with no complement; [18 percent]). Among human recipients, the relative density of Israelite and foreigners is about the same (God to Israelites: 82 percent of humans; humans to Israelites: 80 percent of humans; God to foreigners: 26 percent of humans; humans to foreigners: 29 percent of humans).

Another way to look at the comparison is this: God is slightly harsher than humans, although God's ways of being harsh differ from those of humans. God does more woe, hates, gets angry, shames, and debases more than humans. This is manifested in the realm of effective action as more destruction, punishment, and illness/injury—God acting where people can experience it. God also does more weal than humans, especially healing and reward. In contrast, ethics (bad and good) are primarily in the human domain. Humans are also involved in much destruction, but significantly less than God. In addition, they are involved in more rejection, weakness, non-alertness, and fear than God.

To sum up: God and humans engage in many of the same kinds of activities, although not with equal frequencies. One aspect shared is that they are similar in their amount of emotionality. Further, in SPP, both divine and human activity tends toward the unpleasant; however, the means of achieving this unpleasantness is quite different, so that God and humans do form a definite contrast.

Excursus: What Humans Receive in SPP

The lot for humans in SPP is not very pleasant. Over a third of the actions humans receive are woe, while only 6 percent are weal. The Evaluation for what humans receive is -0.98. Humans receive more illness/injury than healing, more death than life, more destruction than peace, more punishment than reward, more hate than love, more shame than pride, more rejection than agreement, more ethically bad actions than good, and more debasement than exaltation. The only contrast with a higher positive is wealth versus poverty (and both of these are infrequent).

3. Israelite versus Foreigner Activity

Null hypothesis: What ISRAELITES do to ALL in SPP is the same as what FOREIGNERS do to ALL in SPP.

Dominant Metacategories, Categories, Actors, Complements
Significance: *= 0.05 **= 0.01 § and §§ = sig. low

	GOD to ALL in SPP		HUMANS to ALL in SPP	
		%		%
Action	Ethics	32**	Woe	28**
Metacategories	Cognition	19**	Emotions	11
10%+	Emotions	12	Status	11
	Woe	11§§		
Action	Bad ethics	25**	Destruction	19**
Categories	Destruction	10§§	Bad Ethics	7§§
5%+	Good ethics	7**	Punishment	6**
	Rejection	7**	Fear	5*
Actors 10%+	Israelites		Foreigners	
Complements	God	31**	Humans	45**
Recipients	Humans	27§§	Human groups	36**
	Israel	24	Israel	28
10%+	Human groups	12§§	Foreign	26**
	Cultic	11	Military	12**
			Cultic	11

Evaluation

Difference:	+0.34
Significant?	Yes*
Both Evaluations are NEGATIVE	

	ISRAELITES to ALL in SPP	FOREIGNERS to ALL in SPP
Mean	-0.49	-0.83
Std. Dev.	1.81	1.91

ISRAELITES to ALL in SPP—FOREIGNERS to ALL in SPP:
Comparative Frequencies
Significance: *= 0.05 **= 0.01 (§ and §§ = sig. low)

	ISRAELITES to ALL in SPP		FOREIGNERS to ALL in SPP	
Total activity	561		166	
Action/activity	Qty	%	Qty	%
Emotions	66	12	19	11
Joy	7	1	2	1
Sorrow	18	3	5	3
Love	4	0.7	0	0
Hate	6	1	3	2

Pride	4	0.7	0	0
Shaming	12	2	2	1
Anger	2	0.4	0	0
Desire	4	0.7	0	0
Fear	11	2§	9	*5**
Cognition	*105*	*19***	13	*8§§*
Alertness	3	0.5	1	0.6
Non-alertness	13	2	6	4
Knowledge	11	2	1	0.6
Ignorance	19	3	2	1
Obey/agree	18	3	2	1
Rejection	*38*	*7***	1	*0.6§§*
Reason	11	2	2	1
Ethics	*179*	*32***	13	*8§§*
Ethically good	*41*	*7***	2	*1§§*
Ethically bad	*138*	*25***	11	*7§§*
Status	38	7	19	11
Exaltation	4	0.7	2	1
Debasement	12	2	2	1
Wealth	6	1	5	3
Poverty	1	0.2	0	0
Strength	4	0.7	4	2
Weakness	11	2	6	4
Weal	12	2	8	5
Healing	0	0	0	0
Life	1	0.2	2	1
Peace/shalom	8	1§	7	*4**
Reward	3	0.5	0	0
Woe	62	*11§§*	47	*28***
Illness/injury	6	1	4	2
Death	10	2	5	*3**
Destruction	*54*	*10§§*	*31*	*19***
Punishment	9	*2§§*	10	*6***

A comparison of Israelite and foreigner activity will provide aid for a comparison of divine activity with that of Israelites and foreigners.

Israelites and foreigners show only a few similarities. Emotionality and woe appear among the dominant metacategories for both; however, woe-actions are significantly higher for foreigners. While the Evaluation for both is negative, the mean Evaluation for foreigners is significantly harsher.

Israelites are characterized as doing more ethical actions of all types (however, more bad than good). They also engage in more cognitive activities; among these, rejection is a major theme. Israelites (who engage in three times as many actions as do foreigners) direct a far larger share of their actions toward God than foreigners do.

In contrast, foreigners (as reported in these prophecies) focus a large percentage of their actions on humans; that includes a relatively larger number directed toward foreigners.[12] Within woe, foreigners are high in destruction and punishment. They are also high in expressing fear. Surprisingly, foreigners do more peace/shalom, but as a nondominant activity. Foreigners are noticeably lacking in ethically-valued actions.

Thus Israelite activities are characteristically related to value judgments, while foreigners are portrayed as those operating in the physical realm, mainly as envoys of woe (and sometimes of weal).

4. *Divine versus Israelite Activity*

Null hypothesis: What GOD does to ALL in SPP is the same as what ISRAELITES do to ALL in SPP.

Dominant Metacategories, Categories, Actors, Complements
Significance: *= 0.05 **= 0.01 § and §§ = sig. low

	GOD to ALL in SPP		ISRAELITES to ALL in SPP	
		%		%
Action	Woe	35**	Ethics	32**
Metacategories	Emotions	13	Cognition	19**
10%+			Emotions	12
			Woe	11§§
Action	Destruction	25**	Bad ethics	25**
Categories	Punishment	15**	Destruction	10§§
5%+	Illness/Injury	6**	Good ethics	7**
			Rejection	7**
Actors 10%+	God		Israelites	
Complements	Humans	73**	God	31**
Recipients	Israel	60**	Humans	27§§
	Human groups	49**	Israel	24§§
10%+	Foreign	19**	Human groups	12§§
	Cultic	16	Cultic	11

12. Israelites do about the same percentage toward Israelites as foreigners do toward foreigners.

Evaluation

Difference: - 0.21
Significant?   No
Both Evaluations are NEGATIVE

	GOD to ALL in SPP	ISRAELITES to ALL in SPP
Mean	-0.70	-0.49
Std.Dev.	2.01	1.81

GOD to ALL in SPP—ISRAELITES to ALL in SPP:
Comparative Frequencies
Significance: *=0.05 **=0.01 (§ and §§ = sig. low)

	GOD to ALL in SPP		ISRAELITES to ALL in SPP	
Total Activity	366		561	
Action/Activity	Qty	%	Qty	%
Emotions	49	13	66	12
Joy	1	0.3	7	1
Sorrow	5	1	18	3
Love	5	1	4	0.7
Hate	*18*	*5***	6	*1§§*
Pride	1	0.3	4	0.7
Shaming	16	4	12	2
Anger	*6*	*2**	2	*0.4§*
Desire	2	0.6	4	0.7
Fear	0	*0§§*	*11*	*2***
Cognition	34	*9§§*	105	*19***
Alertness	2	0.6	3	0.5
Non-alertness	3	0.8	13	2
Knowledge	6	2	11	2
Ignorance	*5*	*1§*	*19*	*3**
Obey/agree	*3*	*0.8§§*	*18*	*3***
Rejection	*9*	*2§§*	*38*	*7***
Reason	10	3	11	2
Ethics	18	*5§§*	179	*32***
Ethically good	*12*	*3§§*	*41*	*7***
Ethically bad	*6*	*2§§*	*138*	*25***
Status	26	7	38	7
Exaltation	2	0.6	4	0.7
Debasement	*17*	*5**	12	*2§*
Wealth	0	*0§§*	*6*	*1***
Poverty	1	0.3	1	0.2

GOD to ALL in SPP—ISRAELITES to ALL in SPP:
Comparative Frequencies
Significance: *=0.05 **=0.01 (§ and §§ = sig. low)

	GOD to ALL in SPP		ISRAELITES to ALL in SPP	
Strength	4	1	4	0.7
Weakness	3	0.8	11	2
Weal	22	6**	12	2§§
Healing	*4*	*1***	*0*	*0§§*
Life	3	0.8	1	0.2
Peace/shalom	11	3	8	1
Reward	6	2	3	0.5
Woe	*127*	*35***	*62*	*11§§*
Illness/injury	*21*	*6***	*6*	*1§§*
Death	2	0.6	10	2
Destruction	*93*	*25***	*54*	*10§§*
Punishment	*54*	*15***	*9*	*2§§*

God and Israelites both do many actions in the non-Joel prophetic passages chosen, although Israelites do half again as many (God: 366; Israelites: 561). There are major differences among the recipients of divine and Israelite actions. Recipients of divine actions are concentrated among humans, especially Israelites.[13] The main recipients of Israelite actions are roughly equally divided between God and humans.

However, divine activity has a number of similarities with Israelite activity, as it does with human activity in general. God and Israelites both do a wide variety of actions, and they engage in almost all the same types of actions, although not necessarily with the same relative frequency. God and Israelites have similar amounts of emotion and status-related activity. Emotionality, woe, and destruction are dominant for both (although God does significantly more woe and destruction than do Israelites). Both emphasize negative actions; most dominant actions are negatives, except good ethics for Israelites. There is no significant Evaluation difference for God and Israelites, with both Evaluations being mildly negative. In addition, eighteen less-prominent types of actions are not significantly different.

The differences, though, are pointed. God does more woe, especially destruction, punishment, and illness/injury. These actions are not only dominant but significantly high in comparison to Israelite

13. God is not normally a recipient of God's activity (although it does happen once).

activity. God also does more weal than Israelites do, although to a much lesser degree than woe.[14] Less-prominent divine actions which are still high compared to Israelites include debasement,[15] anger, and healing. Unlike Israelites, though, God does not fear and is not involved in wealth-related actions. God also does significantly fewer overtly ethical actions, either good and bad. To sum up: God's highs are all negatives (except weal and its category of healing), and involve altering the state of recipients, their position, and/or having a negative emotional reaction to them.

Unlike divine actions, Israelite dominant actions are highlighted by ethical ones, particularly those ethically bad. Cognitive activity is also prominent and high, including the specific category of rejection. Frequently occurring Israelite actions (other than destruction) thus emphasize volition: bad ethics, good ethics, and rejection. Less-prominent activities by Israelites that are high compared to God's involvement in them are ignorance, fear, obedience, and concern for wealth.[16] Healing, not done at all by Israelites, is a divine trait. Thus, categories in which Israel is high as compared with God involve (besides fear) value-oriented choices: rejection, obedience, good and bad ethics, and possibly wealth.

In sum, the character of the greater part of divine and Israelite activity is different. The main similarities are that both are definitely emotional and more negative than positive. The categorical analysis illustrates that the means of exercising negativity are rather different. God's high negatives emphasize woe categories and antagonistic emotions, while Israelite high negatives emphasize bad ethics and cognitive categories, especially rejection.

5. Divine versus Foreigner Activity

Null hypothesis: What GOD does to ALL in SPP is the same as what FOREIGNERS do to ALL in SPP.

---

14. The only polar opposite that God does significantly more of both is also in the physical realm of weal and woe: healing and illness/injury.

15. Debasement, though listed as 5%, is not a top category. This is because top categories are those actually 5% +, not those rounded to 5%.

16. Israelites do two kinds of polar opposites: high good and bad ethics and keep (obedience)/reject actions.

Dominant Metacategories, Categories, Actors, Complements
Significance: *= 0.05 **= 0.01 § and §§ = sig. low

		GOD to ALL in SPP		FOREIGNERS to ALL in SPP	
		%			%
Action	Woe	35		Woe	28
Metacategories	Emotions	13		Emotions	11
10%+				Status	11
Action	Destruction	25		Destruction	19
Categories	Punishment	15**		Bad ethics	7**
5%+	Illness/Injury	6		Punishment	6§§
				Fear	5**
Actors 10%+	God			Foreigners	
Complements	Humans	73**		Humans	45§§
Recipients	Israel	60**		Human groups	36§§
	Human groups	49**		Israel	28§§
10%+	Foreign	19		Foreign	26
	Cultic	16		Military	12**
				Cultic	11

Evaluation

Difference:	= 0.13
Significant?	No
Both Evaluations are NEGATIVE	

	GOD to ALL in SPP	Foreigners to ALL in SPP
Mean	-0.70	-0.83
Std. Dev.	2.01	1.91

GOD to ALL in SPP—FOREIGNERS to ALL in SPP:
Comparative Frequencies
Significance: *= 0.05 **= 0.01 (§ and §§ = sig. low)

	GOD to ALL in SPP		FOREIGNERS to ALL in SPP	
Total activity	366		166	
Action/activity	Qty	%	Qty	%
Emotions	49	13	19	11
Joy	1	0.3	2	1
Sorrow	5	1	5	3
Love	5	1	0	0
Hate	18	5	3	2

Pride	1	0.3	0	0
Shaming	*16*	*4**	2	*1§*
Anger	6	*2**	0	*0§*
Desire	2	0.6	0	0
Fear	0	*0§§*	*9*	*5***
Cognition	34	9	13	8
Alertness	2	0.6	1	0.6
Non-alertness	3	*0.8§*	*6*	*4**
Knowledge	6	2	1	0.6
Ignorance	5	1	2	1
Obey/agree	3	0.8	2	1
Rejection	9	2	1	0.6
Reason	10	3	2	1
Ethics	18	5	13	8
Ethically good	12	3	2	1
Ethically bad	6	*2§§*	*11*	*7***
Status	26	7	19	11
Exaltation	2	0.6	2	1
Debasement	*17*	*5**	2	*1§*
Wealth	0	*0§§*	*5*	*3***
Poverty	1	0.3	0	0
Strength	4	1	4	2
Weakness	3	*0.8§*	*6*	*4**
Weal	22	6	8	5
Healing	4	1	0	0
Life	3	0.8	2	1
Peace/shalom	11	3	7	4
Reward	*6*	*2**	0	*0§*
Woe	127	35	47	28
Illness/injury	21	6	4	2
Death	2	*0.6§*	*5*	*3**
Destruction	93	25	31	19
Punishment	*54*	*15***	10	*6§§*

God and foreigners do not show as many statistically significant differences as do God and Israelites. This is partially, but not altogether, due to the fact that the number of foreigners' actions are smaller, so that it is harder to reach statistical significance. However, 166 foreigner actions is not a small amount. Both have a somewhat negative (and similar [not significantly different]) Evaluation. They do similar amounts of all emphasized metacategories: emotionality, cognition, ethics, status,[17] weal, and woe activities, and they share woe and

17. Foreigners also have status as a dominant metacategory, which, even though

emotion as their top two dominant metacategories. They also share destruction as the most frequent category. Punishment is another dominant category for both, although God punishes significantly more than
foreigners do. In fact, all dominant categories for both are negative.
A similarity is also indicated by the fact that most differences are among
low-frequency actions.

Differences also exist between divine and foreigner activity in SPP.[18]
God directs a higher percentage of actions toward humans than foreigners do (a quarter of foreigners' activities are intransitive [44]). In
dominant actions, God punishes more than foreigners do. Other actions
of God that are high relative to foreigners' actions are less-prominent
ones: shaming, anger, debasement, and reward. Three of the divine
actions that are relatively high display attitudes or value judgments
(punishment, reward, and anger). Bad ethics and fear are dominant
traits of foreigners,[19] not God. Less-prominent highs for foreigners in
comparison with God appear in their non-alertness, weakness, killing,
and wealth actions. All actions which are significantly high for foreigners (except wealth) have overtly negative connotations.

God is certainly not identical to foreigners. The main differences
seem to be that God more often negatively alters the states of others on
the basis of attitudes (i.e. shaming, anger, punishment, and reward),
while foreigners are viewed without reference to their attitudes.

6. *God to Israelites versus God to Foreigners*

Null hypothesis: What GOD does to ISRAELITES in SPP is the same
as what GOD does to FOREIGNERS in SPP.

Dominant Metacategories, Categories, Actors, Complements
Significance: *= 0.05 **= 0.01 (§ and §§ = sig. low)

		GOD to ISRAELITES in SPP		GOD to FOREIGNERS in SPP	
			%		%
Action	Woe	31§§		Woe	56**
Metacategories	Emotions	14		Emotions	24
10%+	Cognition	13		Status	12
	Weal	11**			

not a dominant one for God, is not significantly different.

18. All foreigner highs are 7% or less, and the only divine high above this is
15%; all other divine highs are 5% or less.

19. They are also traits of Israelites.

Action	Destruction	23§§	Destruction	47**
Categories	Punishment	14	Punishment	19
5%+	Good ethics	6	Illness/Injury	15**
	Debasement	6	Debasement	12
	Peace/Shalom	5	Shaming	12
	Shaming	5	Hate	8
			Reason	5

Actors 10%+	God		God	

Complements Recipients 10%+	Israelites		Foreigners	

Evaluation

Difference:	+1.48
Significant?	Yes**

Both Evaluations are NEGATIVE

	GOD to ISRAELITES in SPP	GOD to FOREIGNERS in SPP
Mean	-0.50	-1.98
Std.Dev.	2.10	1.56

GOD to ISRAELITES in SPP—GOD to FOREIGNERS in SPP:
Comparative Frequencies

Significance: *= 0.05 **= 0.01 (§ and §§ = sig. low)

	GOD to ISRAELITES in SPP		GOD to FOREIGNERS in SPP	
Total activity	204		59	
Action/activity	Qty	%	Qty	%
Emotions	29	14	14	24
Joy	0	0	0	0
Sorrow	3	1	0	0
Love	4	2	0	0
Hate	10	5	5	8
Pride	1	0.5	0	0
Shaming	11	5	7	12
Anger	2	1	2	3

GOD to ISRAELITES in SPP—GOD to
FOREIGNERS in SPP:
Comparative Frequencies
Significance: *= 0.05 **= 0.01 (§ and §§ = sig. low)

	GOD to ISRAELITES in SPP		GOD to FOREIGNERS in SPP	
Desire	0	0	0	0
Fear	0	0	0	0
Cognition	27	13	4	7
Alertness	1	0.5	0	0
Non-alertness	1	0.5	1	2
Knowledge	4	2	0	0
Ignorance	4	2	0	0
Obey/agree	3	1	0	0
Rejection	8	4*	0	0§
Reason	9	4	3	5
Ethics	18	9	2	3
Ethically good	12	6	2	3
Ethically bad	6	3	0	0
Status	18	9	7	12
Exaltation	1	0.5	0	0
Debasement	12	6	7	12
Wealth	0	0	0	0
Poverty	1	0.5	0	0
Strength	3	1	0	0
Weakness	2	1	0	0
Weal	22	*11***	1	2§§
Healing	4	2	0	0
Life	3	1	0	0
Peace/shalom	11	5	1	2
Reward	6	3	0	0
Woe	64	31§§	*33*	56**
Illness/injury	9	4§§	*9*	*15***
Death	1	0.5	1	2
Destruction	46	23§§	28	47**
Punishment	28	14	11	19

It is fairly obvious that God often deals harshly in prophetic literature. Content analysis, however, provides aid to an understanding by quantifying differences between divine treatment of Israelites and foreigners. The contrast between these two groups is not so much in the types of divine actions involved as in the degree to which these are employed. In fact, there are fewer category differences here than in most of the comparisons if the main criterion is the number of categories which are different. God treats Israelites and foreigners similarly, but the Evaluation and significant category differences reveal a harsher treatment of foreigners than of Israelites. While the Evaluation for both is negative, the Evaluation for foreigners is -1.48 harsher (-1.98). Further, while the top divine action toward both groups is woe, it is significantly higher toward foreigners; the same is true about destruction. God punishes, shames, and debases both about the same, but illness/injury are more common in relation to the foreigner. Most of God's dominant actions toward Israelites (four out of six types) are negatives, whereas all of God's dominant actions toward foreigners are inherently deleterious. God does provide weal more frequently to Israelites than to foreigners, although no specific weal categories are high in SPP. The only specific action toward Israelites that is high in comparison with actions toward foreigners is rejection.

It seems that while the lot is bad for God's rebellious people, it is even worse for outsiders. Basically, while God is harsh to Israelites and foreigners, divine treatment of foreigners is considerably less favorable, especially physically.

7. *Divine Activity versus Divine Reception*

Null hypothesis: What GOD does to ALL in SPP is the same as what ALL does to GOD in SPP.

Dominant Metacategories, Categories, Actors, Complements
Significance: *= 0.05 **= 0.01 (§ and §§ = sig. low)

	GOD to ALL in SPP		ALL to GOD in SPP	
		%		%
Action	Woe	35**	Ethics	36**
Metacategories	Emotions	13	Cognition	29**
10%+			Emotions	15
Action	Destruction	25**	Bad ethics	25**
Categories	Punishment	15**	Rejection	14**
5%+	Illness/injury	6**	Good ethics	10**
			Fear	6**
			Obey/agree	5**
Actors 10%+	God		Humans	92
			Israel	84
			Human groups	67
			Cultic	18

Dominant Metacategories, Categories, Actors, Complements
Significance: *= 0.05 **= 0.01 (§ and §§ = sig. low)

		GOD to ALL in SPP		ALL to GOD in SPP	
		%			%
Complements	Humans	73	God		
Recipients	Israel	60			
	Human groups	49			
10%+	Foreign	19			
	Cultic	16			

Evaluation

Difference:	- 0.37
Significant?	YES*

Both Evaluations are NEGATIVE

	GOD to ALL in SPP	ALL to GOD in SPP
Mean	-0.70	-0.33
Std. Dev.	2.01	1.86

GOD to ALL in SPP—ALL to GOD in SPP:
Comparative Frequencies
Significance: *= 0.05 **= 0.01 (§ and §§ = sig. low)

	GOD to ALL in SPP		ALL to GOD in SPP	
Total Activity	366		205	
Action/Activity	Qty	%	Qty	%
Emotions	49	13	30	15
Joy	1	0.3	1	0.5
Sorrow	5	1	7	3
Love	*5*	*1**	*0*	*0§*
Hate	*18*	*5**	*3*	*1§*
Pride	1	0.3	3	1
Shaming	*16*	*4***	*2*	*1§§*
Anger	*6*	*2**	*0*	*0§*
Desire	2	0.6	1	0.5
Fear	*0*	*0§§*	*13*	*6***
Cognition	*34*	*9§§*	*59*	*29***
Alertness	2	0.6	2	1
Non-alertness	3	0.8	1	0.5
Knowledge	6	2	4	2
Ignorance	5	1	6	3
Obey/agree	*3*	*0.8§§*	*11*	*5***

Rejection	9	2§§	29	*14***
Reason	10	3	9	4
Ethics	18	5§§	73	*36***
Ethically good	12	3§§	21	*10***
Ethically bad	6	2§§	52	*25***
Status	26	7	13	6
Exaltation	2	0.6§	6	*3***
Debasement	17	5**	2	1§§
Wealth	0	0	0	0
Poverty	1	0.3	0	0
Strength	4	1	0	0
Weakness	3	0.8	5	2
Weal	22	6*	4	2§
Healing	4	1	0	0
Life	3	0.8	1	0.5
Peace/shalom	11	3	2	1
Reward	6	2	1	0.5
Woe	*127*	*35***	12	6§§
Illness/injury	*21*	*6***	1	0.5§§
Death	2	0.6	1	0.5
Destruction	*93*	*25***	10	5§§
Punishment	*54*	*15***	1	0.5§§

God is both a notable actor and a major complement in the prophets. God does 29 percent and receives 16 percent of all activity in SPP. There are few similarities, though, in the character of what God does versus what God receives. The only similar dominant metacategory is emotionality, and status-related activity is a less-prominent metacategory in which a similarity appears. All other cases in which no significant difference appears are actions that happen infrequently (less than 3 percent).[20] All dominant categories are significantly different, and many emotions are different.

The character of frequent activity in the two situations is dramatically different: eight of the fourteen categories that are significantly different are dominant. The top metacategory of God's activity is woe, while the top metacategory God receives concerns ethics, followed closely by cognition. God's dominant actions are all woe oriented: destruction, punishment, and illness/injury. Less-prominent activities high compare with what God receives are attitudinal in orientation,

---

20. Numbers this small often do not appear significantly different.

and mainly negative: hate, shaming, debasing, anger, and love.[21] What God receives is mainly valuing in nature, and is characterized by ethics and cognition. In particular, God receives bad ethics, rejection, good ethics, fear, and obedience. God is also high relative to others in receiving exaltation, a less-prominent action.

Both Evaluations are negative, but what God does is significantly harsher. The lower Evaluation of divine activity versus divine reception can be explained by the types of negatives. Dominant divine actions are in the physical realm, while the negatives God receives are in the domain of values/decisions/responses. God, who deals physically negatively with others, is not/cannot be easily physically assaulted. God, then, acts in the physical realm but is not approached there.

Three quarters of divine actions are directed toward humans, mainly Israelites. What God receives comes almost exclusively from humans, primarily Israelites. Of human recipients 67 percent are large groups, and 73 percent of human actors are large groups. Human relationship with God in the prophets, as actors and complements, is dominated by the collective.

God does and receives more of both sides of some binary opposites. God does more weal and woe, and more love and hate. God receives more good and bad ethics, and also receives more obey/agree and rejection actions. As for opposites done and received, God does more debasing and receives more exaltation.

To sum up: God acts in the physical realm, but is acted against in the abstract realm of values. God primarily acts negatively, and what God receives involves the rejection of divine values. It seems that harm occurs where it can: God causes physical harm, and receives harm in the form of values.

A future study might bear much fruit by coding time frames and comparing what occurred/occurs with what will occur. My speculation is that much divine activity is a response to what God receives.

8. *God to Humans versus Humans to God*

Null hypothesis: What GOD does to HUMANS in SPP is the same as what HUMANS do to GOD in SPP.

---

21. Collectively, God also does more weal, but no individual weal categories are greater than what God receives.

Dominant Metacategories, Categories, Actors, Complements
Significance: *= 0.05 **= 0.01 (§ and §§ = sig. low)

	GOD to HUMANS in SPP		HUMANS to GOD in SPP	
		%		%
Action	Woe	39**	Ethics	37**
Metacategories	Emotions	17	Cognition	31**
10%+	Cognition	11§§	Emotions	14
Action	Destruction	29**	Bad ethics	27**
Categories	Punishment	17**	Rejection	15**
5%+	Illness/Injury	7**	Good ethics	10*
	Debasement	7**	Fear	7**
	Shaming	6**	Obey/agree	6**
	Hate	6**	Destruction	5§§
Actors 10%+	God		Humans	
Complements Recipients 10%+	Humans		God	

Evaluation

Difference:	- 0.51
Significant?	Yes**
Both Evaluations are NEGATIVE	

	GOD to HUMANS in SPP	HUMANS to GOD in SPP
Mean	-0.89	-0.38
Std. Dev.	2.10	1.87

GOD to HUMANS in SPP—HUMANS to GOD in SPP:
Comparative Frequencies
Significance: *= 0.05 **= 0.01 (§ and §§ = sig. low)

	GOD to HUMANS in SPP		HUMANS to GOD in SPP	
Total activity	257		188	
Action/activity	Qty	%	Qty	%
Emotions	43	17	27	14
Joy	0	0	1	0.5
Sorrow	3	1	7	4
Love	*4*	*2**	*0*	*0*§
Hate	*15*	*6***	*2*	*1*§§
Pride	1	0.4	1	0.5

GOD to HUMANS in SPP—HUMANS to GOD in SPP:
Comparative Frequencies
Significance: *= 0.05 **= 0.01 (§ and §§ = sig. low)

	GOD to HUMANS in SPP		HUMANS to GOD in SPP	
Shaming	16	6**	2	1§§
Anger	6	2**	0	0§§
Desire	0	0	1	0.5
Fear	0	0§§	13	7**
Cognition	29	11§§	58	31**
Alertness	1	0.4	1	0.5
Non-alertness	2	0.8	1	0.5
Knowledge	4	2	4	2
Ignorance	4	2	6	3
Obey/agree	3	1§§	11	6**
Rejection	8	3§§	29	15**
Reason	10	4	9	5
Ethics	18	7§§	69	37**
Ethically good	12	5§	19	10*
Ethically bad	6	2§§	50	27**
Status	23	9	9	5
Exaltation	1	0.4	3	2
Debasement	17	7**	2	1§§
Wealth	0	0	0	0
Poverty	1	0.4	0	0
Strength	3	1	0	0
Weakness	2	0.8	4	2
Weal	22	9**	4	2§§
Healing	4	2*	0	0§
Life	3	1	1	0.5
Peace/shalom	11	4*	2	1§
Reward	6	2	1	0.5
Woe	100	39**	12	6§§
Illness/injury	18	7**	1	0.5§§
Death	2	0.8	1	0.5
Destruction	75	29**	10	5§§
Punishment	43	17**	1	0.5§§

There are only a few minor differences between a comparison that considers 'God to humans versus humans to God' and the previous comparison of 'God to all versus all to God.' The highest ranked dominant metacategories and categories are the same in the two comparisons and have the same amount of significant differences. Some types of actions, however, that are not dominant in God's interaction with all beings are dominant when only the relation with humans is considered. For divine activity toward human beings, the following are dominant (≥5 percent of actions), in addition to those which appear on the dominant list in relation to all beings: debasement, shame (shaming), and hate. In the divine reception of human activity, destruction is a dominant category,[22] but is still significantly low in comparison with what God does to humans. Among less-prominent actions, God is significantly higher in providing than in receiving peace/shalom and healing, but not in receiving (as compared with furnishing) exaltation. In other words, half of the exaltation of God in SPP is unspecified according to source. Evaluations of God-human interactions are a bit harsher than those of actions by God and all beings toward each other, and the respective differences are even more significantly different.

9. *God to Israelites versus Israelites to God*

Null hypothesis: What GOD does to ISRAELITES in SPP is the same as what ISRAELITES do to GOD in SPP.

Dominant Metacategories, Categories, Actors, Complements
Significance: *= 0.05 **= 0.01 (§ and §§ = sig. low)

	GOD to ISRAELITES in SPP		ISRAELITES to GOD in SPP	
		%		%
Action	Woe	31**	Ethics	37**
Metacategories	Emotions	14	Cognition	31**
10%+	Cognition	13§§	Emotions	15
	Weal	11**		
Action	Destruction	23**	Bad ethics	27**
Categories	Punishment	14**	Destruction	16**
5%+	Good ethics	6	Good ethics	10
	Debasement	6**	Fear	6**
	Peace/shalom	5*	Destruction	5§§
	Shaming	5*	Obey/agree	5*
Actors 10%+	God		Israelites	
Complements Recipients 10%+	Israelites		God	

---

22. Types of 'destructive' actions humans do to God in SPP include abandoning, acting treacherously, robbing, and piercing.

Dominant Metacategories, Categories, Actors, Complements
Significance: *= 0.05 **= 0.01 (§ and §§ = sig. low)
GOD to ISRAELITES in SPP   ISRAELITES to GOD in SPP
%   %

Evaluation

Difference:	- 0.08
Significant?	No
Both Evaluations are NEGATIVE	

	GOD to ISRAELITES in SPP	ISRAELITES to GOD in SPP
Mean	-0.50	-0.42
Std. Dev.	2.10	1.85

GOD to ISRAELITES in SPP—ISRAELITES to GOD in SPP:
Comparative Frequencies
Significance: *= 0.05 **= 0.01 (§ and §§ = sig. low)

	GOD to ISRAELITES in SPP		ISRAELITES to GOD in SPP	
Total Activity	204		172	
Action/Activity	Qty	%	Qty	%
Emotions	29	14	25	15
Joy	0	0	1	0.6
Sorrow	3	1	7	4
Love	*4*	*2**	*0*	*0§*
Hate	*10*	*5**	*2*	*1§*
Pride	1	0.5	1	0.6
Shaming	*11*	*5**	*2*	*1§*
Anger	2	1	0	0
Desire	0	0	1	0.6
Fear	*0*	*0§§*	*11*	*6***
Cognition	*27*	*13§§*	*53*	*31***
Alertness	1	0.5	1	0.6
Non-alertness	1	0.5	1	0.6
Knowledge	4	2	4	2
Ignorance	4	2	6	3
Obey/agree	3	1§	9	5*
Rejection	8	4§§	27	16**
Reason	9	4	7	4
Ethics	*18*	*9§§*	*64*	*37***
Ethically good	12	6	17	10
Ethically bad	6	3§§	47	27**

Status	*18*	*9***	5	*3§§*
Exaltation	1	0.5	1	0.6
Debasement	*12*	*6***	2	*1§§*
Wealth	0	0	0	0
Poverty	1	0.5	0	0
Strength	3	1	0	0
Weakness	2	1	2	1
Weal	*22*	*11***	4	*2§§*
Healing	*4*	*2***	0	*0§*
Life	3	1	1	0.6
Peace/shalom	*11*	*5***	2	*1§*
Reward	6	3	1	0.6
Woe	*64*	*31***	11	*6§§*
Illness/injury	*9*	*4***	1	*0.6§§*
Death	1	0.5	1	0.6
Destruction	*46*	*23***	9	*5§§*
Punishment	*28*	*14***	1	*0.6§§*

There are few similarities between divine treatment of Israelites and Israelite treatment of God. Both express about the same amount of emotionality toward each other (although many of the particular emotions are different), do similar amounts of good ethical actions, and have an almost identical mildly negative Evaluation. The amount of category differences, though, indicates that the means of achieving the negative Evaluation are quite different. The wide Evaluation standard deviations for both indicate that their activity has a wide range in regard to this measure, including the extremes.

It is noteworthy that the Evaluation difference in this comparison is not significantly different, while the Evaluation difference when considering God to humans versus humans to God in SPP is significantly different. This is because of God's extremely harsh treatment of foreigners which more than outweighs foreigner's treatment of God, and the fact that God is less harsh to Israelites than to foreigners. (Foreigners actually treat God more positively than Israelites do, although the difference is not significant.)

All dominant metacategories and categories are significantly different, except emotionality in general. God's most frequent type of action toward Israelites is physically harmful: woe, which is manifested through destruction and punishment. Most of God's dominant activity involves the denigration of Israelites—physically, emotionally, and according to status. Specifically, God alters the status of Israelites (9 percent**), while Israelites basically do not alter God's status (3 percent).

God also provides weal for Israelites, enough for this to appear among dominant activities; it includes the furnishing of peace/shalom (a dominant action) and of healing. In other significantly high, but less-prominent, actions, God hates, injures, loves, and heals Israelites, more so than they do to God.

The fact that divine activity itself contains some contrasts illustrates the mixed nature of divine activity. God destroys more and provides more prosperity (peace); God injures and heals more; God hates and loves more. In each of these cases, though, negatives far outweigh the positive counterpart.

In contrast, actions which Israelites do more of are primarily in the realms of ethics and cognition. In particular, the top two kinds of actions Israelites do to God involve bad ethics and rejection. Other highs are fear and obedience. As with God, though, the negative far exceeds the positive. Note that Israelites are never described as loving God in SPP.

In sum, God and Israelites treat each other negatively, but differently. God mainly performs physical harm, while Israelites mainly operate against divine values. As with humans in general, bad ethics are mainly in the domain of Israelites, not in the divine. Neither are completely missing the opposite counterparts, though. Occasionally God blesses, and occasionally Israelites submit to divine authority.

10. *God to Foreigners versus Foreigners to God*

Null hypothesis: What GOD does to FOREIGNERS in SPP is the same as what FOREIGNERS do to GOD in SPP.

Dominant Metacategories, Categories, Actors, Complements
Significance: *= 0.05 **= 0.01 (§ and §§ = sig. low)

		GOD to FOREIGNERS in SPP		FOREIGNERS to GOD in SPP
		%		%
Action	Woe	56**	Emotions	27
Metacategories	Emotions	24	Ethics	27**
10%+	Status	12	Cognition	27*
			Status	13
Action	Destruction	47**	Fear	27**
Categories	Punishment	19*	Bad ethics	13**
5%+	Illness/injury	15*	Good ethics	13

Debasement	12	Exaltation	13**
Shaming	12	Obey/agree	13**
Hate	8	Reason	13
Reason	5	Destruction	7§§
		Rejection	7

| Actors 10%+ | God | Foreigners | |

| Complements Recipients 10%+ | Foreigners | God | |

Evaluation

Difference:	-1.98
Significant?	Yes**

	GOD to FOREIGNERS in SPP	FOREIGNERS to GOD in SPP
Mean	-1.98	0.00
Std. Dev.	1.56	2.27

GOD to FOREIGNERS in SPP—FOREIGNERS to GOD in SPP:
Comparative Frequencies
Significance: *= 0.05 **= 0.01 (§ and §§ = sig. low)

	GOD to FOREIGNERS in SPP		FOREIGNERS to GOD in SPP	
Total activity	59		15	
Action/activity	Qty	%	Qty	%
Emotions	14	24	4	27
Joy	0	0	0	0
Sorrow	0	0	0	0
Love	0	0	0	0
Hate	5	8	0	0
Pride	0	0	0	0
Shaming	7	12	0	0
Anger	2	3	0	0
Desire	0	0	0	0
Fear	0	0§§	*4*	*27***
Cognition	4	7§	4	27*
Alertness	0	0	0	0
Non-alertness	1	2	0	0

GOD to FOREIGNERS in SPP—FOREIGNERS
to GOD in SPP:
Comparative Frequencies
Significance: *= 0.05 **= 0.01 (§ and §§ = sig. low)

	GOD to FOREIGNERS in SPP		FOREIGNERS to GOD in SPP	
Knowledge	0	0	0	0
Ignorance	0	0	0	0
Obey/agree	0	0§§	2	13**
Rejection	0	0	1	7
Reason	3	5	2	13
Ethics	2	3§§	4	27**
Ethically good	2	3	2	13
Ethically bad	0	0§§	2	13**
Status	7	12	2	13
Exaltation	0	0§§	2	13**
Debasement	7	12	0	0
Wealth	0	0	0	0
Poverty	0	0	0	0
Strength	0	0	0	0
Weakness	0	0	0	0
Weal	1	2	0	0
Healing	0	0	0	0
Life	0	0	0	0
Peace/shalom	1	2	0	0
Reward	0	0	0	0
Woe	33	56**	1	7§§
Illness/injury	9	15*	0	0§
Death	1	2	0	0
Destruction	28	47**	1	7§§
Punishment	11	19*	0	0§

Few meaningful statistical comparisons can be made here because of the small amount of actions that foreigners do to God (15).[23] For this reason, immediately following the present comparison another one seeks to determine whether there is much continuity between divine treatment of foreigners and foreigner treatment of Israelites. It is possible that God's reaction to foreigners is more related to foreigners' treatment of Israel than their treatment of God. Indeed, a straight reading

23. The most any particular type of action is done by foreigners to God is four times.

indicates that much divine treatment of foreigners is retribution for their treatment of Israelites.

However, some significant differences between God's actions to foreigners and foreigners' actions toward God can be observed. The former are considerably more harmful. The Evaluation of God's actions is significantly more negative by a factor of -1.98**. God does far more woe, emphasizing destruction, punishment, and illness/injury. Foreigners fear, obey, and exalt God, besides engaging in ethically bad actions. One gets the impression that God's actions here are 'an overwhelming flood' to foreigners, whose largest single process in relation to God is fear.

11. *God to Foreigners versus Foreigners to Israelites*

Null hypothesis: What GOD does to FOREIGNERS in SPP is the same as what FOREIGNERS do to ISRAELITES in SPP.

Dominant Metacategories, Categories, Actors, Complements
Significance: *= 0.05 **= 0.01 (§ and §§ = sig. low)

		GOD to FOREIGNERS in SPP		FOREIGNERS to ISRAELITES in SPP	
			%		%
Action	Woe	56		Woe	41
Metacategories	Emotions	24**		Ethics	11
10%+	Status	12		Weal	11*
Action	Destruction	47		Destruction	30
Categories	Punishment	19		Bad ethics	11**
5%+	Illness/Injury	15		Peace/shalom	11*
	Debasement	12**		Punishment	7
	Shaming	12**			
	Hate	8			
	Reason	5			
Actors 10%+	God			Foreigners	
Complements Recipients 10%+	Foreigners			Israelites	

Evaluation

Difference:	- 0.68
Significant?	No
Both Evaluations are NEGATIVE	

Dominant Metacategories, Categories, Actors, Complements
Significance: *= 0.05 **= 0.01 (§ and §§ = sig. low)

	GOD to FOREIGNERS in SPP	FOREIGNERS to ISRAELITES in SPP
Mean	-1.98	-1.30
Std. Dev.	1.56	1.98

GOD to FOREIGNERS in SPP—FOREIGNERS to ISRAELITES in SPP:
Comparative Frequencies
Significance: *= 0.05 **= 0.01 (§ and §§ = sig. low)

	GOD to FOREIGNERS in SPP		FOREIGNERS to ISRAELITES in SPP	
Total activity	59		46	
Action/activity	Qty	%	Qty	%
Emotions	*14*	*24***	*3*	*7§§*
Joy	0	0	1	2
Sorrow	0	0	1	2
Love	0	0	0	0
Hate	5	8	2	4
Pride	0	0	0	0
Shaming	*7*	*12***	*0*	*0§§*
Anger	2	3	0	0
Desire	0	0	0	0
Fear	0	0	0	0
Cognition	4	7	1	2
Alertness	0	0	0	0
Non-alertness	1	2	0	0
Knowledge	0	0	0	0
Ignorance	0	0	1	2
Obey/agree	0	0	0	0
Rejection	0	0	0	0
Reason	3	5	0	0
Ethics	2	3	5	11
Ethically good	2	3	0	0
Ethically bad	*0*	*0§§*	*5*	*11***

Status	7	12	3	7
Exaltation	0	0	0	0
Debasement	7	*12***	0	0§§
Wealth	0	0	2	4
Poverty	0	0	0	0
Strength	0	0	0	0
Weakness	0	0	1	2
Weal	1	2§	5	*11**
Healing	0	0	0	0
Life	0	0	1	2
Peace/shalom	1	2§	5	*11**
Reward	0	0	0	0
Woe	33	56	19	41
Illness/injury	9	15	2	4
Death	1	2	1	2
Destruction	28	47	14	30
Punishment	11	19	3	7

Essentially, God does unto foreigners as foreigners do unto Israelites in SPP. This is manifested both in terms of categories and Evaluation. Neither treats its complement kindly; the top category for both is destruction, 6/7 of God's dominant categories are negatives, and 3/4 of foreigner dominant categories are negatives. Both scenarios have large amounts of woe. Outside of woe there are no categories of acts or processes with more than 12 percent. In God-to-foreigners relations 20 categories are missing altogether, and in foreigners-to-Israelites relations 19 are missing; they overlap so that 13 are missing from both. The main difference is that foreigners do more weal in general to Israelites than God does to foreigners, especially in the form of peace/shalom (!), as well as more bad ethics (in both cases 11 percent). God is involved in more overall emotion-related activity, and does more shaming and debasing (both 12 percent).[24] Although not to the point that the difference becomes statistically significant (since the absolute numbers are not very large), God is harsher toward foreigners than they are toward Israelites. This is shown by the ratings for destruction (47 percent to 30 percent),[25] punishment (19 percent to 7 percent),[26] illness/injury (15 percent to 4 percent),[27] and Evaluation (-1.98 to -1.30).[28]

24. God's woe is accompanied by emotional intensity.
25. Significance 0.07549.
26. Significance 0.06059.
27. Significance 0.05821.
28. Significance 0.060.

*Excursus: God's Treatment of Foreigners in Zechariah 12–14
Compared with Foreigners' Treatment of Israelites in Zechariah 12–14*

A section in SPP which contains a similar amount of incidents of *both* of these kinds of actions is Zechariah 12–14.[29] As with SPP in general, divine treatment of foreigners is harsh, and foreigner treatment of Israelites is likewise harsh.[30] God, though, does more woe in general, especially destruction (72 percent to 35 percent)[31] and illness/injury (50 percent to 0 percent). The Evaluation for both is quite harsh; although the significance level of this difference does not reach the 0.05 level, God's is harsher by - 0.91 (-2.41 versus -1.50).[32] God's treatment of foreigners in Zechariah 12–14 is similar to foreigners' treatment of Israelites, yet even harsher.

12. *Divine Reception versus Human Reception*

Null hypothesis: What ALL does to GOD in SPP is the same as what ALL does to HUMANS in SPP.

Dominant Metacategories, Categories, Actors, Complements
Significance: *= 0.05 **= 0.01 (§ and §§ = sig. low)

	ALL to GOD in SPP		ALL to HUMANS in SPP	
		%		%
Action	Ethics	36**	Woe	38**
Metacategories	Cognition	29**	Ethics	13§§
10%+	Emotions	15	Emotions	12
Action	Bad ethics	25**	Destruction	30**
Categories	Rejection	14**	Punishment	11**
5%+	Good ethics	10**	Bad ethics	9§§

29. Nahum contains more incidents of God acting toward foreigners, but fewer incidents of foreigners acting toward Israelites.

30. God's treatment of foreigners in Zech. 12–14 is considerably more deleterious than God's treatment of Israelites, which is unlike the rest of SPP.

	God to Israelites	God to Foreigners	Foreigner dif.
Evaluation	+ 0.54	-2.41**	-2.95
Destruction	17%	72%**	+55%
Punishment	0%	11%**	+11%
Illness/injury	0%	50%**	+50%

31. Destruction is also foreigners' top category, but is significantly low in comparison with God's destructiveness.

32. Significance 0.073.

	Fear	6**	Illness/injury	8**
	Obey/agree	5**		
Actors 10%+	Humans	92**	God	45**
	Israel	84**	Humans	40§§
	Human groups	67**	Israel	26§§
	Cultic	18**	Human groups	23§§
			Foreign	13*
Complements Recipients 10%+	God		Humans	

Evaluation

Difference:	+ 0.65
Significant?	Yes**
Both Evaluations are NEGATIVE	

	ALL to GOD in SPP	ALL to HUMANS in SPP
Mean	-0.33	-0.98
Std. Dev.	1.86	2.0

ALL to GOD in SPP—ALL to HUMANS in SPP:
Comparative Frequencies
Significance: *= 0.05 **= 0.01 (§ and §§ = sig. low)

	ALL to GOD in SPP		ALL to HUMANS in SPP	
Total activity	205		576	
Action/activity	Qty	%	Qty	%
Emotions	30	15	67	12
Joy	1	0.5	6	1
Sorrow	7	3	7	1
Love	0	0	6	1
Hate	3	1	19	3
Pride	3	1	4	0.7
Shaming	2	1§	22	4*
Anger	0	0	6	1
Desire	1	0.5	2	0.4
Fear	13	6**	0	0§§
Cognition	59	29**	49	9§§
Alertness	2	1	3	0.5
Non-alertness	1	0.5	7	1
Knowledge	4	2	6	1

ALL to GOD in SPP—ALL to HUMANS in SPP:
Comparative Frequencies
Significance: *= 0.05 **= 0.01 (§ and §§ = sig. low)

	ALL to GOD in SPP		ALL to HUMANS in SPP	
Total activity	205		576	
Action/activity	Qty	%	Qty	%
Ignorance	6	3	8	1
Obey/agree	*11*	*5***	*6*	*1§§*
Rejection	*29*	*14***	*11*	*2§§*
Reason	9	4	12	2
Ethics	*73*	*36***	*74*	*13§§*
Ethically good	*21*	*10***	*25*	*4§§*
Ethically bad	*52*	*25***	*49*	*9§§*
Status	13	6	47	8
Exaltation	*6*	*3**	*4*	*0.7§*
Debasement	*2*	*1§*	*23*	*4**
Wealth	*0*	*0§*	*7*	*1**
Poverty	0	0	1	0.2
Strength	0	0	5	0.9
Weakness	5	2	8	1
Weal	*4*	*2§§*	*37*	*6***
Healing	0	0	4	0.7
Life	1	0.5	5	0.9
Peace/shalom	*2*	*1§§*	*24*	*4***
Reward	1	0.5	8	1
Woe	*12*	*6§§*	*221*	*38***
Illness/injury	*1*	*0.5§§*	*44*	*8***
Death	*1*	*0.5§*	*18*	*3**
Destruction	*10*	*5§§*	*170*	*30***
Punishment	*1*	*0.5§§*	*61*	*11***

There are few similarities between what God receives and what humans receive. The main one of note is that they both receive a similar prominent amount of overall emotions. All particular emotions are similar in the frequency in which they are directed toward God and toward humans, except that God receives a high amount of fear, while humans are shamed more. Less-prominent similarities are status-related activities. (However, within status-related actions there are differences in that exaltation is higher toward God, and debasement and the giving of wealth are higher in relation to humans.)

There are numerous differences between what God receives and what humans receive. The rankings of the dominant metacategories and categories show the differences. God is primarily the recipient of ethical and psychological actions, while humans receive primarily woe actions. That over a third of what God receives pertains to ethics and over a third is psychological (cognitive and emotional) suggests that the prophets conceived God as one who is mainly approached in attitudes and actions based on value judgments, rather than physically.

All dominant categories and metacategories are significantly different—except for the metacategory of emotions. Among particular dominant types of activity (categories), God is the recipient of more ethically bad and ethically good actions (especially the former), as well as of rejection, fear, and obedience/agreement. Sometimes, although not as often, God is exalted. Humans are on the receiving end of destruction, punishment, illness/injury, and actions rated ethically bad (although these last are significantly low in comparison with what God receives). Humans also are provided more weal than God is (particularly peace/shalom) but that is not very frequent. Note that while God receives both more rejection and more obedience than do humans, rejection of God is more frequent than obedience.[33] Further, while the Evaluations of what both God and humans receive are negative, what humans receive is significantly more severe by -0.65**.

There are many differences among the actors involved in these two scenarios. All dominant actors are significantly different, either high or low. While humans, including mainly Israelites and largely societal groups, are among the top actors for both complements, the ratios are quite different: God receives a much larger percentage of actions from the aforementioned types of actors than humans do, while almost half of the activity humans received is from God.

In sum, what God and humans receive is dominated by negatives, but the character of these negatives is different. What God receives is volitional. This is especially so, since the metacategory 'cognition' includes the categories obey/agree, rejection, and reason (which in turn includes decision), so that it might be called 'recognition.' These choices made toward God are mainly (but not always) bad ones. What humans receive more of is physical in character, dominated by woe categories.

33. Significance 0.00232.**

13. *Israelite Reception versus Foreigner Reception*

Null hypothesis: What ALL does to ISRAELITES in SPP is the same as what ALL does to FOREIGNERS in SPP.

Dominant Metacategories, Categories, Actors, Complements
Significance: *= 0.05 **= 0.01 (§ and §§ = sig. low)

	ALL to ISRAELITES in SPP	%	ALL to FOREIGNERS in SPP	%
Action	Woe	34§§	Woe	48**
Metacategories	Ethics	16**	Emotions	12
10%+	Emotions	11	Status	11
Action	Destruction	27§	Destruction	37*
Categories	Bad ethics	11*	Punishment	12
5%+	Punishment	9	Illness/injury	12*
	Illness/injury	6§	Debasement	5
	Good ethics	5*	Shaming	5
	Peace/shalom	5		
Actors 10%+	God	47	Humans	43
	Humans	38	God	40
	Israel	29**	Human groups	35**
	Human groups	19§§	Foreign	29**
			Israel	16§§
Complements	Israelites		Foreigners	
Recipients				
10%+				

Evaluation

Difference:	+ 0.74
Significant?	Yes**

Both Evaluations are NEGATIVE

	ALL to ISRAELITES in SPP	ALL to FOREIGNERS in SPP
Mean	-0.79	-1.53
Std. Dev.	2.02	1.79

ALL to ISRAELITES in SPP—ALL to FOREIGNERS in SPP:
Comparative Frequencies
Significance: *= 0.05 **= 0.01 (§ and §§ = sig. low)

Action/Activity	ALL to ISRAELITES in SPP		ALL to FOREIGNERS in SPP	
Total Activity	437		147	
Action/Activity	Qty	%	Qty	%
Emotions	47	11	18	12
Joy	5	1	1	0.7
Sorrow	6	1	1	0.7
Love	5	1	0	0
Hate	13	3	6	4
Pride	3	0.7	0	0
Shaming	16	4	8	5
Anger	2	0.5	2	1
Desire	2	0.5	0	0
Fear	0	0	0	0
Cognition	40	9	8	5
Alertness	2	0.5	1	0.7
Non-alertness	4	0.9	3	2
Knowledge	4	0.9	1	0.7
Ignorance	7	2	1	0.7
Obey/agree	4	0.9	0	0
Rejection	*11*	*3****	0	0§§
Reason	11	3	3	2
Ethics	*70*	*16****	9	6§§
Ethically good	*24*	*5**	2	1§
Ethically bad	*46*	*11**	7	5§
Status	33	8	16	11
Exaltation	3	0.7	0	0
Debasement	17	4	8	5
Wealth	4	0.9	4	3
Poverty	1	0.2	0	0
Strength	3	0.7	2	1
Weakness	6	1	2	1
Weal	*34*	*8**	5	3§
Healing	4	0.9	0	0
Life	4	0.9	1	0.7
Peace/shalom	22	5	4	3
Reward	*8*	*2**	0	0§

ALL to ISRAELITES in SPP—ALL to FOREIGNERS in SPP:
Comparative Frequencies
Significance: *= 0.05 **= 0.01 (§ and §§ = sig. low)

	ALL to ISRAELITES in SPP		ALL to FOREIGNERS in SPP	
Total Activity	437		147	
Action/Activity	Qty	%	Qty	%
Woe	148	34§§	*71*	*48***
Illness/injury	27	6§	*17*	*12**
Death	13	3	6	4
Destruction	116	27§	*54*	*37**
Punishment	39	9	18	12

A brief contrast between what Israelites receive versus what foreigners receive will help to provide a background for comparisons of each of the two groups as complements to God as a complement.

There are some similarities between what foreigners receive and what Israelites receive. Emotionality, punishment, debasement, shaming, and peace/shalom are received close to equally.

Differences appear in that woe, with its categories of destruction and illness/injury, is significantly higher for foreigners and in that Israelites receive more ethically valued actions (both bad and good), rejection, and overall weal, including reward.

God and humans are the actors similarly often toward both recipients (a little less than half each).[34] Israelites receive more activity from Israelites than do foreigners, foreigners receive more activity from foreigners than do Israelites, and foreigners receive more activity from large groups of people than Israelites do.

14. Divine Reception versus Israelite Reception

Null hypothesis: What ALL does to GOD in SPP is the same as what ALL does to ISRAELITES in SPP.

---

34. God acts somewhat more frequently toward Israelites, while humans are ahead in actions toward foreigners; however, this difference is not statistically significant.

Dominant Metacategories, Categories, Actors, Complements
Significance: *= 0.05 **= 0.01 (§ and §§ = sig. low)

	ALL to GOD in SPP		ALL to ISRAELITES in SPP	
		%		%
Action	Ethics	36**	Woe	34**
Metacategories	Cognition	29**	Ethics	16§§
10%+	Emotions	15	Emotions	11
Action	Bad ethics	25**	Destruction	27**
Categories	Rejection	14**	Bad Ethics	11§§
5%+	Good ethics	10**	Punishment	9**
	Fear	6**	Illness/injury	6**
	Obey/agree	5**	Good Ethics	5§
			Peace/shalom	5**
Actors 10%+	Humans	92**	God	47**
	Israel	84**	Humans	38§§
	Human groups	67**	Israel	29§§
	Cultic	18**	Human groups	19§§
Complements	God		Israelites	
Recipients				
10%+				

Evaluation

Difference:	+ 0.46
Significant?	Yes**
Both Evaluations are NEGATIVE	

	ALL to GOD in SPP	ALL to ISRAELITES in SPP
Mean	-0.33	-0.79
Std. Dev.	1.86	2.02

ALL to GOD in SPP—ALL to ISRAELITES in SPP:
Comparative Frequencies
Significance: *=0.05 **=0.01 (§ and §§ = sig. low)

	ALL to GOD in SPP		ALL to ISRAELITES in SPP	
Total Activity	205		437	
Action/Activity	Qty	%	Qty	%
Emotions	30	15	47	11
Joy	1	0.5	5	1

ALL to GOD in SPP—ALL to ISRAELITES in SPP:
Comparative Frequencies
Significance: *=0.05 **=0.01 (§ and §§ = sig. low)

	ALL to GOD in SPP		ALL to ISRAELITES in SPP	
Total Activity	205		437	
Action/Activity	Qty	%	Qty	%
Sorrow	7	3	6	1
Love	0	0§	5	*1**
Hate	3	1	13	3
Pride	3	1	3	0.7
Shaming	2	1§	16	*4**
Anger	0	0	2	0.5
Desire	1	0.5	2	0.5
Fear	13	*6***	0	0§§
Cognition	59	*29***	40	9§§
Alertness	2	1	2	0.5
Non-alertness	1	0.5	4	0.9
Knowledge	4	2	4	0.9
Ignorance	6	3	7	2
Obey/agree	11	*5***	4	0.9§§
Rejection	29	*14***	11	3§§
Reason	9	4	11	3
Ethics	73	*36***	70	16§§
Ethically good	21	*10**	24	5§
Ethically bad	52	*25***	46	11§§
Status	13	6	33	8
Exaltation	6	*3**	3	0.7§
Debasement	2	1§	17	*4**
Wealth	0	0	4	0.9
Poverty	0	0	1	0.2
Strength	0	0	3	0.7
Weakness	5	2	6	1
Weal	4	2§§	34	*8***
Healing	0	0	4	0.9
Life	1	0.5	4	0.9
Peace/shalom	2	1§§	22	*5***
Reward	1	0.5	8	2
Woe	12	6§§	148	*34***
Illness/injury	1	0.5§§	27	*6***
Death	1	0.5§	*13*	*3**
Destruction	10	5§§	116	*27***
Punishment	1	0.5§§	39	*9***

There is little resemblance between God and Israelites as complements in SPP. This is manifest in terms of actors and activities.

In the SPP the relative frequencies of the entities acting upon God differs from those who act upon Israelites. Humans, mainly Israelites and large groups, constitute most of the actors upon God. On the other hand, almost half (45 percent) of Israelite reception is from God, with the remainder divided primarily among various humans.

The only similar dominant action or process is overall emotionality. All other cases without significant difference are among infrequent categories.

The top two metacategories for what God receives are high relative to what Israelites receive: ethical and cognitive actions.[35] Major parts of these are comprised of bad ethics, followed by rejection, good ethics, fear, and obedience. The Evaluation of what God receives, while negative, is significantly more positive than what Israelites receive by + 0.46**.

All dominant actions toward Israelites are in the weal/woe sphere. One third of what Israelites receive is woe oriented. Woe's particulars (destruction, punishment, and illness/injury, and to a lesser extent, death) are individually frequent—all high compared to what God receives. Weal, though less-prominent, is still relatively high for Israel (including the category peace, frequent enough to be dominant among those Israel receives).[36]

A number of paired extremes appear in these entities' receptions. God is both rejected and obeyed more, and receives more bad and good ethical actions than Israel. Israelites encounter both more destruction and more peace/shalom. In another set, the members of the pair move in different directions: God is exalted more, and Israelites are debased more. Both sides receive more adverse than supporting actions, but the opposite kind is not lacking in either case.

The outcome is that God's reception is characterized by valuing and response categories (mainly negative), while Israelite reception is dominated by physical harm and help (more negative than positive). Comparatively, what God receives is punctuated by the intangible,

---

35. As with other divine reception scenarios, all dominant categories which God receives are significantly high.

36. Israelites also receive high, less prominent amounts of love, shaming, and debasement.

while what Israelites receive emphasizes the concrete (destruction and punishment).

The above indicates that God differs from Israelites as a complement, and not just as an actor. God's otherness is illustrated by the lack of physical reception. God can be 'harmed,' but not through physical means—it is one's ethics and attitudes which affect God.

15. *Divine Reception versus Foreigner Reception*

Null hypothesis: What ALL does to GOD in SPP is the same as what ALL does to FOREIGNERS in SPP.

Dominant Metacategories, Categories, Actors Complements
Significance: *= 0.05 **= 0.01 (§ and §§ = sig. low)

	ALL to GOD in SPP		ALL to FOREIGNERS in SPP	
		%		%
Action	Ethics	36**	Woe	48**
Metacategories	Cognition	29**	Emotions	12
10%+	Emotions	15	Status	11
Action	Bad ethics	25**	Destruction	37**
Categories	Rejection	14**	Punishment	12**
5%+	Good ethics	10**	Illness/injury	12**
	Fear	6**	Debasement	5**
	Obey/agree	5**	Shaming	5**
Actors 10%+	Humans	92**	Humans	43§§
	Israel	84**	God	40**
	Human groups	67**	Human groups	35§§
	Cultic	18**	Foreign	29**
			Israel	16§§
Complements Recipients 10%+	God		Foreigners	

Evaluation

Difference:	+1.20
Significant?	Yes**
Both Evaluations are NEGATIVE	

	ALL to GOD in SPP	ALL to FOREIGNERS in SPP
Mean	-0.33	-1.53
Std. Dev.	1.86	1.79

ALL to GOD in SPP—ALL to FOREIGNERS in SPP:
Comparative Frequencies
Significance: *= 0.05 **= 0.01 (§ and §§ = sig. low)

	ALL to GOD in SPP		ALL to FOREIGNERS in SPP	
Total Activity	205		147	
Action/Activity	Qty	%	Qty	%
Emotions	30	15	18	12
Joy	1	0.5	1	0.7
Sorrow	7	3	1	0.7
Love	0	0§	0	0
Hate	3	1	6	4
Pride	3	1	0	0
Shaming	*2*	*1§§*	*8*	*5***
Anger	0	0	2	1
Desire	1	0.5	0	0
Fear	*13*	*6***	*0*	*0§§*
Cognition	*59*	*29***	*8*	*5§§*
Alertness	2	1	1	0.7
Non-alertness	1	0.5	3	2
Knowledge	4	2	1	0.7
Ignorance	6	3	1	0.7
Obey/agree	*11*	*5***	*0*	*0§§*
Rejection	*29*	*14***	*0*	*0§§*
Reason	9	4	3	2
Ethics	*73*	*36***	*9*	*6§§*
Ethically good	*21*	*10***	*2*	*1§§*
Ethically bad	*52*	*25***	*7*	*5§§*
Status	13	6	16	11
Exaltation	*6*	*3***	*0*	*0§§*
Debasement	*2*	*1§§*	*8*	*5***
Wealth	*0*	*0§§*	*4*	*3***
Poverty	0	0	0	0
Strength	0	0	2	1
Weakness	5	2	2	1
Weal	4	2	5	3
Healing	0	0	0	0
Life	1	0.5	1	0.7
Peace/shalom	2	1	4	3
Reward	1	0.5	0	0

ALL to GOD in SPP—ALL to FOREIGNERS in SPP:
Comparative Frequencies
Significance: *= 0.05 **= 0.01 (§ and §§ = sig. low)

Action/Activity	ALL to GOD in SPP		ALL to FOREIGNERS in SPP	
Total Activity	205		147	
	Qty	%	Qty	%
Woe	12	6§§	71	48**
Illness/injury	1	0.5§§	17	12**
Death	1	0.5§§	6	4**
Destruction	10	5§§	54	37**
Punishment	1	0.5§§	18	12**

There are numerous differences between those who act toward God and those who act toward foreigners. Israelites (mainly their society at large) account for most of those who act toward God. In relation to foreigners, humans are also the main actors, but much less frequently so; God's actions toward foreigners are almost as frequent as those by humans toward foreigners. Most of the human actors toward foreigners are themselves foreigners.[37]

The natures of the actions directed toward God and toward foreigners are quite different. The main similarities of note between them involve overall emotionality and status-related activity (although the specific actions within these metacategories vary.) All the frequent categories of what foreigners receive are negative; the top three are woe oriented, and the next two are negatives involving status and emotion. Specifically, foreigners receive tremendous physical harm and some humiliation. This physical harm is exemplified by an Evaluation which is harsher by -1.20**. (In the present coding, physical harm tends to be evaluated more negatively than cognitive harm.)[38] Among the woes directed toward foreigners (much more so than toward God) are destruction, illness/injury, death, and punishment.[39]

37. This situation is unlike the situation when Israelites are the complement. Most human actors against Israelites are themselves Israelites (see the previous comparison).

38. This appears to have been the trend in Osgood *et al.*, *Cross Cultural Universals*, pp. 422-452.

39. While foreigners and Israelites both receive more woe than God does, foreigners receive much more woe than Israelites do, particularly destruction and illness/injury.

God receives more ethically-valued actions (both bad and good) and such as are cognitive in orientation. Less frequently, but more so than is true for foreigners, God receives rejection, obedience, fear, and exaltation.

God thus mainly receives valuing activity, largely negative but with some positives. Foreigners are mainly lowered in position, physically and emotionally. Overall, foreigners are treated more harshly than God.

16. *Israelites to God versus Foreigners to God*

Null hypothesis: What ISRAELITES do to GOD in SPP is the same as what FOREIGNERS do to GOD in SPP.

Dominant Metacategories, Categories, Actors, Complements
Significance: *= 0.05 **= 0.01 (§ and §§ = sig. low)

	ISRAELITES to GOD in SPP		FOREIGNERS to GOD in SPP	
		%		%
Action	Ethics	37	Emotions	27
Metacategories	Cognition	31	Ethics	27
10%+	Emotions	15	Cognition	27
			Status	13
Action	Bad ethics	27	Fear	27*
Categories	Rejection	16	Bad ethics	13
5%+	Good ethics	10	Good ethics	13
	Fear	6§	Exaltation	13**
	Destruction	5	Obey/agree	13
	Obey/agree	5	Reason	13
			Destruction	7
			Rejection	7
Actors 10%+	Israelites		Foreigners	
Complements Recipients 10%+	God		God	

Evaluation

Difference.	- 0.42
Significant?	No

Dominant Metacategories, Categories, Actors, Complements
Significance: *= 0.05 **= 0.01 (§ and §§ = sig. low)

	ISRAELITES to GOD in SPP	FOREIGNERS to GOD in SPP
	%	%
	ISRAELITES to GOD in SPP	FOREIGNERS to GOD in SPP
Mean	-0.42	0.00
Std. Dev.	1.85	2.27

ISRAELITES to GOD in SPP—FOREIGNERS to GOD in SPP:
Comparative Frequencies
Significance: *= 0.05 **= 0.01 (§ and §§ = sig. low)

	ISRAELITES to GOD in SPP		FOREIGNERS to GOD in SPP	
Total Activity	172		15	
Action/Activity	Qty	%	Qty	%
Emotions	25	15	4	27
Joy	1	0.6	0	0
Sorrow	7	4	0	0
Love	0	0	0	0
Hate	2	1	0	0
Pride	1	0.6	0	0
Shaming	2	1	0	0
Anger	0	0	0	0
Desire	1	0.6	0	0
Fear	11	6§	4	27*
Cognition	53	31	4	27
Alertness	1	0.6	0	0
Non-alertness	1	0.6	0	0
Knowledge	4	2	0	0
Ignorance	6	3	0	0
Obey/agree	9	5	2	13
Rejection	27	16	1	7
Reason	7	4	2	13
Ethics	64	37	4	27
Ethically good	17	10	2	13
Ethically bad	47	27	2	13
Status	5	3	2	13
Exaltation	1	0.6§§	2	13**
Debasement	2	1	0	0

Wealth	0	0	0	0
Poverty	0	0	0	0
Strength	0	0	0	0
Weakness	2	1	0	0
Weal	4	2	0	0
Healing	0	0	0	0
Life	1	0.6	0	0
Peace/shalom	2	1	0	0
Reward	1	0.6	0	0
Woe	11	6	1	7
Illness/injury	1	0.6	0	0
Death	1	0.6	0	0
Destruction	9	5	1	7
Punishment	1	0.6	0	0

The small number of actions by foreigners toward God makes it difficult to reach statistical significance in a comparison. The only statistically significant differences are that foreigners are relatively high in fear and in exaltation of God.

17. *Summary of Activity in SPP*

The preceding analyses examined God as one who acts and one who receives action from a number of angles. This final section of the SPP analysis will consider a few issues which have emerged: whether divine activity more closely resembles that of Israelites or foreigners; whether humans and God in each other's image; whether or not what humans receive is a 'natural' consequence of their actions; and divine treatment of foreigners. Finally, the SPP analyses will be summarized.

a. *Question: Whom does God Resemble More—Israelites or Foreigners?*
A question arises as to whether divine activity resembles more closely that of Israelites or that of foreigners. This section will consider a number of ways to approach the situation: total amounts of significant differences; who is closer for each activity, regardless of significance; and differences among dominant (more common) activity.

As a starting point, the following chart juxtaposes Israelite *and* foreigner activity with that of God in SPP.

Divine Activity Compared to Israelite and Foreigner Activity in SPP

Actor	God		Israelites		Foreigners	
Total words	366		561		166	
Action	Qty	%	Qty	%	Qty	%
Emotions	49	13	66	12	19	11
Joy	1	0.3	7	1	2	1
Sorrow	5	1	18	3	5	3
Love	5	1	4	0.7	0	0
Hate	18	5	6	1§§	3	2
Pride	1	0.3	4	0.7	0	0
Shaming	16	4	12	2	2	1§
Anger	6	2	2	0.4§	0	0§
Desire	2	0.6	4	0.7	0	0
Fear	0	0	11	2**	9	5**
Cognition	34	9	105	19**	13	8
Alertness	2	0.6	3	0.5	1	0.6
Non-alertness	3	0.8	13	2	6	4*
Knowledge	6	2	11	2	1	0.6
Ignorance	5	1	19	3*	2	1
Obey/agree	3	0.8	18	3**	2	1
Rejection	9	2	38	7**	1	0.6
Reason	10	3	11	2	2	1
Ethics	18	5	179	32**	13	8
Good ethics	12	3	41	7**	2	1
Bad ethics	6	2	138	25**	11	7**
Status	26	7	38	7	19	11
Exaltation	2	0.6	4	0.7	2	1
Debasement	17	5	12	2§	2	1§
Wealth	0	0	6	1**	5	3**
Poverty	1	0.3	1	0.2	0	0
Strength	4	1	4	0.7	4	2
Weakness	3	0.8	11	2	6	4*
Weal	22	6	12	2§§	8	5
Healing	4	1	0	0§§	0	0
Life	3	0.8	1	0.2	2	1
Peace/shalom	11	3	8	1	7	4
Reward	6	2	3	0.5	0	0§
Woe	127	35	62	11§§	47	28
Illness/injury	21	6	6	1§§	4	2
Death	2	0.6	10	2	5	3*
Destruction	93	25	54	10§§	31	19
Punishment	54	15	9	2§§	10	6§§

Note: Significance indicators compare Israelites and foreigners to God, not to each other. * = significantly high; § = significantly low.

The number of significant differences with God, as seen above, are totalled in the chart below. The totals themselves have not been subjected to statistical tests, but are provided to indicate the number of metacategories or categories which are or are not significantly different from divine activity.

Totals of Significant Differences Compared to Divine Activity

Dominant[40] and All Metacategories/Categories

	Number of metacategories significantly different from God		Number of metacategories not significantly different from God	
	Israel	Foreign	Israel	Foreign
Dominant Metacategories	4	0	2	6
Dominant categories	14	11	18	21

Totalling metacategories and categories produces an ambiguous picture. God appears to be slightly closer to foreigners than Israelites, in so far as the number of differences is concerned. However, a ratio of 14 to 11 significantly different categories (Israelites and foreigners respectively) is not itself a good measure, for possible infrequent activity is less likely to be significantly different.[41]

A second way of viewing the question is to consider divine activity versus Israelite and foreigner activity in terms of whose percentage is closer to divine activity, regardless of statistical significance.

Divine Activity Compared to Israelite and Foreigner Activity in SPP

Note: Numbers in bold and italics indicate closer in % to divine activity. (Significance indicators are left in this chart to help compare significance to this different measure of similarity, even though this chart does not emphasize significance).

40. 'Dominant' in this chart means that the metacategory or category for at least one actor must be dominant (see earlier charts). In some instances the differences are not significantly different, but one side of the comparison is below the 10% or 5% cutoff.

41. Note that neither Evaluation is significantly different from God's Evaluation (God: - 0.70; Israelites: - 0.49; foreigners: - 0.83).

Actor	God		Israelites		Foreigners	
Total words	366		561		166	
Action	Qty	%	Qty	%	Qty	%
Emotions	49	13	66	12	19	11
Joy	1	0.3	7	1	2	1
Sorrow	5	1	18	3	5	3
Love	5	1	4	0.7	0	0
Hate	18	5	6	1§§	3	2
Pride	1	0.3	4	0.7	0	0
Shaming	16	4	12	2	2	1§
Anger	6	2	2	0.4§	0	0§
Desire	2	0.6	4	0.7	0	0
Fear	0	0	11	2**	9	5**
Cognition	34	9	105	19**	13	8
Alertness	2	0.6	3	0.5	1	0.6
Non-alertness	3	0.8	13	2	6	4*
Knowledge	6	2	11	2	1	0.6
Ignorance	5	1	19	3*	2	1
Obey/agree	3	0.8	18	3**	2	1
Rejection	9	2	38	7**	1	0.6
Reason	10	3	11	2	2	1
Ethics	18	5	179	32**	13	8
Good ethics	12	3	41	7**	2	1
Bad ethics	6	2	138	25**	11	7**
Status	26	7	38	7	19	11
Exaltation	2	0.6	4	0.7	2	1
Debasement	17	5	12	2§	2	1§
Wealth	0	0	6	1**	5	3**
Poverty	1	0.3	1	0.2	0	0
Strength	4	1	4	0.7	4	2
Weakness	3	0.8	11	2	6	4*
Weal	22	6	12	2§§	8	5
Healing	4	1	0	0§§	0	0
Life	3	0.8	1	0.2	2	1
Peace/shalom	11	3	8	1	7	4
Reward	6	2	3	0.5	0	0§
Woe	127	35	62	11§§	47	28
Illness/injury	21	6	6	1§§	4	2
Death	2	0.6	10	2	5	3*
Destruction	93	25	54	10§§	31	19
Punishment	54	15	9	2§§	10	6§§

Totals: Closer to God, without Measure for Significance

	Israelites	Foreigners
Categories	16	13
Metacategories	2	4

If similarity is considered on the basis of the one whose percentage is closest to divine activity, regardless of significance or dominance, then the evidence is once again ambiguous. Israelites are closer in terms of categories, while foreigners are closer in terms of metacategories.[42]

However, the following points indicate more similarity between God and foreigners, rather than God and Israelites:

1. No category where Israelites are closer is above 2 percent of Israelite activity, but three categories where foreigners are closer are above 5 percent of foreigners' activity; one is 19 percent.

2. Israelites are *significantly* different for every metacategory in which foreigners are closer, but foreigners are *not* significantly different for the two metacategories where Israelites are closer.

3. In addition, the categories which are the most frequent for Israelites are not closer to divine activity, whereas the most frequent categories for foreigners are closer to divine activity.

In other words, God is more like foreigners than Israelites when one considers the activities that are most frequent.

Here is where consideration of dominant (i.e. more common) activity is an aid. Practical similarity is based more on what entities do, not what they do not do (see discussion on dominance in the chapter *Application of the Method*, section 2.C.). The question can be clarified as follows: *Who does God resemble more—Israelites or foreigners—in terms of common activity?*

---

42. Viewed another way, though, as with Israelites, divine activity is presented as similarly complex—God and Israelite overlap in 30 types of activities, while God and foreigners share only 23 types of activities. God does all activities except fearing and wealth-related actions; Israelites do all except healing; and foreigners are missing hating, shaming, anger, desire, poverty, healing, and reward.

Comparisons of Dominant[43] Categories

	Number of metacategories significantly different from God		Number of metacategories not significantly different from God	
	Israel	Foreign	Israel	Foreign
Dominant Metacategories	3	0	1	3
Dominant categories	6	3	0	2[44]

The above information suggests that divine activity shows more commonality with foreigners' activity than with that of Israelites, for foreigners show more similarity and fewer differences with God than do Israelites when it comes to frequent activity.

That divine activity has some affinities with foreigner activity in terms of that which is most common brings up some interesting issues. The remoteness of non-Israelites resembles God's remoteness—distant, yet not completely removed from the lives of Israelites. Just as foreigners are perceived as remote and yet influential in the affairs of Israelites, so also is God. As foreigners are not-too-nice, so also is God. However, as instruments of woe foreigners lack (or are low in) some of the personal characteristics of God: anger, shaming, and punishment.[45] Thus God and foreigners share some common traits, but are not identical.

It must be remembered that earlier analyses have shown that God differs in many important ways from Israelites *and* foreigners; God, as an acting agent, is unique.

b. *Question: God in a Human Image?*

A common question is, 'What does it mean to say that humans are created in God's image?' (Cf. Genesis 1.) A similar question which is asked by some is, 'Did humans create God in their image?' God, in these prophetic passages,[46] is not described as an average human or as

43. 'Dominant' in this chart means that the metacategory or category for at least one actor must be dominant.

44. This includes the highest frequency category for God and for foreigners (destruction).

45. It should be remembered that much Israelite activity in the prophets is that of rebellious Israelites. Other literature might present a picture which is quite different.

46. One must bear in mind that the bulk of prophetic literature, especially SPP, is written to/about rebellious humans, which somewhat colors the picture.

just a human on a larger scale, for God is presented as being in major ways quite different from humans. Since God is primarily described in extremely unpleasant terms, God's character is not simply anthropomorphic wishful thinking on the part of the writers, unless the prophets were sadists. If humans and God are said to be reflections of each other, from whatever direction one prefers to view the situation, then it cannot be based on the frequent activities of both as described in the Hebrew prophets.

Yet there are also similarities, for God does many actions which humans also do. Their degree of emotionality perhaps represents the most notable similarity, although the *kind* of emotionality is different. Interestingly, that means that the image of God in humans beings, in so far as it is reflected in these passages, does not concern specifically rationality.

Another possible similarity lies in the exercise of an intentional activity that affects the life of other beings. Human 'ethical' actions to a large extent either give support or (as emphasized in SPP) bring harm to others (human or divine), albeit not necessarily physical. Correspondingly, God's actions often provide weal or woe. However, God's actions are not subject to the same kind of evaluation (i.e., as 'moral'), at least in SPP.

c. *Question: Is What Humans Receive the Natural Consequence of Their Actions?*

From the data one cannot construe that human reception, whether Israelite or foreign, is viewed by the Selected Prophetic Passages as a 'natural' consequence of their actions. According to the prophets, God is integrally involved in the fate of humanity. God is involved in 45 percent of what all humans receive, 47 percent of what Israelites receive, and 40 percent of what foreigners receive. Weal and woe, certainly in the physical realm, account for 42 percent of what God does to Israel and 58 percent of what God does to foreigners. Thus, SPP does not present God as 'wholly other', but quite present—which does not always appear to be desirable.[47]

d. *Reflection: The Treatment of Foreigners by God*

The difference in God's treatment of Israelites and foreigners was

47. This question could be clarified in a future study by adding a time frame to the actions, and/or by including hypertext links which connect causes and effects.

somewhat surprising; I expected more parity. Certainly, there are many similarities in their treatment by God. As for the number of categories which are different, there are fewer differences than most comparisons being considered. However, the differences which exist are extreme, especially when it comes to woe and destruction. The unpleasant things which God does to Israelites are amplified toward foreigners. According to the prophets, then, there must be something even worse about being an 'outsider' than about being a 'sinner' within.

e. *Summary of Divine Activity and Reception versus That of Others*

Divine Activity Compared to Other Acting Agents in SPP

	God Less**	God Less**	Not Sig. Different	God More*	God More**
Emotions			H I F		
Joy			H I F		
Sorrow			H I F		
Love			H I F		
Hate			F		H I
Pride			H I F		
Shaming			I	H F	
Anger				H I F	
Desire			H I F		
Fear	H I F				
Cognition	H I		F		
Alertness			H I F		
Non-alertness		H F	I		
Knowledge			H I F		
Ignorance		I	H F		
Obey/agree	H I		F		
Rejection	I	H	F		
Reason			H I F		
Ethics	H I		F		
Good ethics	I	H	F		
Bad ethics	H I F				
Status			H I F		
Exaltation			H I F		
Debasement				I F	H
Wealth	H I F				
Poverty			H I F		
Strength			H I F		
Weakness		H F	I		

	God Lower**	God Lower*	Not Sig. Different	God Higher*	God Higher**
Weal			F		H I
Healing					H I
Life			H I F		
Peace/shalom			H I F		
Reward			I	H F	
Woe			F		H I
Illness/injury			F		H I
Death		H F	I		
Destruction			F		H I
Punishment					H I F
Evaluation			I F		

Note: H = Humans; I = Israelites; F = Foreigners.

Divine Reception versus Reception by Other Entities in SPP

	God Less**	God Less**	Not Sig. Different	God More*	God More**
Emotions			H I F		
Joy			H I F		
Sorrow			H I F		
Love		I	H F		
Hate			H I F		
Pride			H I F		
Shaming	F	H I			
Anger			H I F		
Desire			H I F		
Fear					H I F
Cognition					H I F
Alertness			H I F		
Non-alertness			H I F		
Knowledge			H I F		
Ignorance			H I F		
Obey/agree					H I F
Rejection					H I F
Reason			H I F		
Ethics					H I F
Good ethics				I	H F
Bad ethics					H I F
Status			H I F		
Exaltation				H I	F
Debasement	F	H I			
Wealth	F	H	I		

Divine Reception versus Reception by Other Entities in SPP

	God Less**	God Less**	Not Sig. Different	God More*	God More**
Poverty			H I F		
Strength			H I F		
Weakness			H I F		
Weal	H I		F		
Healing			H I F		
Life			H I F		
Peace/shalom	H I		F		
Reward			H I F		
Woe	H I F				
Illness/injury	H I F				
Death		F	H I		
Destruction	H I F				
Punishment	H I F				

	God Lower**	God Lower*	Not Sig. Different	God Higher*	God Higher**
Evaluation					H I F

Note: H = Humans; I = Israelites; F = Foreigners

In general, divine action, when compared to the other actors, is distinct in its greater emphasis on physical harm (woe), and its lesser involvement in ethically valued actions (especially in bad ones) and in cognition (primarily less in rejection). Most of God's similarities to other actors concern infrequent activity. In terms of common activity, God most closely resembles foreigners, although God is certainly not identical to them. Emotionality is pretty similarly given out and received in SPP, and emotionality is a fairly integral part of all activity in SPP. None of the major comparisons with God show significant differences in this regard.

On the other hand, divine reception is distinct from other complements in its greater emphasis on the reception of ethical actions (especially bad ones) and cognition (primarily rejection and obedience). It is less mainly in the realm of physical harm: woe. Most of the similarities between what God receives and what other complements receive involve infrequent actions.

Basically, then, what God does more is received by God less, and what God does less is received by God more. God and other actors tend to do and receive many negatives, but the character for each scenario is different. Other actors show negative choices and attitudes, and yet receive physical harm. God, who does far more physical harm, is primarily harmed in the realm of choices and attitudes.

Chapter 8

JOEL

Statistical significance is more difficult to obtain for comparisons in Joel than in SPP because of the smaller extent of the material. However, many significant differences can be tracked.

1. *General Description of Activity in Joel*

This first section presents general information relating to the character of actors, actions, and complements in Joel, paralleling the 'General Description of Activity in SPP' above.

Frequencies of Parts of Speech
Designating Activity in Joel
Total words: 284

Parts of speech used to indicate activity (ranked)

	Qty	%
Verbs	166	58
Verbal instructions	63	22
Substantives	43	15
Adjectives	11	4
Prepositions	1	0.4

Verbal instructions are used far more often in Joel** than in SPP. This indicates that much of the activity is potential rather than realized activity. However, since it is reasonable to assume that the author of Joel believed that these verbal instructions could be carried out, they are included in order to examine the character of all activity, realized or potential.

Actor/Complement Totals in Joel[1]

	God		Humans		Israel		Foreign		Plants		Insects	
	Qty	%	Qty	%	Qty	%	Qty	%	Qty	%	Qty	%
Actions	78	27	109	38	75	26	31	11	7	2	42	15
Receptions	22	8	90	32	71	25	24	8	39	14	10	4

Note: Percentages indicate the percentage of total number of actions in the book of Joel (284), not the percentage of that actor's or recipient's actions.

God does about the same amount of actions as Israelites, but fewer than all humans and more than foreigners. Insects do slightly more actions than foreigners, but receive far less.

The presence of many intransitives in Joel decreases the amount of recipients compared to actors.[2] Humans in general receive a third of the actions. Plants/plant products[3] receive much in Joel, but do very little. God and insects are actors more than three times as often as they receive actions. Israelites do and receive about the same amount of actions.[4]

Actor/Number of Actions/Complement Totals in Joel

Complements/Recipients

Actors	God		Humans		Israel		Foreign		Plants		Insects	
	Qty	%	Qty	%	Qty	%	Qty	%	Qty	%	Qty	%
God	2	0.7	56	20	42	15	17	6	2	0.7	4	1
Humans	19	7	28	10	24	8	6	2	5	2	2	0.7
Israelites	14	5	13	5	12	4	1	0.4	4	1	2	0.7
Foreigners	5	2	14	5	13	5	5	2	2	0.7	0	0
Insects	0	0	1	0.4	4	1	0	0	17	6	1	0.4

1.   Numbers in the chart cannot necessarily be added together, for in a number of instances there are either multiple actors or multiple complements. However, God is not a common actor with any other entities in Joel (this is not true in SPP, where God shares activities with Israelite humans 4 times [3 times with 'human groups' and 2 times with 'nations'], as well as 2 times with 'spirit and one with 'angel' [with 'spirit' and 'angel' overlapping]).

2.   Eight actions (3%) have no actor, while 59 actions (21%) have no complement.

3.   Plants/plant products are a major recipient, but they will only be mentioned in the analyses in connection with insect activity.

4.   If one considers that the agricultural damage affected Israelites, Israelites receive an even greater percentage of the total actions in the book.

Note: Percentages indicate the percentage of total number of actions in the book of
Joel (284), not the percentage of that actor's or recipients actions. Frequencies below
cannot necessarily be added together to obtain totals, nor do the numbers necessarily
equal the preceding chart. This is because of overlapping actors and recipients, as
well as intransitives and passives.

The following observations are noteworthy:

Actors
1. The largest group of actions are done by God toward humans.
   God acts more than twice as often toward Israelites as toward
   foreigners.
2. Humans act most frequently toward other humans, but the
   amount humans act specifically toward Israelites is very close
   to the amount they act toward God.
3. Israelites act about the same percentage toward God as (other)
   Israelites. Israelites act infrequently toward foreigners.
4. Foreigners act most frequently toward humans (almost always
   toward Israelites). Foreigners act infrequently toward God.
5. Insects act mainly on plants.

Recipients
1. God receives most from humans, especially from Israelites.
2. Humans receive most from God, which is twice the amount
   humans receive from (other) humans.
3. Israelites and foreigners receive most from God. God is the
   main actor toward foreigners.
4. Plants receive most from insects.
5. Insects receive most from God.

Comparative Frequencies of Activities by the Major Actors in Joel

	God		Humans		Israel		Foreign		Insects	
Total activities	78		109		75		31		42	
Action/activity	Qty	%	Qty	%	Qty	%	Qty	%	Qty	%
Emotions	10	13	38	35	36	48	1	3	1	2
Joy	0	0	7	6	7	9	0	0	0	0
Sorrow	0	0	19	17	18	24	0	0	0	0
Love	5	6	0	0	0	0	0	0	0	0
Hate	0	0	1	0.9	0	0	1	3	0	0
Pride	4	5	2	2	2	3	0	0	1	2
Shaming	0	0	1	0.9	1	1	0	0	0	0

Anger	0	0	0	0	0	0	0	0	0	0
Desire	1	1	0	0	0	0	0	0	0	0
Fear	0	0	9	8	9	12	0	0	0	0
Cognition	8	10	10	9	6	8	3	10	0	0
Alertness	1	1	3	3	1	1	2	6	0	0
Non-alertness	0	0	1	0.9	0	0	1	3	0	0
Knowledge	0	0	6	6	5	7	0	0	0	0
Ignorance	0	0	0	0	0	0	0	0	0	0
Obey/agree	1	1	0	0	0	0	0	0	0	0
Rejection	0	0	0	0	0	0	0	0	0	0
Reason	6	8	0	0	0	0	0	0	0	0
Ethics	2	3	7	6	2	3	5	16	0	0
Ethically good	2	3	3	3	2	3	1	3	0	0
Ethically bad	0	0	4	4	0	0	4	13	0	0
Status	4	5	5	5	4	5	1	3	1	2
Exaltation	3	4	2	2	2	3	0	0	1	2
Debasement	0	0	1	0.9	1	1	0	0	0	0
Wealth	0	0	0	0	0	0	0	0	0	0
Poverty	0	0	0	0	0	0	0	0	0	0
Strength	1	1	1	0.9	0	0	1	3	0	0
Weakness	0	0	1	0.9	1	1	0	0	0	0
Weal	11	14	4	4	3	4	1	3	0	0
Healing	0	0	0	0	0	0	0	0	0	0
Life	2	3	2	2	2	3	0	0	0	0
Peace/shalom	9	12	2	2	1	1	1	3	0	0
Reward	4	5	0	0	0	0	0	0	0	0
Woe	14	18	8	7	0	0	8	26	14	33
Illness/injury	0	0	0	0	0	0	0	0	0	0
Death	0	0	1	0.9	0	0	1	3	0	0
Destruction	11	14	8	7	0	0	8	26	14	33
Punishment	7	9	4	4	0	0	4	13	0	0

Note: Percentages describe the percentage of an actor's total activity, not the percentage of activity in Joel. See individual comparisons for significant differences.

The following activities which played roles in SPP do not appear in the book of Joel for the major actors: anger, ignorance, rejection, wealth, poverty, healing, and illness/injury.

If one asks which entities devote a high percentage of their activity to a particular activity, as compared with what other entities do (as long as the frequency is five or greater), the following listing provides an answer. (No significance tests are applied at this point.)

1. God: love, cognition (including reason/decision), weal (including peace/shalom).
2. Israelites: emotions (including joy, sorrow, and fear), knowledge.
3. Foreigners: ethics, woe.
4. Insects: destruction.

Comparative Frequencies of Activities Directed Toward
the Major Complements (Recipients) in Joel

	God		Humans		Israelite		Foreigner	
Total activities	22		90		71		24	
Action/activity	Qty	%	Qty	%	Qty	%	Qty	%
Emotions	9	41	10	11	10	14	2	8
Joy	2	9	0	0	0	0	0	0
Sorrow	5	23	0	0	0	0	0	0
Love	0	0	5	6	5	7	0	0
Hate	1	5	0	0	0	0	0	0
Pride	0	0	4	4	4	6	2	8
Shaming	0	0	0	0	0	0	0	0
Anger	0	0	0	0	0	0	0	0
Desire	1	5	1	1	1	1	0	0
Fear	0	0	0	0	0	0	0	0
Cognition	3	14	8	9	3	4	5	21
Alertness	0	0	2	2	1	1	1	4
Non-alertness	0	0	0	0	0	0	0	0
Knowledge	3	14	0	0	0	0	0	0
Ignorance	0	0	0	0	0	0	0	0
Obey/agree	0	0	1	1	1	1	0	0
Rejection	0	0	0	0	0	0	0	0
Reason	0	0	5	6	1	1	4	17
Ethics	3	14	5	6	5	7	0	0
Ethically good	2	9	2	2	2	3	0	0
Ethically bad	1	5	3	3	3	4	0	0
Status	0	0	4	4	3	4	2	8
Exaltation	0	0	4	4	3	4	2	8
Debasement	0	0	0	0	0	0	0	0
Wealth	0	0	0	0	0	0	0	0
Poverty	0	0	0	0	0	0	0	0
Strength	0	0	0	0	0	0	0	0
Weakness	0	0	0	0	0	0	0	0
Weal	0	0	16	18	15	21	1	4
Healing	0	0	0	0	0	0	0	0

Life	0	0	2	2	2	3	0	0
Peace/shalom	0	0	14	16	13	18	1	4
Reward	0	0	4	4	3	4	1	4
Woe	3	14	13	14	5	7	8	33
llness/injury	0	0	0	0	0	0	0	0
Death	0	0	1	1	1	1	0	0
Destruction	3	14	11	12	5	7	6	25
Punishment	3	14	7	8	1	1	6	25

Note: Percentages describe the percentage of an recipient's total reception of activity, not the percentage of activity in Joel. See individual comparisons for significant differences.

The following summary considers the question: which entity receives more of any particular type of action (in terms of percentage of the total they receive) than any other entity (as long as the frequency is five or greater)?[5]

1. God: emotion (including sorrow).
2. Israelites: love, peace/shalom.
3. Foreigners: cognition, woe (including destruction and punishment).

Evaluation of Activity in Joel (Ranked)

Evaluation	Qty	%		
-2	61	21	Mean:	-0.40
-3	61	21	Std. Dev	2.03
+2	58	20	Minimum	-3.0
+1	42	15	Maximum	3.0
0	36	13		
+3	14	5		
-1	8	3		
No score	4	1		

Mean Evaluations in the Book of Joel

	God	Humans	Israel	Foreign	Plants	Insect
Actions	+0.32	-0.31	-0.08	-0.94	+1.00	-1.31
Receptions	-0.45	+0.29	+0.74	-1.17	-1.74	-1.40

42 percent are -2 and -3, 47 percent (close to half) are negative, 13 percent are neutral, 1 percent are no-score, and 40 percent are positive.

5. Actions lacking as far as divine, human, Israelite, and foreigner reception is concerned include: shaming, anger, fear, non-alert, ignorance, rejection, debasement, wealth, poverty, strength, weakness, healing, and illness/injury.

There is a higher evaluation standard deviation in Joel than in SPP.

Foreigner and insect activity and reception are all definitely negative. What God and plants receive is harsher than what they do, while overall humans, especially Israelites, receive better than they give.

Metacategories and Categories:
All Actions in Joel

Action/activity	Qty	%
Emotions	53	19
Joy	8	3
Sorrow	21	7
Love	5	2
Hate	1	0.4
Pride	7	2
Shaming	1	0.4
Anger	0	0
Desire	2	0.7
Fear	9	3
Cognition	19	7
Alertness	4	1
Non-alertness	2	0.7
Knowledge	6	2
Ignorance	0	0
Obey/agree	1	0.4
Rejection	0	0
Reason	6	2
Ethics	9	3
Ethically good	5	2
Ethically bad	4	1
Status	13	5
Exaltation	8	3
Debasement	1	0.4
Wealth	0	0
Poverty	0	0
Strength	2	0.7
Weakness	2	0.7
Weal	19	7
Healing	0	0
Life	4	1
Peace/shalom	15	5
Reward	4	1

Woe		59	21
	Illness/injury	0	0
	Death	1	0.4
	Destruction	56	20
	Punishment	11	4

Ranked Metacategories in Joel[6]

Action/activity	Qty	%
Woe	59	21
Emotions	53	19
Weal	19	7
Cognition	19	7
Status	13	5
Ethics	9	3

Ranked Categories in Joel

Action/activity	Qty	%
Destruction	56	20
Sorrow	21	7
Peace/shalom	15	5
Punishment	11	4
Fear	9	3
Joy	8	3
Exaltation	8	3
Pride	7	2
Knowledge	6	2
Reason	6	2
Love	5	2
Ethically good	5	2
Alertness	4	1
Life	4	1
Reward	4	1
Ethically bad	4	1
Desire	2	0.7
Non-alertness	2	0.7
Strength	2	0.7
Weakness	2	0.7
Death	1	0.4
Debasement	1	0.4

6. As noted in the introduction to SPP, since not all categories are mutually exclusive, totals cannot necessarily be obtained by adding metacategories or categories together.

Ranked Categories in Joel

Hate	1	0.4
Obey/agree	1	0.4
Shaming	1	0.4[7]

The ranking of metacategories is quite different from that in SPP (see the introduction to SPP). Note that emotions are almost as frequent as woe, and ethics is not much of a concern in Joel.

2. *Divine versus Human Activity*

Null hypothesis: What GOD does to ALL in JOEL is the same as what HUMANS do to ALL in JOEL.

Dominant Metacategories, Categories, Actors, Complements
Significance: *= 0.05 **= 0.01 (§ and §§ = sig. low)

	GOD to ALL in JOEL		HUMANS to ALL in JOEL	
		%		%
Action	Woe	18*	Emotions	35**
Metacategories	Weal	14**		
10%+	Emotions	13§§		
	Cognition	10		
Action	Destruction	14	Sorrow	17**
Categories	Peace/shalom	12**	Fear	8**
5%+	Punishment	9	Destruction	7
	Reason	8**	Joy	6**
	Love	6**	Knowledge	6**
	Pride	5		
	Reward	5**		
Actors 10%+	God		Humans	
Complements	Humans	76**	Humans	28§§
Recipients	Human groups	72**	Israel	23§§
	Israel	54**	Human groups	20§§
10%+	Foreign	22**	Destruction	17
	Destruction	15	God	17**
	Land	10	Time	12**

7. The following activities are all missing from Joel: anger, healing, ignorance, illness/injury, poverty, rejection, and wealth-related actions.

Evaluation

Difference:	+ 0.63
Significant?	Yes*

	GOD to ALL in JOEL	HUMANS to ALL in JOEL
Mean	-0.32	-0.31
Std. Dev.	2.16	-1.86

GOD to ALL in JOEL—HUMANS to ALL in JOEL:
Comparative Frequencies
Significance: *= 0.05 **= 0.01 (§ and §§ = sig. low)

Action/activity	GOD to ALL in JOEL		HUMANS to ALL in JOEL	
Total activity	78		109	
	Qty	%	Qty	%
Emotions	10	13§§	38	35**
Joy	0	0§§	7	6**
Sorrow	0	0§§	19	17**
Love	5	6**	0	0§§
Hate	0	0	1	0.9
Pride	4	5	2	2
Shaming	0	0	1	0.9
Anger	0	0	0	0
Desire	1	1	0	0
Fear	0	0§§	9	8**
Cognition	8	10	10	9
Alertness	1	1	3	3
Non-alertness	0	0	1	0.9
Knowledge	0	0§§	6	6**
Ignorance	0	0	0	0
Obey/agree	1	1	0	0
Rejection	0	0	0	0
Reason	6	8**	0	0§§
Ethics	2	3	7	6
Ethically good	2	3	3	3
Ethically bad	0	0§	4	4*
Status	4	5	5	5
Exaltation	3	4	2	2
Debasement	0	0	1	0.9
Wealth	0	0	0	0
Poverty	0	0	0	0

GOD to ALL in JOEL—HUMANS to ALL in JOEL:
Comparative Frequencies
Significance: *= 0.05 **= 0.01 (§ and §§ = sig. low)

Action/activity	GOD to ALL in JOEL		HUMANS to ALL in JOEL	
Total activity	78		109	
Action/activity	Qty	%	Qty	%
Strength	1	1	1	0.9
Weakness	0	0	1	0.9
Weal	*11*	*14***	4	4§§
Healing	0	0	0	0
Life	2	3	2	2
Peace/shalom	*9*	*12***	2	2§§
Reward	*4*	*5***	0	0§§
Woe	*14*	*18**	8	7§
Illness/injury	0	0	0	0
Death	0	0	1	0.9
Destruction	11	14	8	7
Punishment	7	9	4	4

God's character in the book of Joel is not very similar to that of humans. The Evaluation of divine activity is significantly higher, indeed as positive as human deeds are negative. God performs more weal and woe, although none of the individual woe categories are significantly high. In other words, it is the cumulative effect of all woe categories which makes woe high for God.[8] All of the individual categories in which God is significantly high are positive: peace, reason, love, and reward.

The dominant ways in which God and humans are not markedly different include cognitive activity in general, destruction, punishment, and pride. Only destruction is dominant for both God and humans, making destruction the main way in which these actors are similar. Lacking (or rare) for both are anger, obedience (one instance) or rejection, wealth, poverty, healing, and illness/injury.[9]

Humans are characterized in Joel by their high emotionality. Sorrow, fear, and joy are dominant and high in comparison with God. The only

8. The lack of individual category significance for woe categories is not due to small numbers, because weal categories (which have small numbers) *are* significantly different. Rather, it is due to the fact that individual woe categories for humans are just slightly smaller than those for God.

9. Almost two thirds of the categories of activities (21) are infrequent for both.

other processes in humans that are comparatively high are knowledge and bad ethics, although this is not frequent. The cognitive activity characteristic of humans, knowing, is more passive than the cognitive activity in which God is comparatively high, reason. (This is also true for Israelites.) God is not involved in any activity where humans are significantly high, that is the aforementioned ones, with the exception of overall emotionality.

God's emphasis, then, is weal and woe, while the human activity is emotion oriented. As we will see, most of the positive actions God does are to Israelites, while most of the negative ones are done to foreigners.

3. *Israelite versus Foreigner Activity*

Null hypothesis: What ISRAELITES do to ALL in JOEL is the same as what FOREIGNERS do to ALL in JOEL.

Dominant Metacategories, Categories, Actors, Complements
Significance: *= 0.05 **= 0.01 (§ and §§ = sig. low)

	ISRAELITES to ALL in JOEL		FOREIGNERS to ALL in JOEL	
		%		%
Action	Emotions	48**	Woe	26**
Metacategories			Ethics	16*
10%+				
Action	Sorrow	24**	Destruction	26**
Categories	Fear	12**	Bad ethics	13**
5%+	Joy	9*	Punishment	13**
	Knowledge	7	Alertness	6
Actors 10%+	Israelites		Foreigners	
Complements	God	19	Humans	52**
Recipients	Humans	19§§	Israel	42**
	Destruction	17	Human groups	35**
10%+	Time	17	Destruction	19
	Israel	16§§	Military	19**
	Human groups	13§§	Foreign	16*
	Cultic	12	God	16
	Measurement	12	Land	16*

Evaluation

Difference:	+ 0.86
Significant?	Yes*

Both Evaluations are NEGATIVE

Dominant Metacategories, Categories, Actors, Complements
Significance: *= 0.05 **= 0.01 (§ and §§ = sig. low)

	%	%
	ISRAELITES to ALL in JOEL	FOREIGNERS to ALL in JOEL
Mean	-0.08	-0.94
Std. Dev.	1.85	1.77

ISRAELITES to ALL in JOEL—FOREIGNERS to ALL in JOEL:
Comparative Frequencies
Significance: *= 0.05 **= 0.01 (§ and §§ = sig. low)

	ISRAELITES to ALL in JOEL		FOREIGNERS to ALL in JOEL	
Total activity	75		31	
Action/activity	Qty	%	Qty	%
Emotions	36	48**	1	3§§
Joy	7	9*	0	0§
Sorrow	18	24**	0	0§§
Love	0	0	0	0
Hate	0	0	1	3
Pride	2	3	0	0
Shaming	1	1	0	0
Anger	0	0	0	0
Desire	0	0	0	0
Fear	9	*12**	0	0§§
Cognition	6	8	3	10
Alertness	1	1	2	6
Non-alertness	0	0	1	3
Knowledge	5	7	0	0
Ignorance	0	0	0	0
Obey/agree	0	0	0	0
Rejection	0	0	0	0
Reason	0	0	0	0
Ethics	2	3§	5	*16**
Ethically good	2	3	1	3
Ethically bad	0	0§§	4	*13**
Status	4	5	1	3
Exaltation	2	3	0	0
Debasement	1	1	0	0
Wealth	0	0	0	0

Poverty	0	0	0	0
Strength	0	0	1	3
Weakness	1	1	0	0
Weal	3	4	1	3
Healing	0	0	0	0
Life	2	3	0	0
Peace/shalom	1	1	1	3
Reward	0	0	0	0
Woe	0	0§§	8	26**
Illness/injury	0	0	0	0
Death	0	0	1	3
Destruction	0	0§§	8	26**
Punishment	0	0§§	4	13**

The emphasis of the study is divine activity versus the activity of others, rather than comparisons between types of humans. However, a brief analysis of the contrasts between Israelite and foreigner activity in Joel will provide a backdrop against which divine activity can be compared to Israelite and foreigner activity. Further, it will illustrate some of the limitations of combining Israelites and foreigners into 'humans' in Joel.

Israelites and foreigners in Joel act quite differently. Israelites engage in two and a half times as much activity as do foreigners. Israelite activity is primarily emotional in character, while foreigners are involved in woe and ethically charged actions. In particular, Israelites are mainly involved in sorrow, fear,[10] and joy, while foreigners are destroying, acting ethically bad, and punishing.[11] All specific activity that is significantly high for one actor is completely missing for the other: Israelites are not involved in woe at all or in Bad ethics, while foreigners evince no joy, sorrow, or fear.[12] Israelites and foreigners, however, are not markedly different in cognitive activity, status-related activity, and weal—none of which are prominent for either group.[13] The

10. No Israelite fear is directed toward God in Joel. The situation is different in SPP, where all Israelite fear is toward God.

11. Israelites also do non-significantly more knowing, while foreigners do non-significantly more alertness.

12. Foreigners express only one emotion, hate, while Israelites show no hate at all.

13. In the book of Joel neither foreigners nor Israelites are involved in reasoning, love, anger, desire, ignorance, obedience/agreement, rejection, wealth, poverty, healing, reward, or illness/injury.

negative physical nature of foreigner activity makes itself evident by their much lower evaluation.

Many Israelite activities are intransitives, directing toward God and toward humans only one fifth of the time for each.[14] In contrast, over half of foreigner activity is directed at humans, mainly Israelites. Foreigners, further, act more often than Israelites do toward the military, toward (other) foreigners, and toward the land. Israelites and foreigners do act with the same relative frequency toward God.

Israelite activity, then, is mainly emotional in character, while foreigner activity is primarily harmful and directed externally against others.

4. *Divine versus Israelite Activity*

Null hypothesis: What GOD does to ALL in JOEL is the same as what ISRAELITES do to ALL in JOEL.

Dominant Metacategories, Categories, Actors, Complements
Significance: *= 0.05 **= 0.01 (§ and §§ = sig. low)

		GOD to ALL in JOEL	ISRAELITES to ALL in JOEL	
		%		%
Action	Woe	18**	Emotions	48**
Metacategories	Weal	14*		
10%+	Emotions	13§§		
	Cognition	10		
Action	Destruction	14**	Sorrow	24**
Categories	Peace/shalom	12**	Fear	12**
5%+	Punishment	9**	Joy	9**
	Reason	8**	Knowledge	7**
	Love	6**		
	Pride	5		
	Reward	5*		
Actors 10%+	God		Israelites	
Complements	Humans	76**	God	19**
Recipients	Human groups	72**	Humans	19§§
	Israel	54**	Destruction	17
10%+	Foreign	22**	Time	17**
	Destruction	15	Israel	16§§

14. Only 14 of Israel's 75 activities in Joel are directed at God; half of these are emotions.

Land	10	Human groups	13§§
		Cultic	12
		Measurement	12**

Evaluation

Difference:	+ 0.40
Significant?	No

	GOD to ALL in JOEL	ISRAELITES to ALL in JOEL
Mean	-0.32	-0.08
Std. Dev.	2.16	1.85

GOD to ALL in JOEL—ISRAELITES to ALL in JOEL:
Comparative Frequencies
Significance: *= 0.05 **= 0.01 (§ and §§ = sig. low)

	GOD to ALL in JOEL		ISRAELITES to ALL in JOEL	
Total activity	78		75	
Action/activity	Qty	%	Qty	%
Emotions	10	13§§	36	48**
Joy	0	0§§	7	9**
Sorrow	0	0§§	18	24**
Love	5	6**	0	0§§
Hate	0	0	0	0
Pride	4	5	2	3
Shaming	0	0	1	1
Anger	0	0	0	0
Desire	1	1	0	0
Fear	0	0§§	9	*12***
Cognition	8	10	6	8
Alertness	1	1	1	1
Non-alertness	0	0	0	0
Knowledge	0	0§§	5	7**
Ignorance	0	0	0	0
Obey/agree	1	1	0	0
Rejection	0	0	0	0
Reason	6	8**	0	0§§
Ethics	2	3	2	3
Ethically good	2	3	2	3
Ethically bad	0	0	0	0
Status	4	5	4	5
Exaltation	3	4	2	3
Debasement	0	0	1	1

GOD to ALL in JOEL—ISRAELITES to ALL in JOEL:
Comparative Frequencies
Significance: *= 0.05 **= 0.01 (§ and §§ = sig. low)

	GOD to ALL in JOEL		ISRAELITES to ALL in JOEL	
Total activity	78		75	
Action/activity	Qty	%	Qty	%
Wealth	0	0	0	0
Poverty	0	0	0	0
Strength	1	1	0	0
Weakness	0	0	1	1
Weal	*11*	*14**	3	4§
Healing	0	0	0	0
Life	2	3	2	3
Peace/shalom	*9*	*12***	1	1§§
Reward	*4*	*5**	0	0§
Woe	*14*	*18***	0	0§§
Illness/injury	0	0	0	0
Death	0	0	0	0
Destruction	*11*	*14***	0	0§§
Punishment	*7*	*9***	0	0§§

Although Israelite activity differs sharply from that of foreigners, a comparison of divine activity with Israelite activity in Joel is quite similar to the comparison of divine activity and human activity, in good part since Israelites are responsible for 69 percent of human actions.[15]

The most noticeable difference between a comparison of divine with Israelite activity and one that compares divine with human activity generally lies in the fact that Israelites perform no ethically bad actions nor any woe. This contributes to an increase in Evaluation for the Israelites over humans in general.

There are fewer similarities when only Israelite humans are considered (as opposed to all humans). Overall cognition and pride are among the most frequent types of similar actions, and the Evaluation difference becomes insignificant.

God does far more weal *and* woe; destruction and punishment, not

15. The recipient picture is similar to that of God-humans, where the amount of recipients is somewhat low for humans. This is because (as noted in the previous analysis) one third of Israelite activity is intransitive (26 total).

high for God when compared to humans in general, becomes high when compared to Israelite activity. God also does more of the polar opposites of destruction and punishment: peace/shalom and reward respectively. Israelites do hardly any weal actions, and, as noted above, no woe at all.

As with the divine human comparison, psychological activity is quite different, although involvement in cognition and pride—both not very prominent—are similar. Almost half of Israelites' activities are emotions—a 13 percent increase over humans in general—so that God's emotionality is low in comparison. Specifically, Israelites have high amounts of sorrow (almost a quarter of Israelite actions in the book of Joel are sorrow), fear, and joy. The only emotion God expresses significantly more is love. Israel's emotions are response oriented, that is they seem to be in response to external stimuli: sorrow, fear, and joy. God's only comparatively high emotion is choice oriented: love.

As noted above, activity with overt ethical connotations does not play much of a role for either Israelites or God. (Neither does any bad ethical actions;[16] each does two good ones.) Neither Israelites nor God engage in many overall status-related actions, of which they each do the same amount.

In conclusion, God and Israelites are not very similar in terms of their common activity in Joel. This contrast is exemplified by the fact that all highs are also dominant for both scenarios. Divine activity is concentrated in the physical realm, while Israelite activity is focused on the emotional realm.

5. *Divine versus Foreigner Activity*

Null hypothesis: What GOD does to ALL in JOEL is the same as what FOREIGNERS do to ALL in JOEL.

Dominant Metacategories, Categories, Actors, Complements
Significance: *= 0.05 **= 0.01 (§ and §§ = sig. low)

		GOD to ALL in JOEL		FOREIGNERS to ALL in JOEL	
			%		%
Action	Woe		18	Woe	26
Metacategories	Weal		14	Ethics	16**

16. Ethically bad activities occur four times for humans in general; all are done by foreigners.

Dominant Metacategories, Categories, Actors, Complements
Significance: *= 0.05 **= 0.01 (§ and §§ = sig. low)

		GOD to ALL in JOEL		FOREIGNERS to ALL in JOEL	
		%			%
10%+	Emotions	13			
	Cognition	10			
Action	Destruction	14	Destruction	26	
Categories	Peace/shalom	12	Bad ethics	13**	
5%+	Punishment	9	Punishment	13	
	Reason	8*	Alertness	6	
	Love	6			
	Pride	5			
	Reward	5			
Actors 10%+	God		Foreigners		
Complements	Humans	76*	Humans	52§	
Recipients	Human groups	72**	Israel	42	
	Israel	54	Human groups	35§§	
10%+	Foreign	22	Destruction	19	
	Destruction	15	Military	19**	
	Land	10	Foreign	16	
			God	16**	
			Land	16	

Evaluation

Difference:	+1.26
Significant?	Yes**

	GOD to ALL in JOEL	FOREIGNERS to ALL in JOEL
Mean	-0.32	-0.94
Std. Dev.	2.16	1.77

GOD to ALL in JOEL—FOREIGNERS to ALL in JOEL:
Comparative Frequencies
Significance: *= 0.05 **= 0.01 (§ and §§ = sig. low)

	GOD to ALL in JOEL		FOREIGNERS to ALL in JOEL	
Total activity	78		31	
Action/activity	Qty	%	Qty	%
Emotions	10	13	1	3
Joy	0	0	0	0
Sorrow	0	0	0	0

Love	5	6	0	0
Hate	0	0	1	3
Pride	4	5	0	0
Shaming	0	0	0	0
Anger	0	0	0	0
Desire	1	1	0	0
Fear	0	0	0	0
Cognition	8	10	3	10
Alertness	1	1	2	6
Non-alertness	0	0	1	3
Knowledge	0	0	0	0
Ignorance	0	0	0	0
Obey/agree	1	1	0	0
Rejection	0	0	0	0
Reason	6	8*	0	0§
Ethics	2	3§§	5	16**
Ethically good	2	3	1	3
Ethically bad	0	0§§	4	13**
Status	4	5	1	3
Exaltation	3	4	0	0
Debasement	0	0	0	0
Wealth	0	0	0	0
Poverty	0	0	0	0
Strength	1	1	1	3
Weakness	0	0	0	0
Weal	11	14	1	3
Healing	0	0	0	0
Life	2	3	0	0
Peace/shalom	9	12	1	3
Reward	4	5	0	0
Woe	14	18	8	26
Illness/injury	0	0	0	0
Death	0	0	1	3
Destruction	11	14	8	26
Punishment	7	9	4	13

There are few measurable differences between divine activity and foreigner activity in Joel. The Evaluation of activity is different, with God's being +1.26** more positive than that of foreigners. The *only* significant category differences are that God does more reason/ decision, while foreigners do more actions with overtly ethical connotations, specifically more bad ones. However, one can ask, what is emphasized?

The following details, while not statistically significant, are note-worthy. God has the same density of cognitive activity but slightly greater emotionality.[17] Divine emotions include especially love and pride, whereas the only foreigners' emotion is hate. Weal (including the category peace) is dominant for God, but not for foreigners.[18] Woe (including destruction and punishment) is dominant for both God and foreigners, with rather similar percentages of occurrence. God treats Israelites more kindly than foreigners do, although the low frequency of foreigners' actions toward Israel (there are 13 of these) makes statistical comparison difficult.[19]

God, then, is not as harsh as foreigners in Joel, and somewhat more emotion-oriented. Even so, there are similarities between divine and foreigner activity in Joel, especially in that both do many physically harmful actions.

6. *Divine versus Insect Activity*

Null hypothesis: What GOD does to ALL in JOEL is the same as what INSECTS do to ALL in JOEL.

Dominant Metacategories, Categories, Actors, Complements
Significance: *= 0.05 **= 0.01 (§ and §§ = sig. low)

		GOD to ALL in JOEL	INSECTS to ALL in JOEL	
		%		%
Action	Woe	18	Woe	33
Metacategories	Weal	14**		
10%+	Emotions	13*		
	Cognition	10**		

17. Significance 0.098.

18. God does non-significantly more weal and its category peace/shalom (significance for weal: 0.07; significance for peace/shalom: 0.14).

19. The following information is from a *God to Israelites in Joel versus foreigners to Israelites in Joel* comparison. All God's dominant actions are positive (peace/shalom [19%], love [12%], pride [10%], exaltation [7%], reward [7%]), while foreigner activity toward Israelites is mainly negative (destruction [31%]**, ethically bad [23%]**, death [8%], peace/shalom [8%], punishment [8%]). God's evaluation (+1.62) is as positive toward Israelites as the evaluation of foreigners to Israelites is negative (-1.69).**

Action	Destruction	14§	Destruction	33*
Categories	Peace/shalom	12**		
5%+	Punishment	9**		
	Reason	8*		
	Love	6*		
	Pride	5		
	Reward	5		

Actors 10%+	God		Insects	

Complements	Humans	76**	Agriculture	43**
Recipients	Human groups	72	Food-orientated	43**
10%+	Israel	54**	Plants-orientated	40**
	Foreign	22	Land	14
	Destruction	15	Military	12
	Land	10		

Evaluation

Difference:	+1.63
Significant?	Yes**

	GOD to ALL in JOEL	INSECTS to ALL in JOEL
Mean	-0.32	-1.31
Std. Dev.	2.16	1.73

GOD to ALL in JOEL—INSECTS to ALL in JOEL:
Comparative Frequencies
Significance: *= 0.05 **= 0.01 (§ and §§ = sig. low)

Action/activity	GOD to ALL in JOEL		INSECTS to ALL in JOEL	
Total activity	78		42	
	Qty	%	Qty	%
Emotions	*10*	*13**	1	2§
Joy	0	0	0	0
Sorrow	0	0	0	0
Love	5	6*	0	0§
Hate	0	0	0	0
Pride	4	5	1	2
Shaming	0	0	0	0
Anger	0	0	0	0
Desire	1	1	0	0
Fear	0	0	0	0
Cognition	*8*	*10***	0	0§§

GOD to ALL in JOEL—INSECTS to ALL in JOEL:
Comparative Frequencies
Significance: *= 0.05 **= 0.01 (§ and §§ = sig. low)

Action/activity	GOD to ALL in JOEL		INSECTS to ALL in JOEL	
Total activity	78		42	
	Qty	%	Qty	%
Alertness	1	1	0	0
Non-alertness	0	0	0	0
Knowledge	0	0	0	0
Ignorance	0	0	0	0
Obey/agree	1	1	0	0
Rejection	0	0	0	0
Reason	*6*	*8**	0	0§
Ethics	2	3	0	0
Ethically good	2	3	0	0
Ethically bad	0	0	0	0
Status	4	5	1	2
Exaltation	3	4	1	2
Debasement	0	0	0	0
Wealth	0	0	0	0
Poverty	0	0	0	0
Strength	1	1	0	0
Weakness	0	0	0	0
Weal	*11*	*14***	0	0§§
Healing	0	0	0	0
Life	2	3	0	0
Peace/shalom	*9*	*12***	0	0§§
Reward	4	5	0	0
Woe	14	18	14	33
Illness/injury	0	0	0	0
Death	0	0	0	0
Destruction	*11*	*14§*	*14*	*33**
Punishment	*7*	*9***	0	0§§

Insects are a type of actor being considered in the Joel analyses which were not considered in SPP. These creatures are being examined because they are described as Yahweh's army in Joel 2.11, and in view of the fact that they are major actors in the book.[20] Insect activity will initially be compared to divine activity in general. This will be followed

20. Insects perform 42 of the book's 284 actions (7%) in Joel.

by a separate analysis of divine treatment of Israelites versus insect activity.

The foci of divine and insect activity are quite different. Humans are the direct recipient of only one insect action (2 percent), whereas humans receive 59 (76 percent) of God's actions. Instead, that which relates to sustenance (agriculture, food, plants/plant products) is the primary recipient of insect activity. Specifically, plants/plant products receive 40 percent of insect actions (17), while plants/plant products receives only 5 percent of God's actions (4). (This lends support to the idea that Yahweh's army, as depicted in Joel 2, is comprised of insects, not humans or angelic beings.)

Previous analyses have shown that God does large amounts of woe and destruction. Does this make God similar to the insects? Not truly so; unlike insects, God is described as doing almost as much weal as woe; insects do only woe. Furthermore, God's pattern in achieving woe is different; it reflects a conscious choice: God punishes more, whereas insects do not punish at all.

In addition, God is a psychological being who loves and reasons, while insects do not; a quarter (23 percent) of God's actions are psychological (emotions+cognitive), while insects are almost completely non-psychological.[21]

In sum, insects are primarily presented as destructive beings with no other personality traits, whereas God does a larger variety of types of activities.[22]

---

21. A direct examination of the database shows that they do a pride-type action (to do great things; Joel 2.20 [word number 0524]), but it does not mean that they actually express emotions.

22. I also ran a comparison of divine activity to that of divine activity combined with insect activity, recognizing that this might not be a valid statistical procedure. Here is a summary of the analysis.

The main question here concerns whether there is a significant difference when insect actions are added to divine activity versus divine activity alone, noting that the insects are described as Yahweh's instruments (Yahweh's army) in Joel 2. The results are that there are no significant differences between the two scenarios. However, the Yahweh-insect tandem has some non-significant differences with God's activity alone: there are non-significant increases in woe and destruction, and non-significant decreases in all other non-woe metacategories and categories where activity occurs (i.e. which are not missing).

7. *God to Israelites versus Insect Activity*

Null hypothesis: What GOD does to ISRAELITES in JOEL is the same as what INSECTS do to ALL in JOEL.

Dominant Metacategories, Categories, Actors, Complements
Significance: *= 0.05 **= 0.01 (§ and §§ = sig. low)

		GOD to ISRAELITES in JOEL		INSECTS to ALL in JOEL
		%		%
Action	Emotions	24**	Woe	33**
Metacategories	Weal	24**		
10%+				
Action	Peace/shalom	19**	Destruction	33**
Categories	Love	12**		
5%+	Pride	10		
	Exaltation	7		
	Reward	7*		
Actors 10%+	God		Insects	
Complements	Israelites		Agriculture	43
Recipients			Food-orientated	43
10%+			Plants-orientated	40
			Land	14
			Military	12

Evaluation

Difference:	+2.93
Significant?	Yes**

	GOD to ISRAELITES in JOEL	INSECTS to ALL in JOEL
Mean	1.62	-1.31
Std. Dev.	1.40	1.73

GOD to ISRAELITES in JOEL—INSECTS to ALL in JOEL:
Comparative Frequencies
Significance: *= 0.05 **= 0.01 (§ and §§ = sig. low)

	GOD to ISRAELITES in JOEL		INSECTS to ALL in JOEL	
Total activity	42		42	
Action/activity	Qty	%	Qty	%
Emotions	*10*	*24***	1	2§§
Joy	0	0	0	0
Sorrow	0	0	0	0
Love	*5*	*12***	0	0§§
Hate	0	0	0	0
Pride	4	10	1	2
Shaming	0	0	0	0
Anger	0	0	0	0
Desire	1	2	0	0
Fear	0	0	0	0
Cognition	*3*	*7**	0	0§
Alertness	1	2	0	0
Non-alertness	0	0	0	0
Knowledge	0	0	0	0
Ignorance	0	0	0	0
Obey/agree	1	2	0	0
Rejection	0	0	0	0
Reason	1	2	0	0
Ethics	2	5	0	0
Ethically good	2	5	0	0
Ethically bad	0	0	0	0
Status	3	7	1	2
Exaltation	3	7	1	2
Debasement	0	0	0	0
Wealth	0	0	0	0
Poverty	0	0	0	0
Strength	0	0	0	0
Weakness	0	0	0	0
Weal	*10*	*24***	0	0§§
Healing	0	0	0	0
Life	2	5	0	0
Peace/shalom	*8*	*19***	0	0§§
Reward	*3*	*7**	0	0§

GOD to ISRAELITES in JOEL—INSECTS to ALL in JOEL:
Comparative Frequencies
Significance: *= 0.05 **= 0.01 (§ and §§ = sig. low)

Action/activity	GOD to ISRAELITES in JOEL		INSECTS to ALL in JOEL	
	Qty	%	Qty	%
Total activity	42		42	
Woe	0	0§§	*14*	*33**
Illness/injury	0	0	0	0
Death	0	0	0	0
Destruction	0	0§§	*14*	*33**
Punishment	0	0	0	0

The analysis of God to Israelites versus insect activity in general may at first seem to be a strange comparison. However, according to the context, the insects in Joel are God's agents of destruction, Yahweh's army; the eventual recipients of their actions (although not the direct ones) are Israelites. In other words, a question is: how does what God does *directly* to Israel compare to what God does *indirectly* to Israel?

God's direct activity toward Israelites is quite positive and beneficent in Joel. Divine activity is characterized by emotionality and actions of weal. In particular, God directs more peace/shalom, love, and reward toward Israel, while performing no woe at all. (Pride and exaltation of Israel are also dominant but not significantly high.) Further, God's evaluation is +1.62**, which is +2.93 greater than insect activity. God, then, is portrayed as one who is interested in the physical and mental well-being of Israelites. On the other hand, insects are shown to be basically non-thinking destroyers.

Neither engage in ethical or status-related actions. Cognitive activity is high for God only when all its categories are added together (i.e. no individual cognitive categories are significantly different).

The effect is a resulting tension: God is only indirectly responsible for the disaster, yet directly responsible for the recovery and blessing. God is both blamed and not blamed at the same time. The extreme contrast, with God acting so positively for Israel, seems to have the effect of exonerating God.

8. *God to Israelites versus God to Foreigners*

Null hypothesis: What GOD does to ISRAELITES in JOEL is the same as what GOD does to FOREIGNERS in JOEL.

Dominant Metacategories, Categories, Actors, Complements
Significance: *= 0.05 **= 0.01 (§ and §§ = sig. low)

	GOD to ISRAELITES in JOEL		GOD to FOREIGNERS in JOEL	
		%		%
Action	Emotions	24	Woe	47**
Metacategories	Weal	24	Cognition	24
10%+			Emotions	12
Action	Peace/shalom	19	Destruction	35**
Categories	Love	12	Punishment	35**
5%+	Pride	10	Reason	24**
	Exaltation	7	Pride	12
	Reward	7	Exaltation	6
			Peace/shalom	6
			Reward	6
Actors 10%+	God		God	
Complements Recipients 10%+	Israelites		Foreigners	

Evaluation

Difference:	+3.09
Significant?	Yes**

	GOD to ISRAELITES in JOEL	GOD to FOREIGNERS in JOEL
Mean	1.62	-1.47
Std. Dev.	1.40	2.18

GOD to ISRAELITES in JOEL—GOD to
FOREIGNERS in JOEL:
Comparative Frequencies
Significance: *= 0.05 **= 0.01 (§ and §§ = sig. low)

	GOD to ISRAELITES in JOEL		GOD to FOREIGNERS in JOEL	
Total activity	42		17	
Action/activity	Qty	%	Qty	%
Emotions	10	24	2	12
Joy	0	0	0	0
Sorrow	0	0	0	0
Love	5	12	0	0
Hate	0	0	0	0
Pride	4	10	2	12
Shaming	0	0	0	0
Anger	0	0	0	0
Desire	1	2	0	0
Fear	0	0	0	0
Cognition	3	7	4	24
Alertness	1	2	0	0
Non-alertness	0	0	0	0
Knowledge	0	0	0	0
Ignorance	0	0	0	0
Obey/agree	1	2	0	0
Rejection	0	0	0	0
Reason	1	2§§	4	24**
Ethics	2	5	0	0
Ethically good	2	5	0	0
Ethically bad	0	0	0	0
Status	3	7	1	6
Exaltation	3	7	1	6
Debasement	0	0	0	0
Wealth	0	0	0	0
Poverty	0	0	0	0
Strength	0	0	0	0
Weakness	0	0	0	0
Weal	10	24	1	6
Healing	0	0	0	0
Life	2	5	0	0
Peace/shalom	8	19	1	6
Reward	3	7	1	6

Woe	0	0§§	8	47**
Illness/injury	0	0	0	0
Death	0	0	0	0
Destruction	0	0§§	6	35**
Punishment	0	0§§	6	35**

God is involved in two and a half as many actions toward Israelites as toward foreigners. Over half of what Israelites receive is from God (59 percent), and almost three quarters of what foreigners receive in Joel is from God (71 percent). (This is similar to, but not quite the same as, the corresponding distribution in SPP, where 47 percent of what Israelites receive and 40 percent of what foreigners receive is from God.) The low frequency of actions toward each (especially foreigners) means that relative densities must be great to be statistically significant. The following analysis will thus make references to a number of features that do not reach a 0.05 significance level.

God is considerably kinder to Israelites than to foreigners in Joel compared to was the case in SPP. In fact, the Evaluation of divine action toward Israelites is as positive as it is harsh toward foreigners. The resulting difference is extreme: 3.09**.[23]

God does more weal[24] (including peace/shalom[25]) toward Israelites. God also shows more emotion[26] (including love) toward them.[27] In addition to those just mentioned, reward appears among dominant actions.[28] These non-significant highs help explain the far more positive evaluation. God does no woe toward Israelites.

Toward foreigners, God does much woe (including destruction and punishment, which are dominant and significant). In fact, almost half of God's actions toward foreigners involve woe (47 percent); all woe foreigners receive in Joel is from God. Also high and dominant is reason/decision.[29]

---

23. Of positive categories which Israelites receive (regardless of what foreigners receive), the following come completely or mostly from God: all love, pride, desire, alertness, reason, good ethics, exaltation, life, and reward, as well as 10/15 weal and 8/13 peace/shalom actions. Note that God does no negative categories of activity toward Israelites in Joel.

24. Significance 0.08.

25. Significance 0.179.

26. Significance 0.27.

27. Significance 0.058.

28. Other positive actions toward Israelites include good ethics, exaltation, and life.

29. All four instances concern legal reasoning, i.e. judgment.

9. *God to Israelites versus Israelites to God*[30]

Null hypothesis: What GOD does to ISRAELITES in JOEL is the same as what ISRAELITES do to GOD in JOEL.

Dominant Metacategories, Categories, Actors, Complements
Significance: *= 0.05 **= 0.01 (§ and §§ = sig. low)

	GOD to ISRAELITES in JOEL		ISRAELITES to GOD in JOEL	
		%		%
Action	Emotions	24	Emotions	50
Metacategories	Weal	24**	Cognition	21
10%+			Ethics	14
Action	Peace/shalom	19*	Sorrow	36**
Categories	Love	12	Knowledge	21**
5%+	Pride	10	Good ethics	14
	Exaltation	7	Joy	14*
	Reward	7		
Actors 10%+	God		Israelites	
Complements	Israelites		God	
Recipients				
10%+				

Evaluation

Difference:	+1.33
Significant?	Yes*

Both Evaluations are POSITIVE

	GOD to ISRAELITES in JOEL	ISRAELITES to GOD in JOEL
Mean	1.62	0.29
Std. Dev.	1.40	1.82

---

30. Because of the small amount Israelites and foreigners do toward God in Joel there will be no "God to humans versus humans to God" analysis.

GOD to ISRAELITES in JOEL—ISRAELITES
to GOD in JOEL:
Comparative Frequencies
Significance: *= 0.05 **= 0.01 (§ and §§ = sig. low)

	GOD to ISRAELITES in JOEL		ISRAELITES to GOD in JOEL	
Total activity	42		14	
Action/activity	Qty	%	Qty	%
Emotions	10	24	7	50
Joy	0	0§	2	*14**
Sorrow	0	0§§	5	*36***
Love	5	12	0	0
Hate	0	0	0	0
Pride	4	10	0	0
Shaming	0	0	0	0
Anger	0	0	0	0
Desire	1	2	0	0
Fear	0	0	0	0
Cognition	3	7	3	21
Alertness	1	2	0	0
Non-alertness	0	0	0	0
Knowledge	0	0§§	3	*21***
Ignorance	0	0	0	0
Obey/agree	1	2	0	0
Rejection	0	0	0	0
Reason	1	2	0	0
Ethics	2	5	2	14
Ethically good	2	5	2	14
Ethically bad	0	0	0	0
Status	3	7	0	0
Exaltation	3	7	0	0
Debasement	0	0	0	0
Wealth	0	0	0	0
Poverty	0	0	0	0
Strength	0	0	0	0
Weakness	0	0	0	0
Weal	10	24**	0	0§§
Healing	0	0	0	0
Life	2	5	0	0
Peace/shalom	8	*19**	0	0§
Reward	3	7	0	0

GOD to ISRAELITES in JOEL—ISRAELITES
to GOD in JOEL:
Comparative Frequencies
Significance: *= 0.05 **= 0.01 (§ and §§ = sig. low)

	GOD to ISRAELITES in JOEL		ISRAELITES to GOD in JOEL	
Total activity	42		14	
Action/activity	Qty	%	Qty	%
Woe	0	0	0	0
Illness/injury	0	0	0	0
Death	0	0	0	0
Destruction	0	0	0	0
Punishment	0	0	0	0

God and Israelites concentrate on positive types of actions toward each other and have a positive overall Evaluation of their actions. The Evaluation of God's activity, however, is definitely higher than of Israel. God extensively brings weal (including peace/shalom) to Israelites; Israelites do not do so toward God. In fact, God engages in no negative activity at all toward Israelites in the book of Joel (at least directly— but see above for God's acting indirectly through insect activity). The only negative type of process in which Israelites are involved in relation to God is sorrow (which is over a third of their actions to God).

Emotions is the top type of activity of each scenario.[31] Further lacking from both is the performance of any woe.[32] Israelites direct more joy and sorrow toward God. While Israelites are not recorded as acting very frequently toward God (14 actions which is 19 percent of all Israelite actions and 64 percent of all divine receptions in Joel), half of their actions toward God are emotions in the form of joy and sorrow. Although Israelite emotionality toward God is highlighted, one should bear in mind God's emotions toward Israelites. God loves, causes pride (in a positive sense), and desires Israelites.

In the realm of cognition, Israelites have knowledge. Taking account of this as well as emotions, all listed Israelite activity toward God in Joel is psychological, except for two overtly ethical actions. Thus

31. Other similar dominant metacategories and categories are cognition, ethics, love, pride, exaltation, reward, and good ethics.
32. There are no significant ethics, status, or woe differences.

Israelites approach God in the mental realm, not the physical.

10. *God to Foreigners versus Foreigners to God*

Null hypothesis: What GOD does to FOREIGNERS in JOEL is the same as what FOREIGNERS do to GOD in JOEL.

Dominant Metacategories, Categories, Actors, Complements
Significance: *= 0.05 **= 0.01 (§ and §§ = sig. low)

	GOD to FOREIGNERS in JOEL		FOREIGNERS to GOD in JOEL	
		%		%
Action	Woe	47	Woe	60
Metacategories	Cognition	24*	Emotions	20
10%+	Emotions	12	Ethics	20
Action	Destruction	35	Destruction	60
Categories	Punishment	35	Punishment	60
5%+	Reason	24*	Bad ethics	20
	Pride	12	Hate	20
	Exaltation	6		
	Peace/shalom	6		
	Reward	6		
Actors 10%+	God		Foreigners	
Complements Recipients 10%+	Foreigners		God	

Evaluation

Difference:	+1.13
Significant?	No

Both Evaluations are NEGATIVE

	GOD to FOREIGNERS in JOEL	FOREIGNERS to GOD in JOEL
Mean	-1.47	-2.60
Std. Dev.	2.18	0.89

GOD to FOREIGNERS in JOEL—FOREIGNERS to GOD in JOEL:
Comparative Frequencies
Significance: *= 0.05 **= 0.01 (§ and §§ = sig. low)

Total activity	GOD to FOREIGNERS in JOEL		FOREIGNERS to GOD in JOEL	
	17		5	
Action/activity	Qty	%	Qty	%
Emotions	2	12	1	20
Joy	0	0	0	0
Sorrow	0	0	0	0
Love	0	0	0	0
Hate	0	0	1	20
Pride	2	12	0	0
Shaming	0	0	0	0
Anger	0	0	0	0
Desire	0	0	0	0
Fear	0	0	0	0
Cognition	*4*	*24**	0	0§
Alertness	0	0	0	0
Non-alertness	0	0	0	0
Knowledge	0	0	0	0
Ignorance	0	0	0	0
Obey/agree	0	0	0	0
Rejection	0	0	0	0
Reason	*4*	*24**	0	0§
Ethics	0	0	1	20
Ethically good	0	0	0	0
Ethically bad	0	0	1	20
Status	1	6	0	0
Exaltation	1	6	0	0
Debasement	0	0	0	0
Wealth	0	0	0	0
Poverty	0	0	0	0
Strength	0	0	0	0
Weakness	0	0	0	0
Weal	1	6	0	0
Healing	0	0	0	0
Life	0	0	0	0
Peace/shalom	1	6	0	0
Reward	1	6	0	0

Woe	8	47	3	60
Illness/injury	0	0	0	0
Death	0	0	0	0
Destruction	6	35	3	60
Punishment	6	35	3	60

God to foreigners in Joel versus foreigners to God in Joel comprises so few actions that meaningful comparisons are difficult to make.[33] It is noteworthy, however, as with SPP, God does over three times as many actions to foreigners as foreigners do to God (see SPP/Joel comparisons). The distribution of their actions toward each other is similar, both emphasizing woe, including destruction and punishment (the three relevant items are coded both destruction *and* punishment).[34] God is different in reasoning repeatedly.

11. *God to Foreigners versus Foreigners to Israelites*

Null hypothesis: What GOD does to FOREIGNERS in JOEL is the same as what FOREIGNERS do to ISRAELITES in JOEL.

Dominant Metacategories, Categories, Actors, Complements
Significance: *= 0.05 **= 0.01 (§ and §§ = sig. low)

	GOD to FOREIGNERS in JOEL		FOREIGNERS to ISRAELITES in JOEL	
		%		%
Action	Woe	47	Woe	31
Metacategories	Cognition	24*	Ethics	23*
10%+	Emotions	12		
Action	Destruction	35	Destruction	31
Categories	Punishment	35	Bad ethics	23*
5%+	Reason	24*	Death	8
	Pride	12	Peace/shalom	8
	Exaltation	6	Punishment	8
	Peace/shalom	6		
	Reward	6		

33. God to Israelites and vice versa is much greater in terms of absolute frequencies (42:14).

34. That foreigners could do destruction or punishment to God does indeed appear strange. The context concerns recompense in Joel 4.4 [Eng. 3.4]: "And also, what are you to me, O Tyre and Sidon, and all the territories of Philistia? Are you indeed paying Me back? But if you are paying Me back, I will swiftly, *yes*, quickly return your payback on your head".

Significance: *= 0.05 **= 0.01 (§ and §§ = sig. low)

	GOD to FOREIGNERS in JOEL	FOREIGNERS to ISRAELITES in JOEL
	%	%
Actors 10%+	God	Foreigners
Complements Recipients 10%+	Foreigners	Israelites

Evaluation

Difference:	+ 0.22
Significant?	No

Both Evaluations are NEGATIVE

	GOD to FOREIGNERS in JOEL	FOREIGNERS to ISRAELITES in JOEL
Mean	-1.47	-1.69
Std. Dev.	2.18	1.60

GOD to FOREIGNERS in JOEL—FOREIGNERS to
ISRAELITES in JOEL:
Comparative Frequencies
Significance: *= 0.05 **= 0.01 (§ and §§ = sig. low)

	GOD to FOREIGNERS in JOEL		FOREIGNERS to ISRAELITES in JOEL	
Total activity	17		13	
Action/activity	Qty	%	Qty	%
Emotions	2	12	0	0
Joy	0	0	0	0
Sorrow	0	0	0	0
Love	0	0	0	0
Hate	0	0	0	0
Pride	2	12	0	0
Shaming	0	0	0	0
Anger	0	0	0	0
Desire	0	0	0	0
Fear	0	0	0	0
Cognition	4	24*	0	0§
Alertness	0	0	0	0

Non-alertness	0	0	0	0
Knowledge	0	0	0	0
Ignorance	0	0	0	0
Obey/agree	0	0	0	0
Rejection	0	0	0	0
Reason	*4*	*24**	*0*	*0§*
Ethics	*0*	*0§*	*3*	*23**
Ethically good	0	0	0	0
Ethically bad	*0*	*0§*	*3*	*23**
Status	1	6	0	0
Exaltation	1	6	0	0
Debasement	0	0	0	0
Wealth	0	0	0	0
Poverty	0	0	0	0
Strength	0	0	0	0
Weakness	0	0	0	0
Weal	1	6	1	8
Healing	0	0	0	0
Life	0	0	0	0
Peace/shalom	1	6	1	8
Reward	1	6	0	0
Woe	8	47	4	31
Illness/injury	0	0	0	0
Death	0	0	1	8
Destruction	6	35	4	31
Punishment	6	35	1	8

The small number of instances makes comparisons difficult. However, statistical differences appear in reason/decision by God in relation to foreigners and in ethically bad activity by foreigners in relation to Israelites. Noteworthy is the fact that both lines of action are strong in woe. It is logical to conclude that, for Joel, God's negative activity toward foreigners has something to do with the foreigners' destructive actions toward Israelites—a contextual reading certainly bears this out (see Joel 4 [Eng. Joel 3]). Thus Joel presents a picture which is consistent with SPP (see the same comparison for SPP).

12. *Divine Activity versus Divine Reception*

Null hypothesis: What GOD does to ALL in JOEL is the same as what ALL does to GOD in JOEL.

Dominant Metacategories, Categories, Actors, Complements
Significance: *= 0.05 **= 0.01 (§ and §§ = sig. low)

	GOD to ALL in JOEL		ALL to GOD in JOEL	
		%		%
Action	Woe	18	Emotions	41**
Metacategories	Weal	14*	Ethics	14
10%+	Emotions	13§§	Cognition	14
	Cognition	10	Woe	14
Action	Destruction	14	Sorrow	23**
Categories	Peace/shalom	12*	Destruction	14
5%+	Punishment	9	Knowledge	14**
	Reason	8	Punishment	14
	Love	6	Good ethics	9
	Pride	5	Joy	9**
	Reward	5		
Actors 10%+	God		Humans	86
			Human groups	73
			Israel	64
			Foreign	23
Complements	Humans	76	God	
Recipients	Human groups	72		
10%+	Israel	54		
	Foreign	22		
	Destruction	15		
	Land	10)		

Evaluation

Difference:	+ 0.77
Significant?	No

	GOD to ALL in JOEL	ALL to GOD in JOEL
Mean	0.32	-0.45
Std. Dev.	2.16	1.92

GOD to ALL in JOEL—ALL to GOD in JOEL:
Comparative Frequencies
Significance: *= 0.05 **= 0.01 (§ and §§ = sig. low)

	GOD to ALL in JOEL		ALL to GOD in JOEL	
Total activity	78		22	
Action/activity	Qty	%	Qty	%
Emotions	10	13§§	9	41**
Joy	0	0§§	2	9**
Sorrow	0	0§§	5	23**
Love	5	6	0	0
Hate	0	0	1	5
Pride	4	5	0	0
Shaming	0	0	0	0
Anger	0	0	0	0
Desire	1	1	1	5
Fear	0	0	0	0
Cognition	8	10	3	14
Alertness	1	1	0	0
Non-alertness	0	0	0	0
Knowledge	0	0§§	3	14**
Ignorance	0	0	0	0
Obey/agree	1	1	0	0
Rejection	0	0	0	0
Reason	6	8	0	0
Ethics	2	3	3	14
Ethically good	2	3	2	9
Ethically bad	0	0	1	5
Status	4	5	0	0
Exaltation	3	4	0	0
Debasement	0	0	0	0
Wealth	0	0	0	0
Poverty	0	0	0	0
Strength	1	1	0	0
Weakness	0	0	0	0
Weal	*11*	*14**	0	0§
Healing	0	0	0	0
Life	2	3	0	0
Peace/shalom	*9*	*12**	0	0§
Reward	4	5	0	0

GOD to ALL in JOEL—ALL to GOD in JOEL:
Comparative Frequencies
Significance: *= 0.05 **= 0.01 (§ and §§ = sig. low)

	GOD to ALL in JOEL		ALL to GOD in JOEL	
Total activity	78		22	
Action/activity	Qty	%	Qty	%
Woe	14	18	3	14
Illness/injury	0	0	0	0
Death	0	0	0	0
Destruction	11	14	3	14
Punishment	7	9	3	14

There are very few similarities between divine activity and divine reception. God is more of an actor than a recipient—God does 27 percent of all actions in Joel and receives only 8 percent**.

Similarities of note include Evaluation (although God's actions are mildly positive and divine reception is mildly negative), and dominant categories of destruction and punishment.[35] Also the top four recipients of God's actions in Joel are the same as the top four actors of what God receives in Joel. Groups receive from and act toward God considerably more frequently than individuals.

The difference between what God does and what God receives in Joel is quite sharp. God brings weal and peace/shalom, but receives none.[36] God receives joy, sorrow, and knowledge,[37] but is involved in none of these. The amount of emotionality directed toward God is high; it is 41 percent of divine reception.[38]

35. See the explanation in *God to foreigners in Joel versus foreigners to Israelites in Joel.*

36. God also performs more weal and more peace/shalom in SPP than God receives, but unlike Joel, the reception is not completely missing.

37. Since overall divine reception is so low, these significantly high categories do not occur very frequently.

38. Some observations which have not been tested for statistical significance: of the categories that have opposites God does more positive types of categories than negative. God does similar amounts of weal and woe (11: 14). God does more love than hate (5: 1). God does more pride than causing shame (4: 1). God does more alertness than non-alertness (1: 0), and more obedience/agreement than rejection (1: 0). God does more good ethics than bad ethics (2: 0), more exaltation than debasement (3: 0), more strength than weakness (1: 0). God does more life than death

13. *Divine Reception versus Human Reception*

Null hypothesis: What ALL does to GOD in JOEL is the same as what ALL does to HUMANS in JOEL.

Dominant Metacategories, Categories, Actors, Complements
Significance: *= 0.05 **= 0.01 (§ and §§ = sig. low)

		ALL to GOD in JOEL %	ALL to HUMANS in JOEL	%
Action	Emotions	41**	Weal	18**
Metacategories	Ethics	14	Woe	14
10%+	Cognition	14	Emotions	11§§
	Woe	14		
Action	Sorrow	23**	Peace/shalom	16**
Categories	Destruction	14	Destruction	12
5%+	Knowledge	14**	Punishment	8
	Punishment	14	Love	6
	Good ethics	9	Reason	6
	Joy	9**		
Actors 10%+	Humans	86**	God	62**
	Human groups	73**	Humans	31§§
	Israel	64**	Human groups	26§§
	Foreign	23	Foreign	16
			Israel	14§§
Complements Recipients 10%+	God		Humans	

Evaluation

Difference:	- 0.74
Significant?	No

(2: 0), but more destruction than peace/shalom (11: 9), and more punishment than reward (7: 4).

Of the categories that have opposites God receives more negative types of categories than positive. God receives more woe than weal (3: 0). God receives more sorrow than joy (5: 2), and more hate than love (1: 0). God receives no alertness or non-alertness, and more knowledge than ignorance (3: 0). God receives more good ethics than bad ethics (2: 1). God receives more destruction than peace/shalom (3: 0), and more punishment than reward (3: 0).

Dominant Metacategories, Categories, Actors, Complements
Significance: *= 0.05 **= 0.01 (§ and §§ = sig. low)

	ALL to GOD in JOEL	ALL to HUMANS in JOEL
Mean	-0.45	-2.60
Std. Dev.	1.92	2.14

ALL to GOD in JOEL—ALL to HUMANS in JOEL:
Comparative Frequencies
Significance: *= 0.05 **= 0.01 (§ and §§ = sig. low)

	ALL to GOD in JOEL		ALL to HUMANS in JOEL	
Total activity	22		90	
Action/activity	Qty	%	Qty	%
Emotions	9	*41***	10	11§§
Joy	2	9**	0	0§§
Sorrow	5	23**	0	0§§
Love	0	0	5	6
Hate	1	5	0	0
Pride	0	0	4	4
Shaming	0	0	0	0
Anger	0	0	0	0
Desire	1	5	1	1
Fear	0	0	0	0
Cognition	3	14	8	9
Alertness	0	0	2	2
Non-alertness	0	0	0	0
Knowledge	3	*14***	0	0§§
Ignorance	0	0	0	0
Obey/agree	0	0	1	1
Rejection	0	0	0	0
Reason	0	0	5	6
Ethics	3	14	5	6
Ethically good	2	9	2	2
Ethically bad	1	5	3	3
Status	0	0	4	4
Exaltation	0	0	4	4
Debasement	0	0	0	0
Wealth	0	0	0	0
Poverty	0	0	0	0
Strength	0	0	0	0
Weakness	0	0	0	0

Weal	0	0§§	16	18**
Healing	0	0	0	0
Life	0	0	2	2
Peace/shalom	0	0§§	14	16**
Reward	0	0	4	4
Woe	3	14	13	14
Illness/injury	0	0	0	0
Death	0	0	1	1
Destruction	3	14	11	12
Punishment	3	14	7	8

In comparing the figure of God with that of humans, one consideration is how similar or different they are as objects of actions.

God receives more emotions, particularly sorrow and joy, as well as more knowledge (all sorrow, joy, and knowledge are done by Israelites). Humans receive more weal, especially peace/shalom. These actions largely involve Israelites, who receive 15/16 of the weal actions and 13/14 of the peace/shalom actions.[39]

While the evaluation of actions toward God is negative (-0.45) and that of actions toward humans is positive (0.29), the difference is not significant. God receives less weal and an equal percentage of woe.[40]

Divine Reception versus Israelite Reception

If only Israelites are considered among humans, these receive a similar amount of woe as God does (5 actions). The overall evaluation of actions toward Israelites is thus definitely positive (0.74), significantly more so than toward God. (Indirect actions toward Israel, i.e. of insects toward plants, are not taken into account in this.)

14. *Israelite Reception versus Foreigner Reception*

Null hypothesis: What ALL does to ISRAELITES in JOEL is the same as what ALL does to FOREIGNERS in JOEL.

---

39. The absolute figures for actions toward Israelites are included in the chart to follow, which compares these with actions toward foreigners.

40. Actions that God does not receive that humans do: status-related activity (including exaltation), weal, life, peace/shalom, and reward.

Dominant Metacategories, Categories, Actors, Complements
Significance: * = 0.05 ** = 0.01 (§ and §§ = sig. low)

		ALL to ISRAELITES in JOEL		ALL to FOREIGNERS in JOEL
		%		%
Action Metacategories 10%+	Weal	21*	Woe	33**
	Emotions	14	Cognition	21*
Action Categories 5%+	Peace/shalom	18	Destruction	25*
	Destruction	7§	Punishment	25**
	Love	7	Reason	17**
	Pride	6	Exaltation	8
			Pride	8
Actors 10%+	God	59	God	71
	Humans	34	Humans	25
	Human groups	30	Foreign	17
	Foreign	17	Human groups	17
	Israel	17		
Complements Recipients 10%+	Israelites		Foreigners	

Evaluation

Difference:	+1.91
Significant?	Yes**

	ALL to ISRAELITES in JOEL	ALL to FOREIGNERS in JOEL
Mean	0.74	-1.17
Std. Dev.	1.95	2.04

ALL to ISRAELITES in JOEL—ALL to FOREIGNERS in JOEL:
Comparative Frequencies
Significance: *= 0.05 **= 0.01 (§ and §§ = sig. low)

Action/activity	ALL to ISRAELITES in JOEL		ALL to FOREIGNERS in JOEL	
Total activity	71		24	
	Qty	%	Qty	%
Emotions	10	14	2	8
Joy	0	0	0	0
Sorrow	0	0	0	0
Love	5	7	0	0
Hate	0	0	0	0
Pride	4	6	2	8
Shaming	0	0	0	0
Anger	0	0	0	0
Desire	1	1	0	0
Fear	0	0	0	0
Cognition	3	4§	5	21*
Alertness	1	1	1	4
Non-alertness	0	0	0	0
Knowledge	0	0	0	0
Ignorance	0	0	0	0
Obey/agree	1	1	0	0
Rejection	0	0	0	0
Reason	1	1§§	4	17**
Ethics	5	7	0	0
Ethically good	2	3	0	0
Ethically bad	3	4	0	0
Status	3	4	2	8
Exaltation	3	4	2	8
Debasement	0	0	0	0
Wealth	0	0	0	0
Poverty	0	0	0	0
Strength	0	0	0	0
Weakness	0	0	0	0
Weal	15	21*	1	4§
Healing	0	0	0	0
Life	2	3	0	0
Peace/shalom	13	18	1	4
Reward	3	4	1	4

ALL to ISRAELITES in JOEL—ALL to FOREIGNERS in JOEL:
Comparative Frequencies
Significance: *= 0.05 **= 0.01 (§ and §§ = sig. low)

	ALL to ISRAELITES in JOEL		ALL to FOREIGNERS in JOEL	
Total activity	71		24	
Action/activity	Qty	%	Qty	%
Woe	5	7§§	8	*33***
Illness/injury	0	0	0	0
Death	1	1	0	0
Destruction	5	7§	6	*25**
Punishment	1	1§§	6	*25***

Israelites and foreigners do not receive the same types of actions in the book of Joel, even though they come from a similar line-up of actors (God, humans, Human groups, foreigners, and Israel—however, Israelites act toward foreigners only once). Israelite reception is evaluated more positively by 1.91** (this does not take account of insect actions toward Israel's plants). Specifically, over a fifth of what Israelites receive is weal, while a third of what foreigners encounter is woe, especially destruction and punishment.[41]

15. *Divine Reception versus Foreigner Reception*

Null hypothesis: What ALL does to GOD in JOEL is the same as what ALL does to FOREIGNERS in JOEL.

Dominant Metacategories, Categories, Actors, Complements
Significance: *= 0.05 **= 0.01 (§ and §§ = sig. low)

		ALL to GOD in JOEL		ALL to FOREIGNERS in JOEL	
		%			%
Action	Emotions	41**	Woe		33
Metacategories	Ethics	14*	Cognition		21
10%+	Cognition	14			
	Woe	14			

41. Foreigners also receive high cognitive actions (five total actions), including reason (four total actions).

Action	Sorrow	23**	Destruction	25
Categories	Destruction	14	Punishment	25
5%+	Knowledge	14*	Reason	17*
	Punishment	14	Exaltation	8
	Good ethics	9	Pride	8
	Joy	9		
Actors 10%+	Humans	86**	God	71**
	Human groups	73**	Humans	25§§
	Israel	64**	Foreign	17
	Foreign	23	Human groups	17§§
Complements	God		Foreigners	
Recipients				
10%+				

Evaluation

Difference:	+ 0.72
Significant?	No
Both Evaluations are NEGATIVE	

	ALL to GOD in JOEL	ALL to FOREIGNERS in JOEL
Mean	-0.45	-1.17
Std. Dev.	1.92	2.04

ALL to GOD in JOEL—ALL to FOREIGNERS in JOEL:
Comparative Frequencies

Significance: *= 0.05 **= 0.01 (§ and §§ = sig. low)

	ALL to GOD in JOEL		ALL to FOREIGNERS in JOEL	
Total activity	22		24	
Action/activity	Qty	%	Qty	%
Emotions	9	41**	2	8§§
Joy	2	9	0	0
Sorrow	5	23**	0	0§§
Love	0	0	0	0
Hate	1	5	0	0
Pride	0	0	2	8
Shaming	0	0	0	0
Anger	0	0	0	0
Desire	1	5	0	0
Fear	0	0	0	0

Comparative Frequencies
Significance: *= 0.05 **= 0.01 (§ and §§ = sig. low)

	ALL to GOD in JOEL		ALL to FOREIGNERS in JOEL	
Total activity	22		24	
Action/activity	Qty	%	Qty	%
Cognition	3	14	5	21
Alertness	0	0	1	4
Non-alertness	0	0	0	0
Knowledge	*3*	*14**	0	0§
Ignorance	0	0	0	0
Obey/agree	0	0	0	0
Rejection	0	0	0	0
Reason	0	0§	*4*	*17**
Ethics	*3*	*14**	0	0§
Ethically good	2	9	0	0
Ethically bad	1	5	0	0
Status	0	0	2	8
Exaltation	0	0	2	8
Debasement	0	0	0	0
Wealth	0	0	0	0
Poverty	0	0	0	0
Strength	0	0	0	0
Weakness	0	0	0	0
Weal	0	0	1	4
Healing	0	0	0	0
Life	0	0	0	0
Peace/shalom	0	0	1	4
Reward	0	0	1	4
Woe	3	14	8	33
Illness/injury	0	0	0	0
Death	0	0	0	0
Destruction	3	14	6	25
Punishment	3	14	6	25

God and foreigners each receive similar relatively small amounts of actions in Joel (22:24). What God receives is more positive, but not significantly so. The only significant high activity foreigners receive is reason (only four times). Activities directed toward God are relatively high in emotionality (including especially sorrow), knowledge, and ethics. Foreigners receive non-significantly more woe, especially destruction and punishment (all from God).[42] In so far as toward God and foreigners are similar, they show that one aspect of God is that of a conflictual other.

16. *Israelites to God versus Foreigners to God*

Null hypothesis: What ISRAELITES do to GOD in JOEL is the same as what FOREIGNERS do to GOD in JOEL.

Dominant Metacategories, Categories, Actors, Complements
Significance: *= 0.05 **= 0.01 (§ and §§ = sig. low)

	ISRAELITES to GOD in JOEL		FOREIGNERS to GOD in JOEL	
		%		%
Action	Emotions	50	Woe	60*
Metacategories	Cognition	21	Emotions	20§
10%+	Ethics	14	Ethics	20
Action	Sorrow	36**	Destruction	60*
Categories	Knowledge	21	Punishment	60*
5%+	Good ethics	14	Bad ethics	20
	Joy	14	Hate	20
Actors 10%+	Israelites		Foreigners	
Complements	God		God	
Recipients				
10%+				

Evaluation

Difference:	+2.89
Significant?	Yes**

	ISRAELITES to GOD in JOEL	FOREIGNERS to GOD in JOEL
Mean	0.29	-2.60
Std. Dev.	1.82	0.89

42. Except for overall emotionality, all other statistically significant differences between what God and foreigners receive (ethics, sorrow, knowledge, and reason) are absent for the other party.

ISRAELITES to GOD in JOEL—FOREIGNERS to GOD in JOEL:
Comparative Frequencies
Significance: *= 0.05 **= 0.01 (§ and §§ = sig. low)

	ISRAELITES to GOD in JOEL		FOREIGNERS to GOD in JOEL	
Total activity	14		5	
Action/activity	Qty	%	Qty	%
Emotions	7	50*	1	20§
Joy	2	14	0	0
Sorrow	5	36**	0	0§§
Love	0	0	0	0
Hate	0	0	1	20
Pride	0	0	0	0
Shaming	0	0	0	0
Anger	0	0	0	0
Desire	0	0	0	0
Fear	0	0	0	0
Cognition	3	21	0	0
Alertness	0	0	0	0
Non-alertness	0	0	0	0
Knowledge	3	21	0	0
Ignorance	0	0	0	0
Obey/agree	0	0	0	0
Rejection	0	0	0	0
Reason	0	0	0	0
Ethics	2	14	1	20
Ethically good	2	14	0	0
Ethically bad	0	0	1	20
Status	0	0	0	0
Exaltation	0	0	0	0
Debasement	0	0	0	0
Wealth	0	0	0	0
Poverty	0	0	0	0
Strength	0	0	0	0
Weakness	0	0	0	0
Weal	0	0	0	0
Healing	0	0	0	0
Life	0	0	0	0
Peace/shalom	0	0	0	0
Reward	0	0	0	0

Woe	0	0§	*3*	*60**
Illness/injury	0	0	0	0
Death	0	0	0	0
Destruction	0	0§	*3*	*60**
Punishment	0	0§	*3*	*60**

Neither Israelites nor foreigners do much activity toward God in Joel (14:5). A notable difference, however, is that foreigners do more woe (including destruction and punishment), and Israelites express sorrow. The evaluation of foreigner actions (-2.60) is significantly more negative than Israelites (+0.29). While there is not much to compare, it still appears that Israelites treat God differently than foreigners do in Joel, and less negatively.

17. *Summary of Activity in Joel*

In sum, Joel is a book of contrasts, with the various entities having sharply defined characteristics. God is presented as psychological being who brings weal and woe. Israelites are described in terms of their emotional responses (sorrow, fear, and joy). Foreigners are bringers of woe and activity valued ethically bad, with little emphasis on their psychological states and processes. Insects are destroyers of agriculture with no personal characteristics at all.

As for God, the emphasis in Joel is on divine activity, not divine reception. (The SPP–Joel comparisons will show that this is unlike God in SPP.) God is an agent of weal toward Israelites, but a bringer of woe to foreigners. Insects, however, act in a threating fashion, apparently as an army of God.

Chapter 9

SPP COMPARED TO JOEL

The final set of analyses will complete the circle by comparing activity in SPP to that in Joel. As with the preceding analyses, God as an acting and receiving being will be the focal point. The approach will be as follows: first, there is a general treatment of activity in both blocks of literature. Secondly, particular analyses compare various actor/action/complement situations in SPP and Joel. Finally, there are general reflections about these comparisons. Overall, this will serve to indicate many ways in which the prophet Joel is distinct from other prophetic literature.

1. *All Activity*

This section will consider overall similarities and differences between SPP and Joel. These will include style (parts of speech used); main actors and recipients; and activity in general (metacategories, categories, and Evaluation). More detailed comparisons will be in the analyses in other sections, and the conclusion will consider certain types of activity in relation to specific actors and recipients.

a. *Parts of Speech*

	SPP	Joel
All words	3898	959
Total actions	1278	284
Action % of all words	33%	30%

There is no significant difference between the relative density of words used to indicate activity in SPP and Joel (each uses about a third of all words in their respective literature).

Frequencies of Parts of Speech Which Designate Activity

Part of speech	SPP %	Joel %
Verbs	64	58
Substantives	25**	15§§
Verbal instructions	7§§	22**
Prepositions	2*	0.4§
Adjectives	2§	4*
Proper names	0.4	
Prepositional pronoun	0.2	
Particles	0.2	
Interjections	0.2	

While activity comprises a similar amount of words in both blocks of literature, one important difference in Joel is the considerably higher amount of verbal instructions. This indicates that Joel is more prone to giving specific directions, while SPP is more descriptive (past, present, or future). A stylistic difference is that substantives are less likely to be used to indicate activity in Joel. This could be due in part to the greater amount of instructions: substantives probably do not work as well when action is being encouraged as they do when a description is present.

b. *Actors and Recipients (Complements)*
The actor/complement differences, especially among plants/plant products and insects, highlight the agricultural disaster emphasis in the book of Joel.

Actor Totals[1]

Actions	God	Humans	Israel	Foreign	Insect	Plants
SPP	29%	58%**	44%**	13%	0.4%§§	0.7%§§
Joel	27%	38%§§	26%§§	11%	15%**	2%**

Note: Percentages indicate the percentage of the total number all actions in the respective blocks of literature, not the percentage of that actor's total actions.

God is a major actor in SPP and Joel, with similar amounts of activity recorded in both. Humans are the top actors for both SPP and Joel,

---

1.   Numbers in the chart cannot necessarily be added together, for a number of instances there are multiple actors.

but humans, especially Israelites, do significantly more actions in SPP; this is probably due to the addition of insects as major actors in Joel. God and foreigners have similar densities of actions in both.[2] Insects, a major actor in Joel, are virtually a non-factor in SPP. Plants do little in either block of literature, but significantly more in Joel (plants/plant products are major complements in Joel but not major actors).

Recipient (Complement) Totals[3]

Receptions	God	Humans	Israel	Foreign	Insect	Plants
SPP	16%**	45%**	34%**	12%	0.2%§§	4%§§
Joel	8%§§	32%§§	25%§§	8%	4%**	14%**

Note: Percentages indicate the percentage of the total number all actions in the respective blocks of literature, not the percentage of that recipient's receptions. For example, what God receives in SPP is 16 percent of everything received by all recipients in SPP, and foreigners receive 8 percent of everything which is received by all recipients in Joel.

God receives much less activity in Joel than in SPP. Humans are the top recipients in SPP and Joel, but humans, especially Israelites, receive less in Joel than in SPP. Foreigners receive similar amounts in both. While insects (a major actor in Joel) receive little in Joel, they receive far less in SPP. Plants and plant products are the target of considerably more activity in Joel than SPP.

c. *Activity in General: SPP and Joel*

Dominant Metacategories, Categories, Actors, Complements
Significance: *= 0.05 **= 0.01 (§ and §§ = sig. low)

		ALL to ALL in SPP		ALL to ALL in JOEL	
		%			%
Action	Woe	24	Woe		21
Metacategories	Ethics	18**	Emotions		19**
10%+	Cognition	13**			
	Emotions	11§§			
Action	Destruction	19	Destruction		20

2. The addition of insect activity in Joel does not decrease divine activity, even though they are 'Yahweh's army'. Rather, the decrease occurs mainly for Israelites.

3. Numbers in the chart cannot necessarily be added together, for in a number of instances there are multiple complements.

Categories	Bad ethics	13**	Sorrow	7**
5%+	Punishment	6	Peace/shalom	5**

Evaluation

Difference:	- 0.29
Significant?	Yes*

Both Evaluations are NEGATIVE

	ALL to ALL in SPP	ALL to ALL in JOEL
Mean	-0.69	-0.40
Std. Dev.	1.90	2.03

ALL Activity in SPP versus ALL Activity in JOEL
Comparative Frequencies
Significance: *= 0.05 **= 0.01 (§ and §§ = sig. low)

	ALL to ALL in SPP		ALL to ALL in JOEL	
Total activity	1278		284	
Action/activity	Qty	%	Qty	%
Emotions	145	11§§	53	19**
Joy	10	0.8§§	8	3**
Sorrow	30	2§§	21	7**
Love	10	0.8	5	2
Hate	28	2**	1	0.4§§
Pride	9	0.7§	7	2*
Shaming	34	3**	1	0.4§§
Anger	8	0.6	0	0
Desire	7	0.6	2	0.7
Fear	18	1	9	3
Cognition	167	13**	19	7§§
Alertness	8	0.6	4	1
Non-alertness	27	2	2	0.7
Knowledge	20	2	6	2
Ignorance	26	2**	0	0§§
Obey/agree	25	2*	1	0.4§
Rejection	50	4**	0	0§§
Reason	25	2	6	2
Ethics	224	18**	9	3§§
Ethically good	60	5**	5	2§§
Ethically bad	164	13**	4	1§§
Status	100	8*	13	5§
Exaltation	13	1§	8	3*
Debasement	35	3**	1	0.4§§

ALL Activity in SPP versus ALL Activity in JOEL
Comparative Frequencies
Significance: *= 0.05 **= 0.01 (§ and §§ = sig. low)

	ALL to ALL in SPP		ALL to ALL in JOEL	
Total activity	1278		284	
Action/activity	Qty	%	Qty	%
Wealth	*12*	*0.9**	*0*	*0§*
Poverty	2	0.2	0	0
Strength	12	0.9	2	0.7
Weakness	28	2	2	0.7
Weal	*46*	*4§*	*19*	*7**
Healing	4	0.3	0	0
Life	6	0.5	4	1
Peace/shalom	*30*	*2§§*	*15*	*5***
Reward	10	0.8	4	1
Woe	306	24	59	21
Illness/injury	*51*	*4***	*0*	*0§§*
Death	*22*	*2**	*1*	*0.4§*
Destruction	241	19	56	20
Punishment	76	6	11	4

Woe, especially destruction, is a consistent theme in the prophetic literature under consideration, being the most common one in SPP and Joel. Emotionality is also frequent, but considerably more so in Joel than in SPP. SPP has a greater emphasis on overall cognition and ethics (especially bad ethics), while Joel has more sorrow and peace/shalom. The overall Evaluation is significantly less negative in Joel, yet still negative.

There are quite a number of differences among infrequent activity (less than 5 percent). SPP includes a greater emphasis on overall status issues, as well as on hate, shaming, ignorance, obedience, rejection, good ethics, debasement, wealth, Illness/injury, and death. Note that seven of these ten categories are negative in character. In Joel, there is more overall weal (positive), sorrow (negative), pride (ambiguous[4]), and exaltation (positive). Thus, Joel's highs tend to include both positives and negatives, while SPP's highs are mainly, although not exclusively, negatives. These differences reflect to a large extent the

---

4. Pride activity in Joel is positive five times and negative two times.

relatively greater emphasis on ethics and cognitive action in SPP, and on emotions in Joel.

2. *Divine Activity*

Null hypothesis: What GOD does to ALL in SPP is the same as what GOD does to ALL in JOEL.

Dominant Metacategories, Categories, Actors, Complements
Significance: *= 0.05 **= 0.01 (§ and §§ = sig. low)

		GOD to ALL in SPP		GOD to ALL in JOEL	
		%			%
Action	Woe	35**	Woe		18§§
Metacategories	Emotions	13	Weal		14*
10%+			Emotions		13
			Cognition		10
Action	Destruction	25*	Destruction		14§
Categories	Punishment	15	Peace/shalom		12**
5%+	Illness/injury	6**	Punishment		9
			Reason		8
			Love		6*
			Pride		5**
			Reward		5
Actors 10%+	God		God		
Complements	Humans	73	Humans		76
Recipients	Israel	60	Human groups		72**
	Human groups	49§§	Israel		54
10%+	Foreign	19	Foreign		22
	Cultic	16**	Destruction		15**
			Land		10

Evaluation

Difference:	-1.02
Significant?	Yes**

	GOD to ALL in JOEL	GOD to ALL in JOEL
Mean	-0.70	0.32
Std. Dev.	2.01	2.16

GOD to ALL in SPP—GOD to ALL in JOEL
Comparative Frequencies
Significance. *= 0.05 **= 0.01 (§ and §§ = sig. low)

	GOD to ALL in SPP		GOD to ALL in JOEL	
Total activity	366		78	
Action/activity	Qty	%	Qty	%
Emotions	49	13	10	13
Joy	1	0.3	0	0
Sorrow	5	1	0	0
Love	5	1§	5	6*
Hate	18	5**	0	0§§
Pride	1	0.3§§	4	5**
Shaming	16	4**	0	0§§
Anger	6	2	0	0
Desire	2	0.6	1	1
Fear	0	0	0	0
Cognition	34	9	8	10
Alertness	2	0.6	1	1
Non-alertness	3	0.8	0	0
Knowledge	6	2	0	0
Ignorance	5	1	0	0
Obey/agree	3	0.8	1	1
Rejection	9	2	0	0
Reason	10	3	6	8
Ethics	18	5	2	3
Ethically good	12	3	2	3
Ethically bad	6	2	0	0
Status	26	7	4	5
Exaltation	2	0.6§	3	4*
Debasement	17	5**	0	0§§
Wealth	0	0	0	0
Poverty	1	0.3	0	0
Strength	4	1	1	1
Weakness	3	0.8	0	0
Weal	22	6§	*11*	*14**
Healing	4	1	0	0
Life	3	0.8	2	3
Peace/shalom	11	3§§	9	*12***
Reward	6	2	4	5

Woe	*127*	*35***	14	18§§
Illness/injury	*21*	*6***	0	0§§
Death	2	0.6	0	0
Destruction	*93*	*25**	11	14§
Punishment	54	15	7	9

The character of God's activity in Joel has continuity with the situation in SPP, but there are also many differences.

Overall humans, Israelites, and foreigners receive about the same density of divine activity in both sets of literature. God deals more with large human groups in Joel, and less with the cult.

As for common activity, woe and emotions are dominant in both. However, God does only about half as much woe (at least directly) in Joel, particularly less destruction and illness/injury. Destruction, while the most frequent divine action in Joel, is nonetheless low compared to SPP. Punishment is meted out about the same. As for psychological activity, emotions and cognition are among dominant processes[5] and similar. However, God does more love and pride activity in Joel, while no particular cognitive activities are dominant in SPP. Weal is dominant and relatively high, especially the provision of peace/shalom. Further, the Evaluation of divine activity is considerably more beneficial in Joel than in SPP. Although all of God's most common activities in SPP are negative in character, frequently occurring divine activity in Joel includes many positives.[6]

In both cases, actions with strong ethical connotations occupy only a minor role. God does some ethically good actions in each, but does ethically bad actions only in SPP (total of six).[7] (Ethics are mainly a human activity; see comparisons of divine and human activity, and the Evaluation analyses at the end of the chapter.) God does similar amounts of status-related actions in each, but there are two main differences, which involve polar opposites: God does more debasing in SPP, but more exalting in Joel.[8]

---

5.   Cognition is dominant in Joel but not in SPP, but both are so close to the 10% cutoff that they are not significantly different.

6.   As for categories which are inherently positive or negative, all God's highs in SPP are negatives, and all God's highs in Joel are positives.

7.   Five of these are 'curse' in Malachi, and one is 'reject' in Hos. 8.5. It could be argued that these are marginal as far as being 'ethically bad', although 'reject' in Hos. 8.3 and Isa. 1.4 is used in an ethically bad sense to describe human activity.

8.   If insect activity (Yahweh's army) is added to God's activity in Joel, then

The difference, then, between SPP and Joel is that God's activity in Joel, while containing many of the same kinds of negatives as SPP, is seasoned with a heavy dose of physical and psychological positives.

3. *God to Humans*

Null hypothesis: What GOD does to HUMANS in SPP is the same as what GOD does to HUMANS in JOEL.

Dominant Metacategories, Categories, Actors, Complements
Significance: *= 0.05 **= 0.01 (§ and §§ = sig. low)

	GOD to HUMANS in SPP	%	GOD to HUMANS in JOEL	%
Action	Woe	39**	Weal	20*
Metacategories	Emotions	17	Emotions	18
10%+	Cognition	11	Woe	14§§
			Cognition	13
Action	Destruction	29**	Peace/shalom	16**
Categories	Punishment	17	Destruction	11§§
5%+	Illness/injury	7**	Punishment	11
	Debasement	7**	Love	9**
	Shaming	6**	Reason	9
	Hate	6**	Pride	7**
			Reward	7
			Exaltation	5**
Actors 10%+	God		God	
Complements Recipients 10%+	Humans		Humans	

Evaluation

Difference:	-1.62
Significant?	Yes**

	GOD to HUMANS in SPP	GOD to HUMANS in JOEL
Mean	-0.89	0.73
Std. Dev.	2.10	2.18

woe and its category destruction are not significantly different from divine activity in SPP.

GOD to HUMANS in SPP—GOD to HUMANS in JOEL
Comparative Frequencies
Significance: *= 0.05 **= 0.01 (§ and §§ = sig. low)

	GOD to HUMANS in SPP		GOD to HUMANS in JOEL	
Total activity	257		56	
Action/activity	Qty	%	Qty	%
Emotions	43	17	10	18
Joy	0	0	0	0
Sorrow	3	1	0	0
Love	4	2§§	5	9**
Hate	15	6**	0	0§§
Pride	1	0.4§§	4	7**
Shaming	16	6**	0	0§§
Anger	6	2	0	0
Desire	0	0	1	2
Fear	0	0	0	0
Cognition	29	11	7	13
Alertness	1	0.4	1	2
Non-alertness	2	0.8	0	0
Knowledge	4	2	0	0
Ignorance	4	2	0	0
Obey/agree	3	1	1	2
Rejection	8	3	0	0
Reason	10	4	5	9
Ethics	18	7	2	4
Ethically good	12	5	2	4
Ethically bad	6	2	0	0
Status	23	9	3	5
Exaltation	1	0.4§§	3	5**
Debasement	17	7**	0	0§§
Wealth	0	0	0	0
Poverty	1	0.4	0	0
Strength	3	1	0	0
Weakness	2	0.8	0	0
Weal	22	9§	*11*	20*
Healing	4	2	0	0
Life	3	1	2	4
Peace/shalom	11	4§§	9	16**
Reward	6	2	4	7

GOD to HUMANS in SPP—GOD to HUMANS in JOEL
Comparative Frequencies
Significance: *= 0.05 **= 0.01 (§ and §§ = sig. low)

	GOD to HUMANS in SPP		GOD to HUMANS in JOEL	
Total activity	257		56	
Action/activity	Qty	%	Qty	%
Woe	*100*	*39***	8	14§§
Illness/injury	*18*	*7***	0	0§§
Death	2	0.8	0	0
Destruction	*75*	*29***	6	11§§
Punishment	43	17	6	11

Divine treatment of humans in SPP and Joel is far from identical. The top action God does to humans in SPP is woe (specifically destruction and illness/injury), but God's most frequent activity in Joel is weal (especially peace/shalom). Overall psychological treatment (emotionality and cognition) is similar, but specific emotions are different: God shames and hates humans more in SPP, but God directs more love and pride toward humans in Joel. While God debases more in SPP, humans are exalted by God in Joel. Note that all of the above (except illness/injury) are opposites, with all negatives being in SPP and all positives being in Joel. This is also borne out by the significant evaluation difference. What God does to humans in Joel is almost as positive as what God does to humans in SPP is negative. Divine treatment of humans, then, is considerably more favorable in Joel than in SPP.

However, it is not as though God is always beneficent toward humans in Joel. Negatives are still present and stand out, even though they are either low or similar to SPP: woe, destruction, and punishment are all dominant in Joel.

4. *God to Israelites*

Null hypothesis: What GOD does to ISRAELITES in SPP is the same as what GOD does to ISRAELITES in JOEL.

Dominant Metacategories, Categories, Actors, Complements
Significance: *= 0.05 **= 0.01 (§ and §§ = sig. low)

		GOD to ISRAELITES in SPP	GOD to ISRAELITES in JOEL	
		%		%
Action	Woe	31**	Emotions	24
Metacategories	Emotions	14	Weal	24*
10%+	Cognition	13		
	Weal	11§		
Action	Destruction	23**	Peace/shalom	19**
Categories	Punishment	14**	Love	12**
5%+	Good ethics	6	Pride	10**
	Debasement	6*	Exaltation	7**
	Peace/shalom	5§§	Reward	7
	Shaming	5*		
Actors 10%+	God		God	
Complements	Israelites		Israelites	
Recipients				
10%+				

Evaluation

Difference:	-2.12
Significant?	Yes**

	GOD to ISRAELITES in SPP	GOD to ISRAELITES in Joel
Mean	-0.50	1.62
Std. Dev.	2.10	1.40

GOD to ISRAELITES in SPP—GOD to ISRAELITES in JOEL
Comparative Frequencies
Significance: *= 0.05 **= 0.01 (§ and §§ = sig. low)

	GOD to ISRAELITES in SPP		GOD to ISRAELITES in JOEL	
Total activity	204		42	
Action/activity	Qty	%	Qty	%
Emotions	29	14	10	24
Joy	0	0	0	0
Sorrow	3	1	0	0

GOD to ISRAELITES in SPP—GOD to ISRAELITES in JOEL
Comparative Frequencies
Significance: *= 0.05 **= 0.01 (§ and §§ = sig. low)

Total activity	GOD to ISRAELITES in SPP		GOD to ISRAELITES in JOEL	
	204		42	
Action/activity	Qty	%	Qty	%
Love	4	2§§	5	12**
Hate	10	5	0	0
Pride	1	0.5§§	4	10**
Shaming	11	5*	0	0§
Anger	2	1	0	0
Desire	0	0	1	2
Fear	0	0	0	0
Cognition	27	13	3	7
Alertness	1	0.5	1	2
Non-alertness	1	0.5	0	0
Knowledge	4	2	0	0
Ignorance	4	2	0	0
Obey/agree	3	1	1	2
Rejection	8	4	0	0
Reason	9	4	1	2
Ethics	18	9	2	5
Ethically good	12	6	2	5
Ethically bad	6	3	0	0
Status	18	9	3	7
Exaltation	1	0.5§§	3	7**
Debasement	12	6*	0	0§
Wealth	0	0	0	0
Poverty	1	0.5	0	0
Strength	3	1	0	0
Weakness	2	1	0	0
Weal	22	11§	10	24*
Healing	4	2	0	0
Life	3	1	2	5
Peace/shalom	11	5§§	8	19**
Reward	6	3	3	7
Woe	64	31**	0	0§§
Illness/injury	9	4	0	0
Death	1	0.5	0	0
Destruction	46	23**	0	0§§
Punishment	28	14**	0	0§§

The contrast between the divine treatment of Israelites in Joel and the corresponding relation in SPP is striking. While there is little overall psychological difference (emotions and cognition), many other factors are quite different. The top God-to-Israelite activity in SPP is overall woe, mainly comprised of destruction and punishment. That four of the six dominant categories in SPP are negatives contributes to a mildly negative Evaluation. Weal (including peace/shalom) is dominant in SPP, but nevertheless much lower than in Joel. In Joel, God does much weal (including peace/shalom among dominant actions) and is engaged in the generally positive activities of love, pride, and exaltation. In fact, God does not do even one negative action toward Israelites in Joel. These activities contribute to the extremely positive evaluation. There is thus very little similarity between divine treatment of Israelites in SPP and in Joel. God's dealings with Israelites are considerably more positive in Joel than SPP, being much more supportive and helpful.

It should be noted that if insect activity in Joel (as God's agents whose activity affects Israel) is added to the divine treatment of Israelites in Joel, the picture changes, with woe and destruction becoming prominent. However, as noted in the Joel analysis, Joel presents God as only indirectly responsible for the disaster, but directly responsible for the restoration.

5. *God to Foreigners*

Null hypothesis: What GOD does to FOREIGNERS in SPP is the same as what GOD does to FOREIGNERS in JOEL.

Dominant Metacategories, Categories, Actors, Complements
Significance: *= 0.05 **= 0.01 (§ and §§ = sig. low)

	GOD to FOREIGNERS in SPP		GOD to FOREIGNERS in JOEL	
		%		%
Action	Woe	56	Woe	47
Metacategories	Emotions	24	Cognition	24
10%+	Status	12	Emotions	12
Action	Destruction	47	Destruction	35
Categories	Punishment	19	Punishment	35
5%+	Illness/injury	15*	Reason	24*
	Debasement	12	Pride	12**

Dominant Metacategories, Categories, Actors, Complements
Significance: *= 0.05 **= 0.01 (§ and §§ = sig. low)

	GOD to FOREIGNERS in SPP	%	GOD to FOREIGNERS in JOEL	%
	Shaming	12	Exaltation	6
	Hate	8	Peace/shalom	6
	Reason	5§	Reward	6
Actors 10%+	God		God	
Complements Recipients 10%+	Foreigners		Foreigners	

Evaluation

Difference:	- 0.51
Significant?	No

Both Evaluations are NEGATIVE

	GOD to FOREIGNERS in SPP	GOD to FOREIGNERS in JOEL
Mean	-1.98	-1.47
Std. Dev.	1.56	2.18

GOD to FOREIGNERS in SPP—GOD to FOREIGNERS in JOEL
Comparative Frequencies
Significance: *= 0.05 **= 0.01 (§ and §§ = sig. low)

	GOD to FOREIGNERS in SPP		GOD to FOREIGNERS in JOEL	
Total activity	59		17	
Action/activity	Qty	%	Qty	%
Emotions	14	24	2	12
Joy	0	0	0	0
Sorrow	0	0	0	0
Love	0	0	0	0
Hate	5	8	0	0
Pride	0	0§§	2	*12***
Shaming	7	12	0	0
Anger	2	3	0	0

Desire	0	0	0	0
Fear	0	0	0	0
Cognition	4	7	4	24
Alertness	0	0	0	0
Non-alertness	1	2	0	0
Knowledge	0	0	0	0
Ignorance	0	0	0	0
Obey/agree	0	0	0	0
Rejection	0	0	0	0
Reason	3	*5§*	*4*	*24**
Ethics	2	3	0	0
Ethically good	2	3	0	0
Ethically bad	0	0	0	0
Status	7	12	1	6
Exaltation	0	0	1	6
Debasement	7	12	0	0
Wealth	0	0	0	0
Poverty	0	0	0	0
Strength	0	0	0	0
Weakness	0	0	0	0
Weal	1	2	1	6
Healing	0	0	0	0
Life	0	0	0	0
Peace/shalom	1	2	1	6
Reward	0	0	1	6
Woe	33	56	8	47
Illness/injury	*9*	*15**	*0*	*0§*
Death	1	2	0	0
Destruction	28	47	6	35
Punishment	11	19	6	35

There is great continuity between the treatment of foreigners by God in SPP and Joel. Destruction and punishment are the top two categories for both, and the extremely negative evaluation is similar. The only significant differences are that reason (which includes decision) and pride (only twice)[9] are high in Joel, while illness/injury is high in SPP.

In both cases about half of God's actions are explicitly destructive, and many divine actions involve punishment. The evaluation for both is extraordinarily negative: -1.47 (Joel) and -1.98 (SPP).[10]

9. The two instances actually have foreigners as secondary recipients; in these instances Israel will not suffer shame among the nations (Joel 2.17, 19).

10. It is recognized that the small amount of activity God directs toward foreigners

6. *Divine Reception*

Null hypothesis: What ALL does to GOD in SPP is the same as what ALL does to GOD in JOEL.

Dominant Metacategories, Categories, Actors, Complements
Significance: *= 0.05 **= 0.01 (§ and §§ = sig. low)

		ALL to GOD in SPP	ALL to GOD in JOEL	
		%		%
Action	Ethics	36*	Emotions	41**
Metacategories	Cognition	29	Ethics	14§
10%+	Emotions	15§§	Cognition	14
			Woe	14
Action	Bad ethics	25**	Sorrow	23**
Categories	Rejection	14**	Destruction	14
5%+	Good ethics	10	Knowledge	14*
	Fear	6	Punishment	14**
	Obey/agree	5	Good ethics	9
			Joy	9*
Actors 10%+	Humans	92	Humans	86
	Israel	84*	Human groups	73
	Human groups	67	Israel	64§
	Cultic	18	Foreign	23*
Complements Recipients 10%+	God		God	

Evaluation

Difference:	+ 0.12
Significant?	No

Both Evaluations are NEGATIVE

	ALL to GOD in JOEL	ALL to GOD in JOEL
Mean	-0.33	-0.45
Std. Dev.	1.86	1.92

in Joel make statistical differences less likely. However, since dominant activity still shows much continuity with that of SPP, the conclusion still stands: divine treatment of foreigners is similarly harsh in SPP and Joel.

ALL to GOD in SPP—ALL to GOD in JOEL
Comparative Frequencies
Significance: *= 0.05 **= 0.01 (§ and §§ = sig. low)

	ALL to GOD in SPP		ALL to GOD in JOEL	
Total activity	205		22	
Action/activity	Qty	%	Qty	%
Emotions	30	15§§	9	*41**￼*
Joy	1	0.5§	2	*9*￼*
Sorrow	7	3§§	5	*23**￼*
Love	0	0	0	0
Hate	3	1	1	5
Pride	3	1	0	0
Shaming	2	1	0	0
Anger	0	0	0	0
Desire	1	0.5	1	5
Fear	13	6	0	0
Cognition	59	29	3	14
Alertness	2	1	0	0
Non-alertness	1	0.5	0	0
Knowledge	4	2§	3	*14*￼*
Ignorance	6	3	0	0
Obey/agree	11	5	0	0
Rejection	29	*14**￼*	0	0§§
Reason	9	4	0	0
Ethics	73	*36*￼*	3	14§
Ethically good	21	10	2	9
Ethically bad	52	*25**￼*	1	5§§
Status	13	6	0	0
Exaltation	6	3	0	0
Debasement	2	1	0	0
Wealth	0	0	0	0
Poverty	0	0	0	0
Strength	0	0	0	0
Weakness	5	2	0	0
Weal	4	2	0	0
Healing	0	0	0	0
Life	1	0.5	0	0
Peace/shalom	2	1	0	0
Reward	1	0.5	0	0

ALL to GOD in SPP—ALL to GOD in JOEL
Comparative Frequencies
Significance: *= 0.05 **= 0.01 (§ and §§ = sig. low)

	ALL to GOD in SPP		ALL to GOD in JOEL	
Total activity	205		22	
Action/activity	Qty	%	Qty	%
Woe	12	6	3	14
Illness/injury	1	0.5	0	0
Death	1	0.5	0	0
Destruction	10	5	3	14
Punishment	*1*	*0.5§§*	*3*	*14***

Not as much can be said about divine reception as about divine activity, for God receives very little in Joel. This indicates that unlike what happens in the other prophecies, what God receives is not much of a concern in Joel. While God receives 16 percent** of all activity in SPP, God only receives 8 percent §§ of all activity in Joel.

Enough occurs, though, to make a few significant comparisons. The main type of activity God receives in SPP is ethical in orientation, and this specifically involves bad ethics. A related action, also high in comparison with Joel, is rejection. In Joel, in contrast, the main process directed toward God is overall emotionality, especially sorrow. (All other activities occur three times or less.)[11] The Evaluations of what God receives in both blocks of literature is about the same: slightly negative.

7. Humans to God

Null hypothesis: What HUMANS do to GOD in SPP is the same as what HUMANS do to GOD in JOEL.

Dominant Metacategories, Categories, Actors, Complements
Significance: *= 0.05 **= 0.01 (§ and §§ = sig. low)

	HUMANS to GOD in SPP		HUMANS to GOD in JOEL	
		%		%
Action	Ethics	37	Emotions	42**
Metacategories	Cognition	31	Ethics	16
10%+	Emotions	14§§	Cognition	16

11. God receives no weal or status-related activity in Joel.

			Woe	16
Action	Bad ethics	27*	Sorrow	26**
Categories	Rejection	15**	Destruction	16
5%+	Good ethics	10	Knowledge	16*
	Fear	7	Punishment	16**
	Obey/agree	6	Good ethics	11
	Destruction	5	Joy	11**
			Bad ethics	5§
			Hate	5
Actors 10%+	Humans		Humans	
Complements Recipients 10%+	God		God	

Evaluation

Difference:	+ 0.09
Significant?	No

Both Evaluations are NEGATIVE

	HUMANS to GOD in SPP	HUMANS to GOD in JOEL
Mean	-0.38	-0.47
Std. Dev.	1.87	2.06

HUMANS to GOD in SPP—HUMANS to GOD in JOEL
Comparative Frequencies
Significance: *= 0.05 **= 0.01 (§ and §§ = sig. low)

	HUMANS to GOD in SPP		HUMANS to GOD in JOEL	
Total activity	188		19	
Action/activity	Qty	%	Qty	%
Emotions	27	14§§	8	42**
Joy	1	0.5§§	2	11**
Sorrow	7	4§§	5	26**
Love	0	0	0	0
Hate	2	1	1	5
Pride	1	0.5	0	0
Shaming	2	1	0	0
Anger	0	0	0	0
Desire	1	0.5	0	0
Fear	13	7	0	0

HUMANS to GOD in SPP—HUMANS to GOD in JOEL
Comparative Frequencies
Significance: *= 0.05 **= 0.01 (§ and §§ = sig. low)

Action/activity	HUMANS to GOD in SPP		HUMANS to GOD in JOEL	
Total activity	188		19	
	Qty	%	Qty	%
Cognition	58	31	3	16
Alertness	1	0.5	0	0
Non-alertness	1	0.5	0	0
Knowledge	4	2§	*3*	*16**
Ignorance	6	3	0	0
Obey/agree	11	6	0	0
Rejection	29	*15***	0	0§§
Reason	9	5	0	0
Ethics	69	37	3	16
Ethically good	19	10	2	11
Ethically bad	*50*	*27**	*1*	*5§*
Status	9	5	0	0
Exaltation	3	2	0	0
Debasement	2	1	0	0
Wealth	0	0	0	0
Poverty	0	0	0	0
Strength	0	0	0	0
Weakness	4	2	0	0
Weal	4	2	0	0
Healing	0	0	0	0
Life	1	0.5	0	0
Peace/shalom	2	1	0	0
Reward	1	0.5	0	0
Woe	12	6	3	16
Illness/injury	1	0.5	0	0
Death	1	0.5	0	0
Destruction	10	5	3	16
Punishment	1	0.5§§	*3*	*16***

A view of what humans do toward God in Joel and SPP is very close to the analysis of all divine reception which immediately precedes this one. There will therefore not be a separate summary here, but human activity toward God will be considered in terms of 'Israelites to God' and 'foreigners to God'.

8. *Israelites to God*

Null hypothesis: What ISRAELITES do to GOD in SPP is the same as what ISRAELITES do to GOD in JOEL.

Dominant Metacategories, Categories, Actors, Complements
Significance: *= 0.05 **= 0.01 (§ and §§ = sig. low)

	ISRAELITES to GOD in SPP	%	ISRAELITES to GOD in JOEL	%
Action Metacategories 10%+	Ethics	37	Emotions	50**
	Cognition	31	Cognition	21
	Emotions	15§§	Ethics	14
Action Categories 5%+	Bad ethics	27**	Sorrow	36**
	Rejection	16*	Knowledge	21**
	Good ethics	10	Good ethics	14
	Fear	6	Joy	14**
	Destruction	5		
	Obey/agree	5		
Actors 10%+	Israelites		Israelites	
Complements Recipients 10%+	God		God	

Evaluation

Difference:	- 0.71	
Significant?	No	

	ISRAELITES to GOD in SPP	ISRAELITES to GOD in JOEL
Mean	-0.42	0.29
Std. Dev.	1.85	1.82

ISRAELITES to GOD in SPP—ISRAELITES to GOD in
JOEL
Comparative Frequencies
Significance: *= 0.05 **= 0.01 (§ and §§ = sig. low)

Action/activity	ISRAELITES to GOD in SPP		ISRAELITES to GOD in JOEL	
Total activity	172		14	
	Qty	%	Qty	%
Emotions	25	15§§	7	50**
Joy	1	0.6§§	2	14**
Sorrow	7	4§§	5	36**
Love	0	0	0	0
Hate	2	1	0	0
Pride	1	0.6	0	0
Shaming	2	1	0	0
Anger	0	0	0	0
Desire	1	0.6	0	0
Fear	11	6	0	0
Cognition	53	31	3	21
Alertness	1	0.6	0	0
Non-alertness	1	0.6	0	0
Knowledge	4	2§§	3	21**
Ignorance	6	3	0	0
Obey/agree	9	5	0	0
Rejection	27	16*	0	0§
Reason	7	4	0	0
Ethics	64	37	2	14
Ethically good	17	10	2	14
Ethically bad	47	27**	0	0§§
Status	5	3	0	0
Exaltation	1	0.6	0	0
Debasement	2	1	0	0
Wealth	0	0	0	0
Poverty	0	0	0	0
Strength	0	0	0	0
Weakness	2	1	0	0
Weal	4	2	0	0
Healing	0	0	0	0
Life	1	0.6	0	0
Peace/shalom	2	1	0	0
Reward	1	0.6	0	0

Woe	11	6	0	0
Illness/injury	1	0.6	0	0
Death	1	0.6	0	0
Destruction	9	5	0	0
Punishment	1	0.6	0	0

The extreme difference in the number of actions performed in each scenario makes a comparison difficult. (For this reason Israelite activity in SPP and Joel, regardless of recipient, will be viewed in the section following this). Israelites devote a lesser portion of their activity toward God in Joel than in SPP. While there is little Evaluation difference between Israelite actions to God in SPP and Joel, there are differences in the nature of activities. The Israelite highs in SPP suggest rebellion against God, both cognitively (rejection) and non-cognitively (bad ethics); Israelites do not act thus toward God in Joel. Processes relatively high in Joel are all psychological. The emotional opposites, joy and sorrow,[12] imply response to God; knowledge seems to contrast with rebellion in SPP. The difference is an active rejection of God and God's ways in SPP versus positive and negative emotional responses and acknowledgment of God in Joel.

Excursus: Israelite Activity in SPP and Joel

Dominant Metacategories, Categories, Actors, Complements
Significance: *= 0.05 **= 0.01 (§ and §§ = sig. low)

		ISRAELITES in SPP	ISRAELITES in JOEL	
		%		%
Action	Ethics	32**	Emotions	48**
Metacategories	Cognition	19**		
10%+	Emotions	12§§		
	Woe	11**		
Action	Bad ethics	25**	Sorrow	24**
Categories	Destruction	10**	Fear	12**
5%+	Good ethics	7	Joy	9**
	Rejection	7**	Knowledge	7*

Many more Israelite actions are intransitives in Joel** than in SPP;[13]

12. The high sorrow in Joel can be attributed to the lamentation by Israel concerning the locust plague, drought, and wildfires.
13. SPP: 18% (101); Joel: 35% (26).

this accounts in part for the fact that fewer activities are directed toward God there than in SPP. Although emotions are dominant for both, they are considerably higher in Joel. Cognitive activity, though, is much less than in SPP. All dominant activity for Israelites in Joel is psychological—mainly emotional in character. The top two emotions are negatives (sorrow and fear); these are followed by positive processes (joy, knowledge).

Israelite activity in SPP is quite different. The main activity is ethics, particularly those valued as bad. Woe, particularly destruction, is also a major activity for Israelites in SPP. The only dominant activity which is not significantly different is ethically good in character (dominant in SPP only).

9. Foreigners to God

Null hypothesis: What FOREIGNERS do to GOD in SPP is the same as what FOREIGNERS do to GOD in JOEL.

Dominant Metacategories, Categories, Actors, Complements
Significance: *= 0.05 **= 0.01 (§ and §§ = sig. low)

	FOREIGNERS to GOD in SPP		FOREIGNERS to GOD in JOEL	
		%		%
Action	Emotions	27	Woe	60
Metacategories	Ethics	27	Emotions	20
10%+	Cognition	27*	Ethics	20
	Status	13		
Action	Fear	27*	Destruction	60
Categories	Bad ethics	13	Punishment	60**
5%+	Good ethics	13	Bad ethics	20
	Exaltation	13	Hate	20
	Obey/agree	13		
	Reason	13		
	Destruction	7		
	Rejection	7		
Actors 10%+	Foreigners		Foreigners	
Complements Recipients 10%+	God		God	

Evaluation

Difference:	+2.60
Significant?	Yes**

	FOREIGNERS to GOD in SPP	FOREIGNERS to GOD in JOEL
Mean	0.00	-2.60
Std. Dev.	2.27	0.89

FOREIGNERS to GOD in SPP—FOREIGNERS to GOD in JOEL
Comparative Frequencies
Significance: *= 0.05 **= 0.01 (§ and §§ = sig. low)

	FOREIGNERS to GOD in SPP		FOREIGNERS to GOD in JOEL	
Total activity	15		5	
Action/activity	Qty	%	Qty	%
Emotions	4	27	1	20
Joy	0	0	0	05
Sorrow	0	0	0	0
Love	0	0	0	0
Hate	0	0	1	20
Pride	0	0	0	0
Shaming	0	0	0	0
Anger	0	0	0	0
Desire	0	0	0	0
Fear	4	27*	0	0§
Cognition	4	27*	0	0§
Alertness	0	0	0	0
Non-alertness	0	0	0	0
Knowledge	0	0	0	0
Ignorance	0	0	0	0
Obey/agree	2	13	0	0
Rejection	1	7	0	0
Reason	2	13	0	0
Ethics	4	27	1	20
Ethically good	2	13	0	0
Ethically bad	2	13	1	20
Status	2	13	0	0
Exaltation	2	13	0	0
Debasement	0	0	0	0
Wealth	0	0	0	0

FOREIGNERS *to GOD in SPP—FOREIGNERS to GOD in*
JOEL
Comparative Frequencies
Significance: *= 0.05 **= 0.01 (§ and §§ = sig. low)

	FOREIGNERS to GOD in SPP		FOREIGNERS to GOD in JOEL	
Total activity	15		5	
Action/activity	Qty	%	Qty	%
Poverty	0	0	0	0
Strength	0	0	0	0
Weakness	0	0	0	0
Weal	0	0	0	0
Healing	0	0	0	0
Life	0	0	0	0
Peace/shalom	0	0	0	0
Reward	0	0	0	0
Woe	1	7	3	60
Illness/injury	0	0	0	0
Death	0	0	0	0
Destruction	1	7	3	60
Punishment	*0*	*0§§*	*3*	*60***

Foreigners do so little to God that is not possible to make a meaningful statistical comparison; foreigners engage in only fifteen actions to God in SPP and five in Joel.

Excursus: Foreigner Activity in SPP and Joel

Dominant Metacategories, Categories, Actors, Complements
Significance: *= 0.05 **= 0.01 (§ and §§ = sig. low)

		FOREIGNERS to ALL in SPP		FOREIGNERS to ALL in JOEL	
			%		%
Action	Woe		28	Woe	26
Metacategories	Emotions		11	Ethics	16
10%+	Status		11		
Action	Destruction		19	Destruction	26
Categories	Bad ethics		7	Bad ethics	13
5%+	Punishment		6	Punishment	13
	Fear		5	Alertness	6*

The character of foreigners is presented similarly in SPP and Joel. They are destructive creatures of woe, involved in bad ethics and punishment. The only (apparently[14]) statistically significant difference is that foreigners are involved in more activity involving alertness in Joel,[15] but this involves only a small number of activities.

10. *Summary of SPP versus Joel*

This final section of the SPP–Joel comparison contains some discussions from different angles than the preceding analyses.

a. *Question: How Much More Weal or Woe Do Entities Do in SPP and Joel?*

Weal and Woe in SPP and Joel

Actor	SPP				Joel			
	Woe		Weal		Woe		Weal	
	Qty	%	Qty	%	Qty	%	Qty	%
All	306	24**	46	4§§	59	21**	19	7§§
God	127	35**	22	6§§	14	18	11	14
Humans	111	15**	19	3§§	8	7	4	4
Israel	62	11**	12	2§§	0	0	3	4
Foreign	47	28**	8	5§§	8	26**	1	3§§
Insects	2	40	1	20	14	33**	0	0§§

Note: Significance indicators indicate whether weal or woe is higher for each actor in the two blocks of literature. Percentages indicate the proportion of an actors total activity, not a percentage of total activity. Significance indicators do *not* compare SPP and Joel in this chart.[16]

There is much more woe than weal done in SPP and Joel. Israelites in Joel are the only entities to do more weal than woe, although the difference is not significant. In SPP all actors (except insects) do significantly more woe than weal. In Joel, however, God, humans in general, and Israelites seem to be doing similar amounts of woe and weal, whereas foreigners and insects do much more woe than weal. Although

14. Two actions in Joel versus one action in SPP cannot really be considered statistically significant.
15. It is not that they are more alert, but involved in alertness activity: they are to be roused (Joel 4.9, 12 [Eng. 3.9, 12]).
16. Weal and woe can be compared using statistics, for the concepts (as coded in this study) are mutually exclusive. However, many other metacategories and categories cannot be compared this way.

insects do the same raw number of woe actions that God does, the density is greater from the insects. Next to insects, the highest percentage of woe is done by God in SPP, and the least is by Israelites in Joel. The greatest percentage of weal is done by God in Joel, and the least is insects in Joel. Foreigners consistently do more woe than weal.

b. *Question: Are There Significant Differences between the Good and Bad Ethics Performed by Various Entities in SPP and Joel?*

Ethics in SPP and Joel

	SPP						Joel					
Actor	All ethics		Good ethics		Bad ethics		All ethics		Good ethics		Bad ethics	
	Qty	%	Qty	%	Qty	%	Qty	%	Qty	%	Qty	%
All	224	18	60	5§§	164	13**	9	3	5	2	4	1
God	18	5	12	3	6	2	2	3	2	3	0	0
Humans	195	27	44	6§§	151	21**	7	6	3	3	4	4
Israel	79	32	41	7§§	138	25**	2	3	2	3	0	0
Foreign	13	8	2	1§§	11	7**	5	16	1	3	4	13

Note: Significance indicators concern the relationship between good and bad ethics for the particular actor in that particular literature, *not* the relationship between SPP and Joel.

As is obvious from preceding analyses (and from a general knowledge of the prophets), ethical concerns are one of the central themes in most prophetic literature; in this sense Joel's lack of an ethical emphasis is quite different.

Good ethics never occur significantly more than bad ethics in SPP or Joel. Ethics figures for each actor are similar (and infrequent) in Joel. God is the only actor with similar good and bad ethical activity in both sets of literature, and in each case it is infrequent activity.

c. *Question: Do Entities Receive what They 'Give', in Terms of Evaluation?*

Evaluation of Major Entities: Activities and Receptions

Entity	Literature	Activity	Reception	Action-Reception Difference
God	SPP	-0.70	-0.33	-0.37*
	Joel	+0.32	-0.45	+0.77
Humans	SPP	-0.57	-0.98	+0.41**
	Joel	-0.31	+0.29	-0.60*

Israelites	Spp	-0.49	-0.79	+0.30*
	Joel	-0.08	+0.74	-0.82**
Foreigners	SPP	-0.83	-1.53	+0.70**
	Joel	-0.94	-1.17	+0.23

In SPP God performs more negatively than God receives, while humans act more positively than what they receive; so also with Israelites. Foreigners, though, while being harsh, receive even severer treatment. In Joel, humans in general and Israelites in particular perform harsher actions than what they receive, while foreigners are treated non-significantly worse.[17]

d. *Evaluation Relationships in SPP and Joel*

Evaluation Relationships: SPP and Joel

Literature/Actor	All		God		Israelite		Foreigner	
			Recipients (Complements)					
SPP—All	-0.69	1278	-0.33	205	-0.79	437	-1.53	147
Joel—All	-0.40	284	-0.45	22	0.74	71	-1.17	24
SPP—God	-0.70	366			-0.50	204	-1.98	59
Joel—God	0.32	78			1.62	42	-1.47	17
SPP—Israelites	-0.49	516	-0.42	172	-0.50	134	-0.80	25
Joel—Israelites	-0.08	75	0.29	14	0.42	12	-2.00	1
SPP—Foreigners	-0.83	166	0.00	15	-1.30	46	-1.19	43
Joel—Foreigners	-0.94	31	-2.60	5	-1.69	13	-0.40	5

Note: The mean evaluation is stated first, followed by the number of actions for the particular relationship. Tests for significance are not included here.

(The following comments are based solely on mean evaluations, without any statistical tests applied.)

God is much harsher in SPP, treats Israelites consistently better than foreigners, and treats foreigners consistently quite severely. God's Evaluation in SPP is lower than Israelites', but not as negative as foreigners in SPP. In Joel, the divine Evaluation is more positive than either Israelites or foreigners.

Israelites also act more positively in Joel than SPP. Israelite actions toward God in SPP are quite similar to their actions to other Israelites, and more positive than Israelite activity directed at foreigners.

Foreigners average actions never get a positive evaluation. Their

17. God receives so little in Joel that the Evaluation difference would have more extreme to be significant.

actions in Joel are harsher than in SPP, except to other foreigners (opposite of God and Israelites). Foreigners do not treat God consistently.

e. *Issue: A Brief Evaluation Comparison of Divine Treatment of Israelites and Foreigners versus Israelite and Foreigner Treatment of God in SPP and Joel.*

Evaluation Difference

God to Israelites/Israelites to God in SPP	-0.08
God to Israelites/Israelites to God in Joel	+1.33*
God to foreigners versus foreigners to God in SPP	-1.98**
God to foreigners versus foreigners to God in Joel	+1.13

God is nicer to Israelites and foreigners in Joel than they are to God, while in SPP God is harsher to Israelites and foreigners than they are to God.

f. *Who Does or Receives the Most of any Particular Emphasized Action, Regardless of Whether or Not the Differences are Significant?*
God consistently does the most love, reason, weal, and peace/shalom than Israelites or foreigners. Israelites consistently do more sorrow than God or foreigners. Foreigners do not do any emphasized category of action more than God or Israelites in SPP or Joel.

As for receptions which are consistent with SPP and Joel, God receives the most overall emotions and sorrow; Israelites receive the most love and peace/shalom; and foreigners receive the most woe, especially destruction and punishment.

g. *Reflections on the SPP—Joel Comparison*
Joel shares many concerns with other prophetic literature. God is presented as extremely active in the life of Israel, and bad things happen to God's people. It also shares the view that foreigners are a destructive folk who will themselves experience God's wrath.

However, it is unlike other prophetic literature in that ethics (good or bad) are of little concern, while the emotional state of the nation stands out. God is also not presented as a bringer of bad tidings to Israel, but as an envoy of prosperity.

Chapter 10

CONCLUDING DISCUSSION

1. *Purpose and Procedure*

One of the most fundamental ideas expressed in the Old Testament is that Yahweh acts—defining *act* in the ordinary sense of the word: *a specific deed performed by an agent.*[1] The purpose of the present study is to obtain a clearer picture of the image of God as an acting agent. Although it does not cover the entire prophetic corpus, much less the entire Old Testament, it is likely that the implications of the study reach beyond the particular texts studied.

This analysis has examined God's activity in five 'Selected Prophetic Passages' (SPP: Isa. 1.1–4.1; Hos. 4–8; Nahum; Malachi; and Zech. 12–14) which provide a certain, although not perfect, cross-section of prophetic materials—and, more particularly, in Joel. In the process, it gave attention to the way in which God's image differs from images for human beings (including those for Israelites and foreigners) and for insects (in Joel).

The results of the present content analysis often augmented, confirmed, or contradicted other methods of study. Some observations made are similar to those that have been obtained through other means; these have been confirmed and made more precise by the present study.[2] Other observations suggest conclusions which have not been reached through other means.

Specifically, the present study differs methodologically from most others in several ways. First, the choice of categories focuses on those which illuminate the characters of the agents, including God. Secondly,

1. Cf. G. Kaufman, 'On the Meaning of "Act of God"', in *idem*, *God the Problem* (Cambridge, MA: Harvard University Press, 1972), pp. 125-26.

2. The presence of conclusions which have also been obtained through other methods can serve the purpose of 'validation' (see R.P. Weber, *Basic Content Analysis* [Beverly Hills: Sage Publications, 1985]), p. 71.

the human profile too—with which the divine is compared—is taken from the literature itself, rather than from general assumptions about what humans do. Thirdly, activities are tallied, and divine–human comparisons are based on the relative frequencies of activities. The questions are, 'To what degree do humans and God resemble each other?' and, 'In what areas does God's activity resemble that of humans, and in what areas is this not true?' Fourthly, statistics provide a control on the significance of the various kinds of comparisons made.

In order to keep the analysis within bounds, the present study does not attempt to deal with all possible types of actions, but focuses on those activities which appear important for determining personality characteristics of the various actors. The two groups of activity which are emphasized are: *psychological activity*, and *activity with strong helpful/harmful connotations*.[3] Omitted are references to general movement, physical states and processes, institutional activity, and to communication processes, since these involve personality less directly. However, a numeric scale, *Evaluation* is applied to all activities; it tracks the relative beneficence of activity (+3 [helpful] to minus 3 [harmful]). It should be noted that Evaluation figures are derived from all activity, not just from those categories that are specifically described (so-called 'emphasized' ones).

This final chapter summarizes some of the major findings of the study, compares results to those of other approaches, and considers some of the implications of the study, especially those concerning the character of God in the prophets.

2. Approaches by Others

The idea of drawing a picture of God's character on the basis of what God is reported to do in the Hebrew Bible is not a novel one, but there is much uncertainty about how it is to be interpreted. In fact, G. Hasel

---

3. God's personality is usually discussed only in psychological terms (cf. O. Baab, *The Theology of the Old Testament* [New York: Abingdon Press, 1949], p. 29; D. Patrick, *The Rendering of God in the Old Testament* [Philadelphia: Fortress Press, 1981], pp. 38, 119). However, God's other activities—especially those with helpful and harmful connotations—also say much about the personality of God. (So also E. Cherbonnier, 'The Logic of Biblical Anthropomorphism', *HTR* 55 [1962], p. 204, who says that if God is to be known, it is 'through word and deed').

found it necessary to encourage this kind of interest[4] in the face of criticisms that have been directed toward descriptions of God's activity in the so-called 'Biblical Theology' movement.[5]

When God's activity in the Hebrew Bible has been examined in somewhat recent works, it has usually been in a way that describes God's saving acts,[6] God as creator,[7] or the love and justice of God.[8] Often the emphasis is on the foundation of Israel's relationship with God[9] or a treatment of God's demands,[10] rather than a description of God's character as an acting agent.[11] Thus there is a distinct lack of a systematic treatment of the *wide* variety of divine activities in the Old Testament, especially those which relate to God's personality.

While treatments of the personality of God are infrequent,[12] they are not altogether lacking.[13] Authors who emphasize God's personality in the Old Testament tend to describe God in terms which are

---

4. G.F. Hasel, *Old Testament Theology: Basic Issues in the Current Debate* (Grand Rapids: Eerdmans, 4th edn, 1991), p. 168.

5. Cf. L. Gilkey, 'Cosmology, Ontology, and the Travail of Biblical Language', *JR* 41.3 (1961), pp. 194-205; J. Barr, *The Semantics of Biblical Language* (London: Oxford University Press, 1961).

6. Cf. C. Westermann, *Elements of Old Testament Theology* (Atlanta: John Knox, 1978).

7. Cf. G.E. Wright, *The Old Testament and Theology* (New York: Harper & Row, 1969); and B.S. Childs, *Biblical Theology of the Old and New Testaments* (Minneapolis: Fortress Press, 1992).

8. Cf. E. Jacob, *Theology of the Old Testament* (London: Hodder & Stoughton, 1958).

9. E.g. E. Nicholson, *God and His People* (Oxford: Clarendon Press, 1986); and W. Zimmerli, *Old Testament Theology in Outline* (Atlanta: John Knox, 1978).

10. G. von Rad, *Old Testament Theology* (New York: Harper & Row, 1965).

11. W. Eichrodt's view (*Theology of the Old Testament* [2 vols.; Philadelphia: Westminster Press, 1961, 1967]) can be seen as a synthesis of such observations.

12. For instance, J. Scullion ('God', *Anchor Bible Dictionary*) notes many of God's activities in the Old Testament, but makes little reference to God's psychological activities except for noting that God loves and is all-knowing.

13. M. Burrows, *An Outline of Biblical Theology* (Philadelphia: Westminster Press, 1946), p. 61; Baab, *Theology of the Old Testament*, pp. 28-29, 33; Cherbonnier, 'Anthropomorphism', pp. 187-88; D. Clines, 'The Image of God in Man,' *TynBul* 19 (1968), pp. 70-71; Patrick, *Rendering of God*, pp. 38, 119; T.E. Fretheim, *The Suffering of God* (Philadelphia: Fortress Press, 1984), p. 6; H.D. Preuss, *Theologie des Alten Testaments*, Band I (Stuttgart: Verlag W. Kohlhammer, 1991), p. 280.

also appropriate for humans (i.e. those which could be called 'anthropomorphic'). Thus, A. Heschel describes God's *pathos* according to categories from Aristotle (*Nicomachean Ethics*, 1105b): '... desire, anger, fear, confidence, envy, joy, friendly feeling, hatred, longing, jealousy, pity; and generally those states which are accompanied by pleasure or pain.'[14] T. Fretheim, in many ways following Heschel, says 'The vast majority of metaphors for God in the Old Testament... are drawn from the sphere of the humans...'[15] E. Cherbonnier argues that the presentation of God in the Bible is quite unlike that of mystical philosophy, with the Bible presenting God in extremely personal terms.[16] D. Patrick, emphasizing a literary approach to the Old Testament, notes many anthropomorphic aspects of God, especially that God is presented as a 'concrete personality.'[17]

Nevertheless, there is also a tendency among theologians to stress Yahweh's differences from human beings (God's other-ness).[18] Some of the characteristics contrasting with human ones, emphasized in Christian theology, are omniscience, omnipotence, transcendence, etc.[19] A tension therefore occurs between a description of God as an acting agent and a view of God as wholly other; as a result, many theologies say little about God's characteristics as an agent, especially about those that have affinities with human activity.[20]

Although Heschel drew on categories by which Aristotle described human beings for his own presentation of God's image in the prophets, he said, 'It is of extreme importance that theology should endeavor to operate with categories indigenous to the insights of depth-theology

14. A.J. Heschel, *The Prophets* (New York: Harper & Row, 1962), II, p. 4.

15. Fretheim, *The Suffering of God*, pp.13ff; esp. pp. 25-26.

16. Cherbonnier, 'Anthropomorphism', pp. 187-209.

17. Patrick, *Rendering of God*, p. 40.

18. Cherbonnier ('Anthropomorphism', p. 190) and Heschel (*The Prophets*, pp. 6-7) both argue that this is due in part to an influence of Greek philosophical concepts on Christianity.

19. Baab, *Theology of the Old Testament* (p. 38) notes that 'the so-called attributes of God demanding discussion in any theological treatise—and this includes the idea of divine goodness—are at the best arbitrary and highly artificial symbols of the reality called God.'

20. Fretheim (*The Suffering of God*, p. 17) offers a similar criticism of Old Testament scholarship: '. . . God is understood in terms of traditional categories: freedom, immutability, omniscience, and omnipotence; if not explicitly stated, they are commonly assumed'.

instead of borrowing its categories from speculative philosophy or science.'[21] The present study is in line with this demand by comparing the image of God with an image of human life—as it appears in the same body of literature and according to the same criteria.

Past theologies have often focused on the use of such terms as 'heart', 'soul', and 'spirit' in descriptions of God.[22] Here, we deal with characteristics of God according to a different set of categories: emotionality, thinking, and helpful/harmful activities.

3. *The Character of God in Prophetic Materials*

a. *God as an Actor*
The Psychological Portrayal of God. Psychological processes depicted include emotionality[23] and cognition.[24]

In the prophets, God is pictured as an emotional and calculating being rather than as a dispassionate and non-rational force.[25] Specifically, psychological processes constitute over a fifth (22 percent) of divine activity in SPP and Joel combined; this is only slightly lower than for humans (28 percent).[26]

God's overall emotionality in SPP is similar to that of humans and is broadly distributed among all types of emotions, except that God does not fear at all. However, the frequencies of divine and human activities are different. Specifically, God is involved in more hate[27] and anger,[28] while humans tend toward sorrow[29] and fear. In fact, there is

21. Heschel, *The Prophets*, p. 45. Cherbonnier ('Anthropomorphism', pp. 196, 202) suggests a similar approach.

22. These are common categories in Old Testament theologies; see Eichrodt, *Theology of the Old Testament*, II, pp. 131-50; Baab, *Theology of the Old Testament*, pp. 65-68.

23. Joy, sorrow, love, hate, pride, shaming, anger, desire, and fear.

24. Alertness, non-alertness, knowledge, ignorance, obey/agree, rejection, and reason.

25. For a historical survey of views which reject the idea of a God with passions, see Heschel, *The Prophets*, esp. pp. 27-47, 55.

26. There is very little overlap between emotionality and cognition in this study. Only 13 of 371 psychological actions are classified as both, and none of God's psychological activity in either Joel or SPP overlaps the two metacategories.

27. According to Heschel (*The Prophets*, p. 32), Spinoza held that 'strictly speaking, God does not love or hate.'

28. While anger is not a high frequency emotion in SPP, God is the main one to

little evidence in the material covered for a 'suffering' God, spoken of by Fretheim.[30] Rather, God's emotional relationship with Israelites and foreigners in SPP is that of an adversary.[31]

Non-emotional psychological states and processes ('cognition') by God are likewise broadly distributed in SPP. Reason/decision stands out as a relatively frequent cognitive feature, although it does not appear much more often than for humans.[32] Rejection also occurs, but less frequently than for humans.[33] Humans in SPP are more involved in rejection, obedience/agreement, and non-alertness. Indeed, God's overall cognitive characterization is somewhat lower than for humans (9 percent versus 17 percent), although one must consider the fact that some of the human characterizations in this area are negative (non-alertness, ignorance).

In Joel, a similar overall pattern of emotionality and rationality appears, but specific elements of it differ.

Emotionality for God occurs similarly often as in SPP. It is, however, positive, especially in the form of love; in fact, none of the major actors in Joel—including God—express anger. Unlike the situation in SPP, God's emotionality does contrast in amount with that of humans (chiefly Israelites), who are strongly involved in emotions, particularly sorrow and fear.

---

express it. Jacob (*Theology of the Old Testament*, p. 114) rightly points to the frequency of God's wrath in the prophets.

29. Humans are involved in more sorrow (3% to 1%), but this difference is not statistically significant.

30. In SPP, love and sorrow comprise only 1% each of all divine activity. God's compassion does occur in Joel: sorrow is not present, although love is a notable action (5%).

31. Heschel (*The Prophets*, pp. 59-78) rightly points out that God's 'anger is by no means regarded as an attribute, as a basic disposition, as a quality inherent in the nature of God, rather as a mood, a state of mind or soul' (*The Prophets*, p. 77). For a similar view, see also Patrick, *Rendering of God*, p. 38.

32. S.E. Balentine's analysis (*The Hidden God: The Hiding of the Face of God in the Old Testament* [Oxford: Oxford University Press, 1983]) of God hiding from Israel relates to two categories in this study: non-alertness and rejection.

33. Balentine (*The Hidden God*, esp. pp. 136-37; 143-44; cf. 115-76) discusses God in terms which relate to cognition, specifically 'rejection' and 'ignorance': God, who makes conscious choices, actively forgets and rejects God's people ('hides the face'). The idea of God as one who hides from God's people is also mentioned by Fretheim, *The Suffering of God*, pp. 65-66; and W. Brueggemann, 'Presence of God, Cultic', *IDBSup*, p. 682.

God's involvement in cognitive activity in Joel is similar to what it is in SPP as well. This includes the fact that the most common cognitive activity by God in both is reason/decision. Since the cognitive activity of human actors is less here than in SPP (where human cognitive activity is higher than God's), divine and human cognitions are similar in overall amount. In Joel, the reduction in human cognitions—namely, an almost complete absence of the themes of obedience, rejection, and even ignorance—is related to the low level of explicit ethical concerns (see 'Ethics' below).

Activity with Strong Helpful/Harmful Connotations. The prominence of God's activity directed toward humans indicates that God is an active participant in the realm of humanity.[34] The prophets believe that people do not reap the consequences of their actions in a mechanistic or fatalistic fashion but that God is integrally involved in the alteration of their circumstances.[35]

Specifically, the prophets are concerned with a few major types of helpful/harmful activities and states. They involve positional well-being (status), physical well-being (weal/woe), and moral well-being (ethics); the latter two are the most common in the prophetic literature being examined.

Status. Although status-related activity is not a common theme in SPP (8 percent), God and humans are involved in a similar percentage of overall activity of this type.[36] They do differ in the specific kinds of status activity. God's main status activity is debasement, while human status activity is fairly evenly distributed among the various status categories.

Status activity is likewise infrequent in Joel, for God and all other actors, but some distinctions can be drawn, which illustrates a dissonance between the two blocks of literature. While debasement is a trait of SPP, its opposite, exaltation, is a more common theme in Joel. God does most of the exalting in Joel, but Israelites are also involved in it.

---

34. God does 29% of all activity in SPP.

35. This is also made evident by the high degree of punishment and reward on the part of God—activities which presuppose valuing decisions.

36. Foreigners are mentioned a little more frequently in connection with status items than are Israelites or God, but the difference is not statistically significant.

Weal and Woe. The idea that God is a being of wrath, vengeance, destruction, and punishment (which is a problem for some)[37] is ever-present in the prophets. God is a being who, according to the descriptions afforded God in the literature under consideration, can strike terror into the hearts of whoever encounters this being by acting upon God's negative attitudes. Granted, God also acts in a beneficent manner, but these gracious acts are far less common in both Joel and SPP.[38] In this literature it is appropriate to say, 'Yahweh your God is a consuming fire' (Deut. 4.24; cf. Heb. 12.29).

God's total woe and weal activity eclipses God's psychological activity in both SPP and Joel. This indicates that the prophets envisioned God not only as having thoughts or feelings, but even more so as One who acts in the physical realm (especially toward humans), presumably in connection with those thoughts and feelings.

The production of weal or woe is far more characteristic of divine activity than of human. Woe accounts for the largest block—over a third—of all divine activity in SPP, with destruction and punishment (two subdivisions of woe) being God's two most common types of actions.[39] The destruction is primarily directed toward humans, with much more destructive activity being directed toward foreigners than toward Israelites (see below).

In Joel, the total frequency of woe is similar to what is in SPP, but the distribution of woe among the various actors in Joel is different.[40] In particular, God's direct woe activity in Joel is much lower than in SPP,

---

37. For instance, Fretheim (*The Suffering of God*, p. 1) reacts strongly against what he views as an over-emphasis on portrayals of the God of the Old Testament as a God of wrath. To Fretheim's credit, he does acknowledge the wrath of God (pp. 29-30, 41), as well as stating that his study has a narrow focus which does not encompass all Old Testament views (p. 12).

38. SPP: 24% to 4%; Joel: 21% to 7%.

39. For a discussion concerning the connection between bad ethics and divine punishment, see P.D. Miller, *Sin and Judgment in the Prophets* (Chico, CA: Scholars Press, 1982).

40. Only foreigners show consistency, with woe comprising a quarter of their activities in both blocks of literature. Woe is also common for Israelites in SPP (but to a much lesser degree than for God in SPP), but Joel contains no instances of Israelites doing woe. The activity of insects (who are the most destructive beings in Joel), drought, and wildfires compensates for the lesser woe in Joel on the part of God and Israelites.

accounting for only a sixth of God's activity. However, punishment is a similarly frequent divine activity in both SPP and Joel.[41]

Weal is not completely absent in SPP, but it is eclipsed by woe activity. When weal occurs, God is the main one doing it. God's most frequent weal activities affect that which surrounds humans (peace/ shalom and reward), rather than the body itself (life and healing).

Weal is a major feature of God's activity in Joel. In fact, it is almost as common there as is God's woe activity. This indicates a greater interest in God's beneficence in Joel than in SPP. However, God's beneficence in Joel is tempered when God's indirect activity is taken into account, a matter to which we will return.

Weal and woe: God's direct dealings with Israelites and foreigners: God's activity toward foreigners is different from that toward Israelites. God disproportionately deals with Israelites, and acts with different attitudes and activities toward Israelites than toward foreigners. This favoritism exists even when Israelites are what could be termed 'rebellious' or 'sinful'. This section will consider some trends which have emerged when humans are divided into Israelites and foreigners.

Since God is more involved with Israelites than with foreigners in both SPP and Joel, and most of what God does in SPP is toward humans, a detailed summary of God's treatment of Israelites would be redundant. Suffice it to say that God's treatment of Israelites in SPP tends to be physically harmful, emphasizing destruction and punishment, while weal activities seldom occur.

In Joel, God's treatment of Israelites is quite different from what it is in SPP. While God's main approach to Israel in SPP is through destruction and punishment, God metes out peace and love to Israel in Joel. In other words, God is not merely less harsh to Israelites in Joel than to foreigners, but God is actually kind to Israelites, doing no negative activities at all toward them.[42]

One of the few consistencies between SPP and Joel involves God's harsh treatment of foreigners—a treatment which is consistently worse than Israelites in both sets of literature. Specifically, while 31 percent of God's activity toward Israelites in SPP is oriented toward woe, 56 percent of what God does to foreigners is physically harmful.

41. Reward occurs similarly often as a divine activity in both sets of literature, but to a much lesser degree than punishment.

42. It should be noted that Israelite activity varies greatly between SPP and Joel, while foreigner activity is consistent.

The situation is not very different for foreigners in Joel, where 47 percent of what they receive from God is harmful.[43]

Cause/effect relationships were not specifically examined in the present study; this would have required a temporal indicator. However, one apparent association was noted: divine treatment of foreigners does not mirror what foreigners do to God. Rather, God treats foreigners in the same way they treat Israelites, but in an 'eye for a tooth' manner— God's treatment of foreigners is even harsher than their treatment of Israelites.[44]

T. Fretheim offers a thesis that there is equality in God's dealings with Israelites and foreigners, both positively and negatively.[45] However, when calculated numerically, Fretheim's view does not hold true for the prophetic literature under consideration. These prophets, who are often critical of Israelites (Joel excepted), betray God's favoritism of Israelites by describing a different, less negative/more positive treatment of them than that of foreigners.

Ethics. Good and bad ethics are manifestations of helpful/harmful states and processes which could be termed *righteous* or *wicked*. God does very few actions which are coded as either good or bad ethics;[46] normally God's activities are not subject to such an assessment. Instead, ethics (good and bad) is a major feature of human activity in SPP. This is especially true for Israelite actions, one third of which are ethical ones (most frequently bad ethics).

The situation is different in Joel; its interests lie elsewhere than in ethics.[47] If one believes the view that literature without an emphasis

43. The Evaluation scale also supports this thesis (see the Evaluation chart below).

44. This is also reminiscent of Gen. 12.3: 'I will bless those who bless you, and I will curse those who curse you.'

45. So Fretheim (*The Suffering of God*, p.137), who says, 'That God is represented as mourning over the fate of non-Israelite peoples as well as Israelites demonstrates the breadth of God's care and concern for the sufferers of the world, whoever they might be. Israel has no monopoly on God's empathy. All people everywhere have *experienced* the compassion (and judgment) of God, even though they may not realize that fact.'

46. While God does more good than bad ethical activity, most of God's ethically bad activity could possibly be coded as destructive activity which does not actually involve ethics (as defined in this study).

47. R. Simkins (*Yahweh's Activity in History and Nature in the Book of Joel* [Lewiston, NY: Edwin Mellen Press, 1991]), pp. 171-82, who holds (as does the

on ethics is valueless, then Joel is a valueless book. Such a view, though, would mean that deliverance from oppressors (e.g. natural disasters and human enemies) is of little value, as well as a concern for the emotional well-being of God's people.[48]

b. *God as a Recipient*
Divine activity is not an uncommon theme in literature about the Bible, but little is said about divine reception. However, as Heschel[49] and Fretheim have also noted, not only is God an actor in the prophets, but God can also be acted upon and affected by the activities and attitudes of others. (The present study examines divine reception with the aid of categories that are the same as those that have been used to describe divine activity.)

In SPP, close to half of all activity directed toward God is psychological in orientation. Within this set, non-emotional processes are especially common, particularly rejection[50] and, although to a lesser degree, obedience and reason/decision. Emotional responses to God are less frequent than are cognitive ones; they are dominated by fear and sorrow. Thus God not only acts, but even more so is approached, in a psychological way.

In addition, while God is not often involved in activity with overtly ethical connotations, much of what God receives is in the ethical realm: one third of what God receives is ethically valued, mainly ethically bad (25 percent).[51]

As for woe and weal, God receives very little of either in SPP and Joel—which is quite different from what humans receive.

The alteration of God's status is not much of a concern in SPP.

author) that Israel is not accused of sin in Joel, summarizes many attempts to identify the 'sin' of the people that brought on the disaster.

48. Joel does express sensitivity to ethically bad activity by foreigners, but this is probably only because these activities harm Israelites.

49. Heschel, *The Prophets*, pp. 3-4.

50. Fretheim (*The Suffering of God*, p. 109) discusses how rejection causes God to suffer.

51. Ethically bad activities which God receives (without frequency counts) are: abomination, act treacherously, be arrogant, desecrated, evil, negated faithfulness, negated fear, negated good, negated heed, iniquity, negated keep, be led astray, lie/deceit, plan, profane, prostitute, prostitution, rebel/revolt, refuse, reject, negated repent, rob, negated serve, sin, sinful, stray, be stubborn, test, turn aside, and wickedness.

Noteworthy, though, is that half of the exaltation God receives in SPP (three of six) has an unspecified source.[52]

In Joel, divine reception of *any* type of activity is not much of a concern. This may indicate that 'threats' to God (e.g. bad ethics, rejection) are either unimportant for Joel or not considered to be serious.

The little that God does receive in Joel has a different orientation from what God receives in SPP. Unlike SPP, where ethics comprise a large part of Israel's way of relating to God, Israel's relation to God in Joel is almost exclusively mental (10/14) and is comprised of emotions. Sorrow and joy account for the bulk of psychological activity directed toward God, while cognition is much lower. Nevertheless, Joel is similar to the other prophets in that God receives no love.

In short, God is pictured as being affected primarily by the attitudes and value-laden actions of humans: ethics, cognition, and emotions.[53] In SPP and Joel, these processes have strong negative connotations, particularly manifested by bad ethics (especially), rejection, and fear. (The negative character of what God receives is also displayed by the Evaluation scale—see below.)

Since God is not generally acted upon physically, these Israelite prophets apparently do not believe that one can do much directly to God outside the psychological and valuing realm. This does not mean that God is unaffected by humans; on the contrary—most of what God receives is from humans.

c. *Evaluation*

The Evaluation scale has provided a tool for gauging the relative beneficence of activity in prophetic literature. Cutting across all categories under consideration, this scale provides some insights that categories as such do not. For instance, if one party is involved in bad ethics, and the other is involved in destruction, Evaluation may demonstrate that there is a correspondence between their actions. A second advantage is that it furnishes not just a 'yes' or 'no' analysis, but indicates degrees of

---

52. These are passives, but Mal. 1.5 implies Israelites and foreigners as common actors. Stated actors who exalt God are all in Malachi; twice those who exalt God are foreigners, and once they are Israelites.

53. Heschel (*The Prophets*, pp. 3-4) likewise states that God is 'moved and affected by what happens in the world, and reacts accordingly. . . He is not conceived as judging the world in detachment.' Fretheim (*The Suffering of God*, p. 3) offers a similar view.

negativity or positivity; thus, if one party is involved in more severe woe than another one, Evaluation shows the difference.

Evaluation Relationships: SPP and Joel

	All		God		Humans		Israel		Foreign	
Literature/Actor					*Recipient (Complements)*					
SPP—ALL	-0.69	1278	-0.33	205	-0.98	576	-0.79	437	-1.53	147
JOEL—ALL	-0.40	284	-0.45	22	+0.29	90	+0.74	71	-1.17	24
SPP—GOD	-0.70	366			-0.89	257	-0.50	204	-1.98	59
JOEL—GOD	+0.32	78			+0.73	56	+1.62	42	-1.47	17
SPP—HUMN	-0.57	734	-0.38	188	-0.84	229	-0.81	167	-1.11	63
JOEL—HUMN	-0.31	109	-0.47	19	-0.57	28	-0.71	24	-0.50	6
SPP—ISRL	-0.49	516	-0.42	172	-0.60	150	-0.50	134	-0.80	25
JOEL—ISRL	-0.08	75	+0.29	14	+0.23	13	+0.42	12	-2.00	1
SPP—FRGN	-0.83	166	0.00	15	-1.36	74	-1.30	46	-1.19	43
JOEL—FRGN	-0.94	31	-2.60	5	-1.43	14	-1.69	13	-0.40	5

Locust Evaluations

JOEL—LOCUSTS	-1.31	42
JOEL—GOD + LOCUSTS	-0.25	120
JOEL—DROUGHT + LOCUSTS	-1.62	64
JOEL—DROUGHT + LOCUSTS + GOD	-0.53	142

Note: The mean Evaluation is stated first, followed by the number of actions for that particular relationship. Tests for significance are not included here.

The overall Evaluation of activity in SPP is negative (-0.69), indicating that the sense of evil is strong. God and humans display differing versions of negativity (God primarily woe, humans primarily bad ethics), but the Evaluation scale indicates a continuity. In this sense God is shown to be similar to both Israelites and foreigners (in terms of their total activity).[54] However, God's activities are shown to be significantly more negative than God's receptions. (Some of this difference can probably be attributed to the fact that woe activities [physically harmful] tended to be coded a point more negatively than bad ethical activities whose harm is not also classified as woe.)

In Joel, the overall Evaluation is also negative, but less so than in SPP. In particular, God's (direct) activity is positive, while that of Israel is neutral, and only that of foreigners and insects is negative.

54. These evaluations are not significantly different.

As for God's treatment of specific human groups, God is (directly) kinder to Israelites in Joel[55] than in SPP, but God treats foreigners quite harshly in both bodies of literature. Thus the difference between the Evaluation of God's activity in Joel and SPP reflects a different treatment of Israelites, not of foreigners.[56]

d. *Reflections: God as an Actor and Recipient*
In both SPP and Joel, a very large part of divine and human activity concerns well-being or its opposite, especially for humans. Emotions, too (hate, anger, fear, sorrow) are closely related to this issue. In other words, the prophetic materials have a strong pragmatic orientation. Thus, in so far as 'history' is a relevant category,[57] it is not simply one of 'objective' or 'interesting' events, but one in which weal/joy or woe/sorrow—that is those things which are pleasant or unpleasant— take place.[58]

Divine activity in the prophets is dominated by activity in the physical realm (although psychological activity is fairly common), while what God receives is primarily in the mental and valuing realm. Since most of what God does is toward humans, and most of what God receives is from humans, then it can be said that what God does to humans is more tangible than what they do to God.

The fact that divine activity is oriented toward weal/woe (in SPP and Joel), while human activity often involves ethics (in SPP), constitutes an important difference between them. If one, however, considers that much of ethics involves the production of aid or harm to someone, a parallel can be seen between this and the woe/weal activities of God. The possibility of a correspondence between them is confirmed by the Evaluation scale: the average for both God and humans is negative and not significantly different in SPP.[59] While the current study has not dealt with the issue of temporal or causal relations, nevertheless, God's woe-dealing, especially in SPP, can be viewed as a

55. Combined with insect activity, +0.15.
56. This is also borne out by the category system.
57. As noted earlier, a major interest in prior discussions of God's activity has been God's action 'in history'.
58. Heschel (*The Prophets*, p. 76) says that 'Anger, too, is a form of [God's] presence in history.'
59. It should be remembered that positive or negative connotations of activities are indicated not only by the Evaluation scale, but by many categories as well.

response to bad (deleterious) ethics on the part of human beings.

4. *God and Natural Forces: God's Indirect Activity*

a. *Introduction*

So far we have considered only how God compares with human beings. Joel, however, contains extensive references to agents that are neither human nor divine—especially locusts.

In Joel, God's main similarity to locusts is that the top activity for both is woe, especially destruction. However, there are numerous differences: God acts psychologically (with emotions and cognitions) and punishes, while insects do not do so. While destruction is the most common activity for both, insects devote more of their activity to destructive ends than God does. Further, the focus of divine activity is humanity, while the focus of direct insect activity is plants.

Especially noteworthy, however, is that while the activity of these 'natural forces' is shown to be different from God's direct activity, it also represents God's character. The locusts' activity (along with drought and wildfires) is described as an indirect activity of God's: they are called 'the army of Yahweh' (Joel 2.11, 25) and their actions are described as a 'Day of Yahweh' (Joel 1.15; 2.1-2, 11).

The importance of the matter is this: if direct divine activity is considered apart from indirect divine activity, then God appears considerably kinder in Joel than in SPP, especially toward Israelites (although God is consistently harsh toward foreigners). Including the activities of the locusts, drought, and wildfires as part of God's actions in Joel results in a presentation of God which is almost as harsh as in other prophetic literature; the main difference is a lack of negative attitudes on God's part.

b. *The Days of Yahweh in the Hebrew Bible*

The 'Day of Yahweh' in the Hebrew Bible refers to various kinds of divine visitations often involving wrath and judgment,[60] not necessarily

---

60. There are a variety of theories concerning the origin of the term or concept, the 'Day of Yahweh.' G. von Rad ('The Origin of the Concept of the Day of Yahweh,' *JSS* 4 [1959], pp. 97-108 [repeated in *Old Testament Theology* [Edinburgh: Oliver & Boyd, 1965], II, pp. 119-25) has articulated the position that the Day of Yahweh comes out of the idea of holy war. Another view, as proposed by S. Mowinckel (*He That Cometh* [Nashville: Abingdon Press, 1965], p. 145), sees the origin in a cultic

a final eschatological one. There are two applications of the term: judgment against God's people, and judgment against the enemies of God's people.

The 'Day of Yahweh' often has military overtones in the Bible. However, it is not necessarily connected with holy war,[61] and it can include other types of disasters (although the military similes in Joel are especially fitting for an 'invasion' of locusts). This is not only true in the Hebrew Bible, but elsewhere in other ancient Near Eastern literature. Parallels have been noted by Cerny, Buss, and Loretz, concerning texts which speak of gloom or terror, including agricultural disaster, as part of a 'day' of ancient Near Eastern deities.[62]

Joel[63] contains two events which are called the 'Day of Yahweh':[64]

Day of Yahweh, specifically the Enthronement festival, finding ANE parallels. L. Cerny (*The Day of Yahweh and Some Relevant Problems* [V Praze: Nakladem Filosoficke Fakulty Univ. Karlovy, 1948]) and O. Loretz (*Regenritual und Jahwetag im Joelbuch* [Altenberge: CIS-Verlag, 1986]) see its origin in non-Yahwistic ANE traditions. Many have followed in the steps of both of these views; a synthesis of holy war and cultic day has also been offered by F.M. Cross (*Canaanite Myth and Hebrew Epic* [Cambridge, MA: Harvard University Press, 1973], pp. 243-46). The advantage of M. Buss's approach (*The Prophetic Word of Hosea: A Morphological Study* [BZAW, 111; Berlin: Töpelmann, 1969], pp. 93-95) is that it does not specifically tie the Day of Yahweh to a cultic day or to holy war.

For these and other views on the Day of Yahweh, see A.S. Kapelrud, *Joel Studies* (Uppsala: Lundeqvist, 1948), pp. 55-56, 72, 78; Cerny, *Day of Yahweh*; G. von Rad, 'The Origin of the Concept of the Day of Yahweh'; Mowinckel, *He That Cometh*, p. 145; Buss, *Prophetic Word of Hosea*, pp. 93-95; G. Ahlström, *Joel and the Temple Cult of Jerusalem* (Leiden: Brill, 1971), pp. 69-70; Cross, *Canaanite Myth and Hebrew Epic*, pp. 243-46; A.J. Everson, 'Days of Yahweh', *JBL* 93 (1974), pp. 329-37; J. Gray, 'The Day of Yahweh in Cultic Experience and Eschatological Prospect', *SEÅ* 39 (1974), pp. 5-37; H. Wolff, *Joel and Amos* (Philadelphia: Fortress Press, 1977), pp. 33-34; Y. Hoffmann, 'The Day of the Lord as a Concept and a Term in the Prophetic Literature', *ZAW* 93 (1981), pp. 37-50; H. Barstad, *The Religious Polemics of Amos* (Leiden: Brill, 1984), pp. 82-111; Loretz, *Joelbuch*; Simkins, *Yahweh's Activity*, pp. 201-80. See Loretz, *Joelbuch*, pp. 77-79 for a more complete bibliography.

61. See the studies cited in the preceding note.

62. Buss, *Prophetic Words of Hosea*, pp. 93-95; Cerny, *Day of Yahweh*, pp. 9-17; and Loretz, *Joelbuch*, pp. 77-81.

63. For a recent survey of many issues related to the book of Joel, see Simkins, *Yahweh's Activity*.

64. I have argued in an unpublished essay that Joel 1.2–2.17 was designed be an instruction manual in the event of natural disaster. On the basis of a central theological

the disaster caused by the locust plague,[65] drought, and wildfires (Joel 1.15; 2.1-2, 11),[66] and God's judgment against the nations (Joel 4.14 [Eng. 3.14]);[67] neither of these should be understood eschatologically.[68]

confession concerning Yahweh's faithfulness and mercy, Joel argues that it is possible to get Yahweh to change Yahweh's mind and bring about restoration.

65. The locusts in Joel 1 are literal, rather than symbols for human armies, and the beings in Joel 2.1-11 are locusts, not an eschatological army (contra von Rad, 'Origin', p. 101; and Wolff, *Joel and Amos*, pp. 39-43), for the following reasons: (1) The similes are in the direction from the locusts to armies—locusts are *like* armies. This must be said against the view that Joel refers to a *human* army, defended by D. Stuart (*Hosea-Jonah* [Waco, TX: Word Books, 1987], p. 226); P.C. Craigie (*Twelve Prophets* [Philadelphia: Westminster Press, 1984], pp. 85-100); and D. Garrett ('The Structure of Joel', *JETS* 28 [1985], pp. 289-97). Armies may have been compared to locusts in other Old Testament passages, but not here. Garrett ('Structure', p. 293), though, (unconvincingly) argues that k does not necessarily equal *like* in all instances, especially in Joel. (2) Agricultural elements are prominent in the passage, even in 2.1-11, which focuses on a description of the destroyers. (3) All the damage listed is agricultural. All calls to lamentation concern agricultural damage which affects particular groups in society. (4) There is no indication that any destruction comes upon cities, fortifications, the Temple, or people (for a contrast see Zephaniah 1). The only term with the connotation *kill* (cut off, *krt*) is directed at produce and rejoicing, not human lives, and does *not* occur in the military section. (5) All the restoration is agricultural: the destroyers have been destroyed, the rains have come, the plants have grown, and the produce has been used. Modern western interpreters would do well to bear in mind that a famine, whatever its cause, is a calamity on the level of a military conflict. (S.R. Driver, [*The Books of Joel and Amos* (Cambridge: Cambridge University Press, 1907), p. 30] made a similar observation.) (6) It is not unprecedented to have ANE literature which concerns imploring a god to eliminate a locust plague. V. Hurowitz ('Joel's Locust Plague in light of Sargon II's Hymn to Nanaya', *JBL* 112 [1993], pp. 597-603) argues for some parallels between Joel and an ANE hymn relating to a locust plague, without relating it to a 'day' of a god.

Loretz (*Joelbuch*, p.125), who proposes Ugaritic parallels to Joel, notes that Keret's army is described as being like locusts. However, the comparison falters, for the simile in Joel goes the other direction: the beings are 'like' armies.

66. Simkins (*Yahweh's Activity*, p. 154) argues that Joel 1 speaks of a different locust plague than Joel 2. His interpretation, if accepted, would have little effect on the results presented herein.

67. Note that the activity of these destructive elements is called the Day of Yahweh, while the activities of foreigners in Joel are not even indirectly associated with God.

68. Contrary to the view that Joel treats a catastrophic event as a 'harbinger of the Day of Jehovah which he sees approaching. . . ', for Joel the disaster *is* the Day of

The former concerns indirect activity of God against Israelites, while the latter concerns God's direct activity toward foreigners.

c. *God's Indirect Activity in Joel*

It is the indirect activity of God (Joel 1–2) which is of interest here. This is because the activity of non-human/non-divine destructive entities (i.e. locusts, drought, and wildfires) in Joel 1–2, when added to direct divine activity toward Israelites (since Israelites are those affected by the disaster), alters the positive picture of God-to-Israelite activity.[69] This indirect activity, focused against agriculture, results in much suffering, sorrow, and fear on the part of Israelites.

The impersonal nature of indirect divine activity, combined with the complete absence of any ethically bad activity on the part of Israelites, gives the impression that there is no particular reason for the visitation of the Day of Yahweh upon Israel as described in Joel 1–2. Unlike SPP, where the bad ethics and the rebellion of Israelites can be seen as a catalyst for divine judgment (punishment involves a value judgment), and where the divine judgment is accompanied by negative attitudes (anger, hatred, and rejection), there are no charges against Israel[70] in Joel, and no accompanying negative attitudes on the part of God—which makes God appear somewhat capricious.[71] Thus Joel does not affix the

Yahweh. (Cf. Driver, *Joel and Amos*, p. 10; J.A. Bewer, *The Book of the Twelve Prophets* [New York: Harper & Brothers, 1949], II, p. 81; D.R. Jones, *Isaiah 56-66 and Joel* [London: SCM Press, 1964], p. 138; L.C. Allen, *The Books of Joel, Obadiah, Jonah, and Micah* [Grand Rapids: Eerdmans, 1976], p. 30; Stuart, *Hosea-Jonah*, p. 231; Craigie, *Twelve Prophets*, pp. 85-100; W.S. Prinsloo, *The Theology of the Book of Joel* [Berlin: de Gruyter, 1985], p. 48; Kapelrud, *Joel Studies*, p. 178; Wolff, *Joel and Amos*, p. 17; and R.P. Carroll, 'Eschatological Delay in the Prophetic Tradition [Isa. 11.25; 59; Hab. 2.3; Joel 2.1; Hag. 1]', *ZAW* 94 [1982], p. 53.)

69. Simkins (*Yahweh's Activity*, pp. 167, 200, 258) views the Day of Yahweh in Joel as Yahweh's victory over the locusts, rather than locusts doing Yahweh's bidding. While this view is not accepted by the present author (Yahweh sent the 'army' of locusts [Joel 2.11, 25]), if Simkins is correct, then Yahweh's activity toward Israelites in Joel is *extremely* positive.

70. The expression 'turn' or 'return' in Joel 2.12 does not necessarily imply repentance from sin.

71. Contra Fretheim, *The Suffering of God*, p. 11. Fretheim rightly notes that God is not involved in many human activities (e.g. sex, crime, lack of wisdom). However, his contention that 'capriciousness' cannot be attributed to God does not appear to hold true in this case.

cause of the disaster to activities by Israelites,[72] nor does Joel present the disaster as rejection of any sort by God.[73] In other words, while the disaster is indirectly attributed to God, the issue of a reason for the disaster is not addressed.[74]

There are some important differences between this indirect divine activity and God's direct activity. First, unlike what God does to all in SPP, and unlike what God does to foreigners in all the prophets under consideration, there is no punishment. This is significant because punishment is a woe-oriented activity which presupposes reflection on the part of the punisher. Secondly, psychological activities are virtually missing from God's indirect activity: there is no anger or hatred present. Thus God's indirect activity is without any discernible attitude, a fact which underlines the purposelessness of the locust plague.

The result is a tension of blame—God is not (directly) responsible for the disaster and yet indirectly so. Without these secondary agents, God does no negative activities toward Israel; God's beneficent activities toward Israel are direct, without an intermediary.[75] Yet the event is a 'Day of Yahweh' (Joel 1.15; 2.1-2, 11), executed by Yahweh's army (Joel 2.11, 25).

d. *Reflections: Indirect Activity and Biblical Theology*
The inclusion of insect activity with divine activity brings up some intriguing possibilities and some serious questions. Since the Bible presents God as acting both directly and indirectly, the consideration of both kinds of acts as acts of God is appropriate for constructing a biblical theology of God. What would a theology of the indirect acts of God look like? For instance, outside of Joel, if the activity of non-Assyrian foreigners in Nahum (part of SPP) were to be included as

72. Contra Barstad (*Polemics*, p.83), who argues that the disaster is 'a consequence of the moral and religious behaviour of the Israelites. . . [particularly] the worship of gods other than Yahweh and the disobedience of his divine laws.' In our study, idolatry was coded as ethically bad, and yet this is not present in Joel 1–2.

73. Joel 1.2-3 indicates that the first major part of Joel (chs 1 and 2 [Eng. 1.1–2.27]) was explicitly written for the benefit of future generations, rather than for the generation which experienced the disaster. Joel's interests appear to be concentrated in showing people their involvement in the rectification of future disasters, not explaining why these disasters will occur.

74. So also Simkins, *Yahweh's Activity*, p. 182; see also p. 130.

75. This situation can be contrasted with that in SPP, where God's harmful activity toward Israelites is direct, while God's beneficial actions are not frequent.

indirect divine activity,[76] the result would be an even harsher picture of God in SPP.

Similarly, the Bible sometimes presents God as being affected by what happens to people, so that indirect reception of activity by God is also an appropriate topic of inquiry. While the present study did not address this question—except to note that God treats foreigners as foreigners treat Israelites—it could be justified by some passages in SPP (Hos. 4.1,6; Isa. 1.2-4) where activities directed by humans toward humans are characterized as violations of God's law. If SPP were examined in this light the result would be an even more extensively negative picture of the human–God relationship.

5. The 'Image of God' and Anthropomorphic Conceptions of God in the Old Testament

The expression 'image of God,' used in this study in the title and in the question, 'What does it mean to say that humans are created in God's image?' is a play on words, based on Gen. 1.26,[77] and should not be understood to constitute an exegesis of that passage.[78] Rather, an issue for this study is the idea ever-present in the Old Testament (presumably also in some way in Gen. 1.26) that God and humans share many characteristics.[79] I will address this topic now directly, in conversation with previous studies.

76. The actions of Assyrian foreigners were not distinguished from those of non-Assyrian foreigners when Nahum was coded. However, I would estimate that God would be credited with 20 additional woe activities, increasing the overall amount of divine woe in SPP to 40%.

77. For summaries and interpretative suggestions, see J.M. Miller, 'In the 'Image' and 'Likeness' of God', *JBL* 91 (1972), pp. 289-304; C. Westermann, *Genesis 1–11* (Minneapolis: Augsburg, 1984), pp. 147-58; and Clines, 'Image of God', pp. 53-104.

78. The author is in agreement with the interpretation of many that the emphasis of Gen. 1.26 is that humans were made to physically resemble God (cf. J.M. Miller, 'In the 'Image' and 'Likeness' of God', pp. 289-304; contra Clines, 'Image of God'). I also agree, in general, with the notion that since the Hebrew conception of human nature was holistic, the 'image of God', by default, would have included psychological aspects as well (e.g. Vriezen, von Rad, Barth; see Westermann, *Genesis 1–11*, p. 150; and Clines, 'Image of God', p. 61).

79. Both Heschel (*The Prophets*, p. 40) and Fretheim (*The Suffering of God*, pp. 10-11) argue that humans should be regarded as 'theomorphic', rather than God as anthropomorphic.

a. *Rationality and Emotionality*

Some interpreters have indicated that the area in which human beings are similar to God—and thus God to humans—is the psychological, especially rationality. According to Jacob Jervell, early Jewish traditions held that 'The image of God is the ability to know good and evil. This includes freedom of the will.'[80] According to J. Pelikan, for the early Christian theologian Gregory of Nyssa, 'to be made according to the image of God and therefore to be authentically human meant to be rational', and 'reason... was superior... to the passions and emotions...' Emotions were understood to be 'shared by human nature with the irrational creatures...' and thus not a part of the image of God.[81] For Augustine, the image involved memory, perception/ understanding, and love.[82] A number of interpreters, from ancient to recent ones, have stressed the phenomena of 'understanding, the will and its freedom, self-consciousness, intelligence...'[83]

Much in these views can be affirmed, but only in so far as rationality is not seen as the exclusive or even primary feature of God's image in humanity. First, God and humans are involved in almost all the same kinds of activity (according to the categories employed in this study, but not according to the frequencies of the various activities); much of this activity is other than psychological in orientation. Secondly, with the notable exceptions of a few authors—especially Heschel, Fretheim, and Cherbonnier—previous interpreters have given too little attention to emotionality. We have seen that God and human beings are similar in overall emotionality, although the specifics are quite different, with love being infrequent for both (contra Augustine).[84] Thirdly, since in the material covered, animals are not marked by emotionality, and yet God is,[85] it is not likely that the writers thought of emotionality in

80. J. Jervell, *Imago Dei* (Göttingen: Vandenhoeck & Ruprecht, 1960), p. 27.

81. J. Pelikan, *Christianity and Classical Culture* (New Haven: Yale University Press, 1993), p. 129.

82. Clines, 'Image of God', p. 54; see also p. 86.

83. Thus Westermann, *Genesis 1–11*, p. 149, on opinions by Philo, B. Jacob, P. Bratsiotis, G. Söhngen.

84. However, if emotionality is to be associated with the 'unreasoning creatures' (cf. Gregory of Nyssa), then a great part of God's character in the Bible resembles that of animals.

85. Only one of the 55 activities by wild creatures, 'languishing' (Hos. 4.3), could be considered an emotional activity.

humans as forming a continuity with animals rather than with God (contra Gregory of Nyssa).

b. *God and Humans Compared: The Question of Anthropomorphic Conceptions of God*

The issue of anthropomorphic conceptions of God often involves a number of elements not treated here, such as physical characteristics (e.g. hands, eyes, arms, theophanies which describe God in a form resembling humans[86]) and communicative activities of God. However, the issue can be addressed on a theoretical level.

Opinions about the use of anthropomorphisms have varied. Some interpreters note that Israelites held anthropomorphic views; some consider this type of Old Testament view to be a valuable one,[87] while others present it as a flaw.[88] Still others express doubt that anthropomorphic statements were meant to be taken literally by the ancient writers.[89] Heschel envisions a partially anthropomorphic view: 'The prophets... seem to have had no apprehension that the statements of divine pathos might impair their understanding for the one, unique, and transcendent God.'[90] However, as Fretheim has said, 'Anthropomorphic metaphors have tended to be depreciated, even denigrated, in the history of Judaeo-Christian thought and Old Testament scholarship in particular.'[91]

In one way, the present study acknowledges and underscores the anthropomorphic presentation of God in the prophets. The Old Testament writers, including the prophets, applied the same language constructions

---

86. E.g. Preuss (*Theologie*, p. 280) notes some anthropomorphic representations of God in the Old Testament: face, mouth, eyes, heart, hands, ears; remorse, hate, anger, sorrow, grief. See also Jacob, *Theology of the Old Testament*, p. 40.

87. Preuss, *Theologie*, p. 281; Cherbonnier, 'Anthropomorphism'; Heschel, *The Prophets*.

88. Burrows (*Outline of Biblical Theology*, p. 61) refers to anthropomorphisms as 'naïve' and 'crude'.

89. Burrows (*Outline of Biblical Theology*, p. 61) states that 'in view of... the obviously figurative nature of many anthropomorphic expressions, it is only reasonable to suppose that the statements attributing to him human thoughts and emotions partake of the same character.'

90. Heschel, *The Prophets*, pp. 48-49.

91. Fretheim, *The Suffering of God*, p. 6.

to God and humans.[92] This fact (which made it possible to code activity without making any conceptual distinction based solely on actors or recipients[93]) has allowed us to illuminate the anthropomorphic nature of God's activity in the prophets.[94] We have seen that God and humans are involved in all of the same types of activity under examination with the following exceptions: God does not fear at all and is involved in no wealth-related activity.[95]

In another way, the study also calls into question the notion of anthropomorphism in the Bible. If 'anthropomorphism' includes the idea that the various activities occur with a similar frequency (and thus with similar emphases) for God and for humans, then the prophetic presentation of God is far from being anthropomorphic, for the relative frequencies of most of the specific activities are different.[96]

---

92. So also Cherbonnier ('Anthropomorphism', p. 202), who states that 'the Bible does apply a common language to both men and God. . . '

93. The main exception does not regard coding, but the interpretations of a particular pair of categories: KEEP (obey/agree) and RJCT (rejection). KEEP was generally viewed as obedience when performed by humans toward God, but as agreement when performed by God. Likewise, rejection was more likely to be viewed as including rebellion when performed by a human toward God, and rejection when God did it toward humans. However, both instances involved the relative acquiescence to another's desires.

94. One would surmise that if God, Israelites, foreigners, and insects were replaced in the database with W, X, Y, Z, it would not be immediately obvious who were the actors and recipients. Rather, it would take a knowledge of the normal ratios of particular activities of each—information which does not exist outside the present study—to determine which is which. The most obvious would be insects, who act frequently on agricultural elements and exhibit no psychological traits. (This procedure is called 'masking'; see C. Osgood, 'The Representational Model and Relevant Research Methods', in I. Pool (ed.), *Trends in Content Analysis* [Urbana: University of Illinois Press, 1959]), pp. 43-45.

95. The removal of 'wealth' is coded as 'poverty'.

96. Indeed, Heschel argues that describing God as having thoughts and emotions is not anthropomorphic, for much of what is said about divine pathos involves emphases which are not human ones: 'Nowhere in the Bible is man characterized as merciful, gracious, slow to anger, abundant in love and truth, keeping love to the thousandth generation' (*The Prophets*, pp. 50-51). The difference for Heschel, then, is not whether God and humans have pathos, but whether the pathos is the same pathos. (Cf. Heschel, *The Prophets*, p. 55, 'My pathos is not your pathos.')

6. *Ways in which the Method Used*
Aided the Reaching of Conclusions[97]

Since many others have considered God's image in the Bible, it should not be surprising that the present study does not present a completely new picture of God. Nevertheless, the use of content analysis has allowed another avenue for an examination of the topic, as well as some new insights concerning God's image.

Contributions of the method itself include the fact that it demands that one formulate fairly clear questions and apply consistent, clear criteria to answer these questions. In fact, a large part of the work has consisted in the formulation of questions (what do I want to know), and in the construction of the criteria to answer these questions (especially the so-called 'categories'). To be sure, there can always be improvements in the categories themselves (construction and definition), as well as in the actual coding of the texts. However, it is unnecessary and possibly even dangerous to modify the categories or specific coding in midstream. It is unnecessary because, while content analysis demands a high degree of accuracy, minor database changes would have no significant effect on the results. It is dangerous because of the possibility of modifying the data to suit one's desired conclusions (e.g. if they were not supported by the initial results).

The use of the category system illuminated the wide variety of divine activities. Many of these divine processes have either been passed over by numerous theologians throughout history, or have been denied as being attributes of the God of the Bible.

The organization of concepts into 'categories' and 'metacategories' (grouped categories) was useful in that it helped to clarify similarities and differences. For example, the metacategory 'emotionality' facilitated a comparison of God to other beings (humans, animals, etc.) according to overall emotionality, regardless of the specific types of emotions. A result was that God is seen to be similar to humans as far as an emphasis on emotions is concerned, while the specific emotional makeup of each, as described by the categories, is different.

Using the actor/action/complement system (who does what to whom?) offered the opportunity to make explicit some ideas which may have

---

97. See the first section in this chapter, 'Purpose and Procedure', for a brief summary of the main steps employed.

been implicit elsewhere, as the following examples will show. (1) It made it clear that most divine activity in the prophets is specifically directed toward humans, rather than being intransitive. (2) It forced the recognition that God is frequently acted upon, especially by humanity. (3) While God acts directly and indirectly, the character of these activities varies. This insight was driven by a recognition that insect-to-human activity formed a circle of its own and yet was attributed to God, in that the insects were described as God's 'army'. (4) God's activity toward humans is mainly physical in nature, while human activity toward God is primarily valuing (ethically bad) and mental. Again, while this notion has been known to some degree, this study clarifies the notion that, according to the prophets, humans seldom have any physical effect on God.

The numerical aspect of the work—counting the frequency of categories and determining average Evaluations—offered the opportunity to examine degrees of involvement. These answer such questions as: is divine and human activity similarly negative? (yes, on the whole); does God treat Israelites and foreigners with parity? (no, foreigners are treated worse); does God's activity closely resemble human activity? (no, they are quite different).

The consideration of the relative frequency of activities made it possible to be more precise than Heschel has been about the God of the prophets being an emotional being, while confirming much of his work. Fretheim's thesis regarding God as someone who suffers was able to be tested, and was shown not to apply in this prophetic literature; however, the study did support Fretheim's idea that God is strongly affected by human attitudes.

This study applied formal procedures to determine the statistical significance of numerical assessments. Fortunately, the study is set up in such a way so that readers unfamiliar with formal statistical procedures should nevertheless be able to follow the analyses intuitively. Except in rare instances, the observations of the present study are based on data that reach the level of statistical significance at least at the level of 0.05 (i.e., there is a chance of less than one in twenty that the data are mere 'accidents').

This measure of significance indicates whether something is worth considering seriously. What the nature of this significance is—how and in what way it is significant—is a matter of reflective judgment. The present work has accordingly explored some of the theoretical implication of the results, although a thorough examination of the relevant issues is beyond the scope of a limited study.

These observations illustrate the relation of the method to the conclusions reached. They are only illustrations, since the conclusions cannot all be repeated. Since formal content analysis, however, is relatively new to biblical studies, it is worthwhile to describe how it helped the study as well as to explain how the procedure itself has been employed.

The work is presented as an early step in a journey. It is hoped that other studies will apply the method to other biblical texts (and to other issues within these texts), apply still more accurate and sophisticated procedures, and consider more deeply the import of the results.

7. Summary of Highlights

In the prophetic materials examined, God is described as one who feels and thinks, as well as acting in ways which affect the well-being of humanity. God shares a similar overall emphasis on emotions as humans, although the emphases on specific emotions are different (for instance, God does not fear). Divine involvement in non-emotional cognitive activity is common but less pronounced than it is for humans. (In both of these respects, God is different from animals mentioned, i.e. insects, which do not feel or think.) God's effective actions primarily involve altering the physical circumstances of humans, especially in a negative fashion.

God is also acted upon, mainly by humanity. God receives thoughts and feelings (chiefly negative ones), but, unlike humans, rarely weal or woe. Instead, the human counterparts to God's physical weal-or-woe actions are righteousness and wickedness, especially the latter. As with divine activity, the predominant form of what humans do is thus hurtful, but in relation to God this hurt can rarely be termed 'physical'.

The God–human relationship is frequently negative, but there is a detectable difference between how God treats various groups of people, with favoritism being shown to Israelites over foreigners. God takes a more destructive and especially a less supportive stance toward foreigners than toward Israelites.

In Joel, God's relation to Israelites can be looked at two ways. On the one hand, God's direct physical and psychological activities are completely beneficial for Israel. On the other hand, there is much indirect activity on God's part in an agricultural disaster: locusts, drought, and wildfires. No motive is given for this, and it is not described as a punishment (which appears to be related to the fact that Israel is not accused of sin). The presence of this negative indirect activity means that the presentation of God's figure in Joel is not as different from that given in prophetic literature as it would be without that aspect.

The comparison of God and humanity shows both continuity and discontinuity. They are involved in almost the same kinds of physical and mental processes, but to considerably different degrees. In other words, God is not the 'wholly other' of some theologies, but is also not merely the personification of the average human.

APPENDIX A: PREVIOUS STUDIES

(Referenced in the 'Introduction')

The following are summaries of my previous studies which employed various forms of content analysis. These represent the evolution of the method as applied by me, and served to help lay the theoretical groundwork for this book.

1. *God Said (1984)*

The goal[1] was to determine the various modes of primary communication from God to humans.[2] It found that:

1. God is depicted as communicating in a wide variety of manners (37 ways plus 'not stated');
2. God's communication is usually in private (76 per cent), although sometimes public (13 per cent; the remaining 11 per cent contain either questionable or incomplete information);
3. The highest category of communication mode is *not stated* (48 per cent), followed by *personal appearances* (17 per cent), *visions* (12 per cent), and *dreams* (3 per cent).
4. While only 9 per cent state there was a voice, most references have quotation terminology (65 per cent, not including 'voice').
5. Conversation is recorded in only 22 per cent of instances.

1.　The study was requested by Dr Mark McLean; the means of obtaining the information was designed by my wife (Terry) and myself.

2.　The procedure was to classify and categorize a sampling of 285 Old and New Testament passages.

2. *Consumption of Alcoholic Beverages*
in the Old Testament (1985)

The analysis was conducted to provide information for a denominational report on alcohol consumption. It showed that:

1. Alcohol is most frequently viewed neutrally (40 per cent), followed by negatively (31 per cent) and positively (29 per cent). Nine per cent of positive references explicitly consider wine a blessing.
2. Consumption is usually viewed either positively or neutrally.
3. Drunkenness is usually viewed negatively.
4. An unexpected observation: many assassinations took place while leaders were drunk.

3. *An Identification and Comparison of*
Elements in Zechariah 1–8 (1988)

The Zechariah study was transitional, in that it was the first of mine to emphasize words and phrases in one block of material.[3] The purpose was to determine redactional layers in Zechariah 1–8. My conclusions were that Zechariah 1–8 can be broken down into various layers: A (1.1-7); B (1.8–ch. 6); and C (Zech. 7–8). B can be divided up into three layers (B1, B2, and B3) so that the message material (B3) is separated from the vision material (B1B2). By comparison of the various elements in Zechariah 1–8, the message material (B3) appears to be an integral part of the introductory and concluding framework (AC). Zechariah 1–8 contains two main layers of literature: AB3C and B1B2. B1B2 is a collection of visions which relate to exilic and early postexilic concerns. These have been placed within the theological framework of AB3C, in most cases modifying the original significance of the visions. The message of Zechariah 1–8 to the postexilic community, in its present form, is that (1) wrath came because of rebellion against Yahweh; (2) restoration is coming; therefore (3) live in a just, upright manner in the restored land.[4]

---

3. The study was for a seminar with Paul Hanson.
4. The relationship of B1 to B2 was not examined.

The next three studies were conducted concurrently.

4. *Hosea 5.11–7.7 (1989)*

As part of a directed study on Hosea I conducted an analysis of Hos. 5.11–7.7. The analysis involved a combination of classifications: grammatical, some of my own (emphasizing emotional and sociological aspects), and Osgood's semantic differential scales. Osgood's scales showed that the passage was low in activity, but that high activity words were mainly negative in evaluation. The movement of the passage is slow, producing a depressing, hopeless tone. My classifications showed that about one third of the nouns and verbs are not literal (with many similes used), and that the passage was quite low in imperatives. The conclusion was that Hos. 5.5–7.7 is primarily a descriptive statement about Israel's depressing condition; Israel is both wounded and one who wounds, doing that which is detrimental to its own health.

5. *Zephaniah 1 (1989)*

The Zephaniah study employed similar classifications and categories as the Hosea one (including Osgood's scales), with the addition of indicators of the time frame and agent (human or divine) of verbs. Here are the results:

1. Yahweh's present actions are to speak; Yahweh's future actions are to destroy and kill. The people's past actions are mainly violence and improper worship; their future actions will mainly be lamentation. In the past the people were the active agents; in the future Yahweh will be the active agent. The implication is that wrong *actions* in the past will lead to a *state* of destruction.
2. Unlike Hosea 5–7, Zephaniah 1 moves at a swift pace. It does not call for repentance, nor does it only describe Judah's state, but it calls for the people to be appalled at the thorough destruction which will swiftly arrive.
3. Violence is a major theme in the passage. Judah commits violence, and therefore violence will be done to Judah.
4. Improper worship and pain are associated. A major message is that *improper worship will result in punishment from Yahweh*. Most terms of worship could be positive in other con-

texts (and were classified as such), but in Zephaniah 1 they are spoken of in a pejorative sense: worship is being conducted in an improper manner.

6. *Joel's Theology of Natural Disaster (1989)*

The purpose was to determine the realm of life from which the symbolism of Joel 1–2 was drawn, examine the interrelationship of subdivisions of the passage, and extract the instructions contained within the text—all with the view of explicating the major intent of the passage as a whole. The types of terminology contained in the various subdivisions indicated that an agricultural disaster had overtaken the land, and that the cult functioned as a means to get people from all walks of life to call upon Yahweh for mercy. Further, all terminology which involved direct acts of violence were directed at plants; none at humans. The restoration described in the final subdivision was an agricultural restoration, not a cultic one. The first three subdivisions are interlocking—and yet incomplete in and of themselves—and all point to the fourth (restoration). However, in spite of all the descriptive elements, the passage is focused on the future, with a large number of imperatives. In short, my conclusion was that Joel 1–2 was an instruction manual for times of natural disaster; what worked in his day would also work in the reader's day.

7. *Who Was Israel in the Eighth Century BCE? (1990)*

Terminology used by eighth-century prophets was examined in order to determine the self-designations of the Northern and Southern kingdoms at that time.[5] The results are as follows:

1. The Northern Kingdom may be designated Israel, Jacob, Samaria, or Ephraim.
2. The Southern Kingdom may be designated Israel, Jacob, Jerusalem, or Zion.
3. Israel often refers to the people without reference to the political structure.

---

5.   All passages in Hosea, Amos, Micah, and 1 Isaiah (233 verses) were coded considering the designations of the following terms: Israel, Judah, Samaria, Jerusalem, Ephraim, Zion, and Jacob.

4. Northern and southern prophets used different terminology. Amos, Hosea, Isaiah, and Micah each make clear distinctions between the two kingdoms in the eighth century, but in different ways. There is, at best, a lack of consistent terminology in their writings; that which exists is found in references to the Northern Kingdom as Ephraim and Samaria, and the *territory* of the Southern Kingdom as Judah with its capital at Jerusalem. *Israel* and *Jacob* are ambiguous at best, with the regional prophets using them to refer to the territory in which their messages were delivered. The Judah-Israel dichotomy is mainly present in the Northern prophets.

The conclusions were threefold:

1. Both kingdoms perceived themselves to be 'Israel'.
2. The peoples of the two kingdoms viewed themselves as a united people with separate governments.[6]
3. The traditional designations 'Israel' and 'Judah', while convenient for our purposes, do not accurately reflect the self-perceptions of the two kingdoms in the eighth century BCE.

8. *Nahum: A Thesaurus of Violence (1990)*

The study was intended to demonstrate a number of ways content analysis could be used to analyze biblical texts. The main classifications were grammatical, universal distinctions, political, terms of violence and death, and two of Osgood's scales (activity and potency). The main results and conclusions were that Nahum's low root use average and high use of violence terminology was representative of a creative attempt to give an extremely thorough description of the destruction of Nineveh; the literary effect was that all causes and effects of violence would overwhelm defenses against it. Osgood's scales showed extremes in activity. This is explained by the highly active violent actions which result in the low activity states of its results, that is, death and destruction.

---

6. Cf. the following modern examples: East and West Germany, North and South Korea, North and South Vietnam.

APPENDIX B. CATEGORY DICTIONARIES

1. *Emphasized Action Category Dictionary*

The following should be noted concerning this category dictionary:

1. These are English root translations of words coded as activities.
   a. These words/phrases represent the root of the Hebrew words.
   b. Many words are abbreviated/truncated.
   c. Words which are not coded as activities do not appear here.
2. Since words were often coded with more than one category, many words occur under more than one category.
3. The presence of some substantives and other non-verb parts of speech is due to the fact that over a third of all activity was indicated by non-verbs.
4. Frequencies of the various words are not indicated.
5. For the study, words which were negated had an opposite category applied (when opposite categories exist).
6. Coding which may appear incorrect can be justified by the context.

a. *Emotionality*

Joy: אשר call fortunate, גיל rejoice, הלל praise, חג celebrate, חפץ delight, פוש spring about, שׂמח rejoice, שׂשׂון rejoicing.

Sorrow: אבל mourn, אוי woe!, אלה wail, אמלל languish, אנה mourn, אנח groan, אנקה crying, אשׁם guilty<be>, אשׁם suffer, בכה weep, בכי weeping, דמעה tears, זעק cry out, חול anguish, חלחלה anguish, ילל wail/lament, לין spend the Night, מנהג moan, מספד wailing, מרר bitter<be>, מתפפת beating, נוד grieve, ספד wail, ספד wailing, צום fast, קדרנית mourners<as>, קרע rend, שׂק sackcloth, תקע clap.

Love: אהב love, חוס pity, חמל have pity, חמל spare/have Pity, חן favor, חנון gracious, חנן show favor, נחם comforter, נחם compassionnate, רצון favor, שׂוב turn.

Hate: בוז despise, בזה despised, נפח sniffInContmpt, נקם take revenge, שבע full, שנא hate, שיב repay, שלם repay, שקוץ detested thing, תלאה weariness.

Pride: בנה build up, גאון exaltation, גבה proud, גדל do great thngs, גדל magnify above, חזק arrogant<be>, חשב esteemed<be>, יטב better than, כבד honor, לבן white<be>, נשא raise/lift up, שגב exalted<be>.

Shaming: אדם red<be>, בוש ashamed<be>, גלה uncover/liftUp, חפר ashamed<be>, חרפה reproach, לעג mocking, מהל diluted, מערה nakedness, משל saying/byword, נבל make a fool, סיג dross, ערה naked<be>, פרש dung, פתה foolish, קלון dishonor, קלל of no account, קרחה bald spot, ראה spectacle, שחח humbled<be>, שחח humbled<is>, שני scarlet, שפל humbled<be>, שפל humbled<is>.

Anger: אף anger, אפה anger, זעם indignant, זעם indignation, חרה angry<burn>, עברה anger.

Desire: חמד desire, חפץ delight, טוב pleasant, ערב pleasing<be>, ערג long for, קנא zealous, רצה take delight.

Fear: אפלה darkness, חול anguish, חלחלה anguish, חרד terror causer, חשך darkness, חתת in awe<be>, ירא fear, ירא fearer, ירא revere/fear, מהומה panic, נורא feared, נורא terrifying, נמס melt, ענן cloud, ערפל darkness/gloom, ערץ causeToTremble, פארור glow, פחד dread, פיק tottering, קבץ gather, רגז tremble.

b. Cognition

Alertness: זכר remember, עור arouse, עור rouse, עור rouse oneself, קיץ awake, שחר look early, שכם start early.

Non-alertness: בוך wander, בלע confuse, הלל act as aMadman, חלה weak<be>, ישן smolder, כשל stumble, לקח take away, נם sleep, נפל fall, סבא drunkard, פיק tottering, פתה foolish, רעל staggering, שגעון madness, שכח forget, שכן settle/lieDown, שכר drunk<be>, שתה drink, תמהון bewilderment, תעה lead astray.

Knowledge: אור light, אמת truth, גבה proud, דעת knowledge, זכר remember, זמה wicked plan, חזן vision, חלם dream, ידע know, יסר train, למד learn, שוב turn unto, שמר preserve.

Ignorance: שכח forget.

Obey/agree: אבה willing<be>, אמן faithful, בקש require, היה belong to, הלך walk, זכר remember, חסד faithfulness, חתת in awe<be>, יאל determined<be>, ירא fear, ירא fearer, ירא revere/fear, כבד honor, לקח accept, נורא feared, נשא bear<endure>, עבד serve, פנה regard, קשב give heed, קשב pay attention, רצה accept, שום put/set, שוב repent, שוב repent<make>, שוב return, שלם pay, שמע hear, שמע listen, שמר heed, שמר keep, שמר take heed, שמר watch/beCarefl.

Rejection: אמן refuse, בוז despise, דבר speak, זד insolent, זור stranger<be> a>, זנח reject, זר strange thing, חזק arrogant<be>, חלץ withdraw, חשב one who plans, מאס spurn/reject, מרה rebel, נאץ reject, נדד stray, נשא protest, סור turn aside, סרה rebellion, סרר rebel, סרר stubborn<be>, פשע rebel/revolt, ריב contender.

Reason: אמר think, בחן test, בחר choose, בין discern, דין judge, חרוץ decision, חשב one who plans, חשב plan, חשב regard, חשב thinkers, יאל determined<be>, יכח decide, יכח reason, ירה teach, לבב heart {undrstdg}, משפט judgment, נחם change mind, נשא regard, פנה regard, ראה distinguish, רדף pursue, ריב lawsuit, שום put/set, שוב turn, שנה change, שפט judge.

c. Ethics

Ethically good: אור light, אמן faithful, אמת truth, ברית covenant, דבר word, הלך go/walk, הלך walk, זכה clean yourself, חסד faithfulness, חתת in awe<be>, טהר purify, טוב go well, טוב good, יטב good, ירא fear, ירא fearer, ירא revere/fear, לבן white<be>, מזרק bowl, מישור uprightness, מצוה commandment, מקור spring, משפט justice, נדר vow, נורא feared, נקיון innocence, עבד serve, צדק righteousness, צוה command, צמר wool, צדקה righteousness, קדש holy, קדש sanctify, רחץ wash off, ריב contend, ריב contend for, שוב repent, שוב repent <make>, שוב return, שוב turn unto, שמר heed, שמר keep, שמר preserve, תורה law/teaching.

Ethically bad: אדם red<be>, און iniquity, אלה swearing, אמן refuse, ארב ambush, ארר cursed, אשם guilty<be>, בגד actTreachersly, בחן test, בלע confuse, גאל defile, גאל desecrated, גבה proud, גזל stolen, גנב stealing, דם bloodshed, זבח sacrifice, זד insolent, זמה wicked plan, זנה prostitute, זנה prostitution, זנות prostitution, זנח reject, חבר unite/join,

חזק arrogant<be>, חטא sin, חטא sinful, חכה lie in waitFor, חלל profane, חמס violence, חן charming one, חרם curse, חשב plan, טמא defile, טפף mince steps, כזב lie/deceit, כחש lie/deceit, כחש lie/deceive, כשל causeToStumble, כשף seduction, לקח take, מרה rebel, נאף adulterer, נאף adultery, נאץ reject, נדד stray, נדה impurity, נטה turn aside, נשא showPartiality, סדם Sodom, סוג displacer, סור turn aside, סרה rebellion, סרר rebel, סרר stubborn<be>, עבר transgress, עולה injustice, עון iniquity, עכס shake bangles, עמרה Gomorrah, ענן soothsayer, עקב tracked, עשה do, עשה make, עשה work, עשק oppressor, פרד go apart, פשט raid, פשע rebel/revolt, צו worthlessness, קבע rob, קטר offer incense, רמיה lie/deceit, רע evil, רעה wickedness, רעע evildoer, רצח murder, רצח murderer, רשע wicked, רשע wickedness, שקר tossSedctvGlnc, שבע swearer, שגל rape<be>, שחד bribe, שחט depravity, שחת act corruptly, שחת corrupt, שלח divorce, שלמן reward, שפך shed, שקר lie/falsehood, שתה bow down/wrshp, שתה worship, תועבה abomination, תנה rcvPrsttutPay, תעה lead astray, תעה led astray<be>.

d. *Status*

Exaltation: בנה build up, גאון exaltation, גבה proud, גדול great, גדל do great thngs, גדל great, גדל magnify above, חזק arrogant<be>, חשב esteemed<be>, יטב better than, כבד honor, לבן white<be>, נשא raise/lift up, ראש chief{of mtns}, רב great, שגב exalted<be>.

Debasement: אדם red<be>, בוש ashamed<be>, גלה uncover/liftUp, חפר ashamed<be>, חרפה reproach, לעג mocking, מהל diluted, מערה nakedness, נבל make a fool, סיג dross, ערה naked<be>, פרש dung, פתה foolish, קלון dishonor, קלל of no account, קרחה bald spot, ראה spectacle, שחח humbled<be>, שחח humbled<is>, שני scarlet, שפל humbled<be>, שפל humbled<is>, שק sackcloth.

Wealth: בזז plunder, גזלה plunder, מכר seller, נחל inheritance, פרק plunder, שחד bribe, שלמן reward, שסס plunder, תנה rcvPrsttutPay.

Poverty: די need, עשק oppressor, שק sackcloth.

Strength: אבן stone, אלהים God, אמץ strong<be>, גבור warrior, דויד David, חזק strengthen, חיל strength, יכל able<be>, יכל endure, כול endure, כח strength, כלכל endure, מלאך angel, עמד endure, עצום mighty, עצמה might, קום endure.

Weakness: אשה woman, בוך wander, חלה weak<be>, טרח burden, יגע weary, כבד weighed down, כשל stumble, לאה weary<be>, מהל diluted, מעמסה heavy, נער lad, עמס lift a load, פיק tottering, תאנה fig tree, תלאה weariness.

e. Weal

Healing: גהה cure<mkDepart>, זור press out, חבש bandage, חבש binderOfWounds, כבה quench, כהה alleviation, מפרא healing, מתם soundness, נחם comforter, רכך softened, רפא heal.

Life: חיה he make usLive, חיה life, חיה live, מחסה refuge, מעוז refuge, פליטה escaper, שריד survivor.

Peace/shalom: אשר call fortunate, בטח security, בצע advantage, ברכה blessing, ברכה pool, גשם rain, חלק divide, חמל spare/havePity, טוב go well, טוב pleasant, ירד pour down, ישב dwell, ישע save/deliver, מורה rain, מחסה refuge, מעוז refuge, נצל deliverer, עזב leave, ערב pleasing<be>, פלא wondrously act, פרי fruit, רעה tend, שבע satisfied/full, שבר break, שוב restore, שוק overflow, שלח send, שלם at peace, שלם peace.

Reward: בצע advantage, מלט escape, נקה lv unpunished, שוב give back, שלם repay, שלמן reward.

f. Woe

Illness/injury: דוי sick, חבורה stripe, חזק seize, חלי sickness, חצב hew, טרי raw wound, טרף tear, יד from your hand, כי scar, מגפה plague, מכה injury, מכה strike, מכה wound, מקק rot, נגף plague, נגף strike, נכה strike, נכה wound, סבך entangled, עורון blindness, פצע bruise, קרחה bald spot, רקב rottenness, רשש beaten down<be>, שפח afflict, שרט injured<be>, שבבים pieces, שבר breaking.

Death: ארב ambush, גויה dead body, גוע perish, דם bloodshed, דקר pierce, הרג kill, חלל slain ones, חנק strangle, כרת cut off, נפל fall, עקב tracked, פגר corpse, קבר grave, רטש dash in pieces, רצח murder, רצח murderer, שפך shed.

Destruction: אבד destroyed<is>, אין there is not, אכל consume, אכל consumed, אכל devour, אכל eat, אמלל wither, אסף gather against, אפר ashes, ארב ambush, ארבה locust B, אש fire, באש stench, בגד

actTreachersly, בוקה waste, בזז plunder, בלע swallow up, בלק waste,
בער burn, בער consume, בקע split<be>, בקק devastate, גבור warrior,
גוב locust E, גוע perish, גזז sheared off, גזלה plunder, גמל recompense,
גנן defend, גער rebuke, דוי sick, דכא crush, דם bloodshed, דמה destroy,
דמם destroy, דקר pierce, הרג kill, הרס tear down, הרס torn
down<are>, זרה spread, זרק sprinkled<are>, חבורה stripe, חזק seize,
חטא punishment, חלה severe, חלי sickness, חלף pass on/away, חלק
divide, חמה wrath, חמס violence, חנק strangle, חצב hew, חרב destroy,
חרד terror causer, חרם destruction, חשף strip bark frm, טחן grind,
טרי raw wound, טרף tear, יבש dry up, ירד tread, כי scar, כלה destroy,
כלה destruction, כלה finished<be>, כפיר lion, כרת cut down, כרת cut
off, כשל causeToStumble, כשל stumble, לבט thrust down<be>, לבן
strip, להט set ablaze, לחם fight, לכד capture, מבוקה devastation, מגפה
plague, מהומה panic, מהפכה overthrow, מוג melt, מכה injury, מכה
strike, מכה wound, מלחמה battle, מנע withheld<are>, מעמסה heavy,
מצור siege, מקק rot, נבל wither&fall, נגף plague, נגף strike, נגש
oppressed<be>, נגש oppressor, נוע shaken<be>, נחם relieved of<be>,
נטה turn aside, נטר maintain, ניצוץ spark, נכה strike, נכה wound, נמס
melt, נמש abandon, נערת tinder, נפל fall, נצר besieged, נקה avenge,
נקה deserted, נקם take revenge, נשא lift up, נשא raise/lift up, נשא
upheaved, נתן set, נתץ broken down, נתק tear apart, סבך entangled,
סדם Sodom, סור turn aside, עבר pass away, עבר pass over, עבר pass
through, עבר remove, עבש shrivel, עגה bread-cake, עורון blindness,
עזב abandon, על against, עלה go up, עמרה Gomorrah, ענה oppress,
עסס tread down, עש moth, עשק oppressed<be>, עשק oppressor, פיק
tottering, פצע bruise, פקד punish, פרץ do violence, פרק plunder, פשט
raid, פשט strip off, צחנה stench, קבע rob, קבץ gather, קבר grave,
קרחה bald spot, קש stubble/chaff, רגז shake, רהב assail/pester, רטש
dash in pieces, רעה calamity, רעל shaken<be>, רעש quake, רצח
murder, רצח murderer, רצץ crushed<be>, רקב rottenness, רשש beaten
down<be>, שפה afflict, שרט injured<be>, שבבים pieces, שבר breaking,
שבר crushed<be>, שגל rape<be>, שד destruction, שדד laid waste, שדד
ruined<is>, שוב turn<against>, שוק overflow, שחל lion, שחת corrupt,
שחת ruin, שטף flood, שיב repay, שכל bereave, שלח divorce, שלך
throw, שלם repay, שמד destroy, שמה waste, שמם desolate<are>, שממה
desolation, שסס plunder, שפט judge, שפך shed.

Punishment: אל against, אף anger, אפה anger, ארר cursed, אשר reprove, גלה exile, גמל recompense, גער rebuke, זעם indignant, זעם

indignation, זעף fetter, חטא punishment, חמה wrath, חרה angry<burn>,
חרם curse, ידד cast lot, יכח reprove, יסר chastise, מוט bar of yoke,
מוסר chastise, משפט judgment, נגש oppressed<be>, נגש oppressor, נחם
relieved of<be>, נטר maintain, נקה avenge, נקם take revenge, נשא
carry away, עברה anger, עד witness, על against, עלה carry away, ענה
oppress, עשק oppressed<be>, עשק oppressor, פזר scatter, פקד punish,
רדף pursue, רהב assail/pester, רעה calamity, רתק bind, שפח afflict,
שבי captivity, שוב return, שוב turn<against>, שיב repay, שכל bereave,
שלם repay, שפט judge.

2. *Activity Evaluation Dictionary*

The following should be noted concerning this category dictionary:

1. These are English root translations of words coded as
   activities.

   a. These words/phrases represent the root of the Hebrew
   words.

   b. Many words are abbreviated/truncated.

   c. Words which are not coded as activities do not appear
   here.

2. When the same English word is listed under more than one
   evaluation number, it may be there for one of two reasons.

   a. One English word represents more than one Hebrew
   word.

   b. The literary context justifies different evaluations for
   the same word.

3. The presence of some substantives and other non-verb parts of
   speech is due to the fact that over a third of all activity was
   indicated by non-verbs.

4. Frequencies of the various words are not indicated.

5. For the study, words which were negated had the opposite
   Evaluation applied.

Evaluation +3

אהב love, ברכה blessing, גדל do great thngs, גהה cure<mkDepart>, גשם
rain, גנן defend, זור press out, שוב restore, שלם at peace, שלם peace,
שתח worship, חבש bandage, חבש binderOfWounds, חיה he make
usLive, חיה life, חיה live, חנן gracious, טוב pleasant, ישע save/deliver,
יסד found/establsh, יצר form, כבה quench, כהה alleviation, מלאך angel,

מפרא healing, מתם soundness, נחל inheritance, נחם comforter, נחם compassionnate, נטה stretch out, נצל deliverer, נקה lv unpunished, ערב pleasing<be>, פלא wondrously act, קרב in the midst, רוח Spirit, רכך softened, רפא heal, רצה take delight.

Evaluation +2

אבה willing<be>, אב father, אור light, אשה woman, אשר call fortunate, אכל eat, אכל feed, אמן faithful, אמץ strong<be>, אמת truth, אסף take away, את plowshare, בשל ripen, בטח security, בנה build, בנה build up, בעל marry, בצע advantage, ברא create, ברית covenant, ברכה pool, גאון exaltation, גדול great, גדל great, גדל magnify above, גדל raise {a child}, גיל rejoice, דבר word, דויד David, דשא sprout, דעת knowledge, היה belong to, הלך flow, הלך go/walk, הלך walk, הלל praise, זבח sacrifice, זבח sacrificer, זכה clean yourself, זקק refine, זרע sow, שאב draw {water}, שבר break, שוב repent<make>, שוב repent, שוב return, שוב turn unto, שוק overflow, ששון rejoicing, שכן dwell, שלח send, שלם repay, שמע report, שמר heed, שמר keep, שמר preserve, שפט do justice for, שקה water, שריד survivor, שתח worship, חבר companion, חגג mkPilgrimage, חג celebrate, חוס pity, חזק strengthen, חשב esteemed <be>, חיל strength, חלק divide, חמד desire, חמל have pity, חמל spare/ havePity, חמץ leavened, חן favor, חנן show favor, חסד faithfulness, חפץ delight, חתת in awe<be>, טהר purifier, טהר purify, טוב good, טוב go well, טרף food, יאל determined<be>, ידע know, ישב dwell, יטב better than, יטב good, יכל endure, ילד bear<child>, יסר train, יצא go forth, ירא fear, ירא fearer, ירא revere/fear, ירה teach, ירה water, כבד honor, כבס laundryman, כון established<be>, כח strength, כתת beat, לבב heart{undrstdg}, לבן white<be>, לוש knead, לון lodge, מורה rain, מזמרה pruning knife, מזרק bowl, משפט justice, מחסה refuge, מישור uprightness, מים water, מלט escape, מנחה grain offering, מעוז refuge, מעשר tithe, מצוה commandment, מקור spring, נגש offer/brngNear, נגש present, נדר vow, נורא feared, נחם change mind, נטף drip, נצר guard, נקיון innocence, נשא bear<fruit>, נשא raise/lift up, נתן give, נתן set, נתן utter, סור remove, עבד serve, עגה bread-cake, עוש lend aid, עולה injustice, עזרה helper, פדה ransom, פדה ransomed<be>, פוש spring about, פליטה escape, פליטה escaper, פקח guard, פרי fruit, פתח open, צדקה righteousness, צוה command, צמר wool, צרף refiner/smeltr, צדקה righteousness, קדש consecrate, קדש holy, קדש sanctify, קום raise, קשב give heed, קנא zealous, קציר harvest, קצר harvest, ראה distinguish, ראש chief{of mtns}, רדף pursue, רחץ wash off, ריב contend, ריב contend for, ריק pour out, רעה tend, רצרץ favor, שבע satisfied/full, שׂגב exalted<be>, שׂום put/set, שׂמח rejoice, תאנה fig tree, תורה law/teaching, תפלה prayer, תרומה offering.

Evaluation +1

אור kindle fire, אזן give ear, אמר say, אמר think, אסף gather, אסף lose, בוא bring, בוא come, בחן test, בין discern, בקשׁ require, בקשׁ seek, דבר speak, דבר word, דרשׁ seek, הלך come, הלך come on!, הלך go/walk, הפך turn over, זכר remember, זרח rise, זרע scatter, שׁאל inquire, שׁאר leave, שׁאר remain, שׁבע swear, שׁוב give back, שׁוב restore, שׁוב return, שׁחר look early, שׁית appoint, שׁלח send, שׁלם pay, שׁם name, שׁמע hear, שׁמע hearer, שׁמע listen, שׁמר take heed, שׁמר watch/beCarefl, שׁפט judge, שׁפך pour out, שׁתה drink, חגר girded, חזה see, חזן vision, חשׁב regard, חשׁב thinkers, חלה entreat, חלם dream, חנן supplication, חסה refuge seeker, ידע make known, ישׁב remain, ישׁב situated, יכח decide, יכח reason, יכל able<be>, ילד bear<child>, יסף add to, יצא go forth, יתר leave over, יתר remain, כבד multiply, כול endure, כון appointed, כון set up, כלכל endure, כנען trader, כתב write, לבשׁ clothe, למד learn, לקח accept, ל you have, משׁל rule, מלאך messenger, מלך appoint a king, מלך king, מצא find, נאם declaration, נבא prophesy, נבט look, נביא prophet, נגד tell, נדר vow, נהר flow, נוח leave alone, נצב established<is, נשׂא raise/lift up, נשׂא regard, נתן allow, נתן produce, סבב surrounding, ספר tell, עוף fly, עור rouse, עור rouse oneself, עזב leave, עלה go up, על go up, עמד endure, עמס lift a load, ענה answer, עצום mighty, עצמה might, עצרה assembly, עשׂה do, עשׂה produce, פנה regard, פנה return, פרץ increase, פרשׂ spread out, פתח open, צוה command, צפה keep watch, צרף refiner/smeltr, צרף smelt, קבץ assemble, קבץ gather, קבץ gatherer, קול sound, קום endure, קשׁב pay attention, קשׁת bow, קיץ awake, קצין ruler, קרא call, קרא call upon, קרא proclaim/call, קרב bring near, ראה see, ראם rise, רבב increase, רבב multiply, רבה multiply, רב many, רב multiplied, רצה accept, שׂום appoint.

Evaluation Zero

אדם red, בוא bring, בוא come/enter, בוא come, בוא enter, בחר choose, גדול great, הלך come, הלך go/walk, הלך go, הלך go away, הלך walk, שׁבת cease, שׁוב return, שׁוב turn, שׁלח send, שׁנה change, שׁפך pour out, שׁקק run, חדל cease, חמם become hot, חנה descend, ישׁב sit, יכל able<be>, יסף do again, יצא going forth, יצא go forth, ירד pour down, כון sure<be>, לקח take, מושׁ depart, מור change, משׁך stretch out, מלא fill/full, מלא filled with<be>, מלא full, נגשׁ draw near, נגשׁ present, נגע

reach, נחת bring down, נטה stretch out, נפל fall, נתן make, סבב surround, עבט change course, עור stir up <fire>, עלה climb, עלה go up, עמד stand, עמד stop, ערך arrange, עשה do/act, עשה do, עשה make, עשה perform, עשה prepare, פנה prepare, פרש spread out, פתח open, קום arise, קצה end/limit, קרב approach, קרב go near, ראה appear, רב great, רום bring up, רוץ run, שבע full, שום make, שום put/set, תלע clad inScarlet.

Evaluation -1

אבן stone, בדד alone<be>, בוא come, בוא enter, בוך wander, בשל boil, בלל mix, בצע break ranks, בקע split<be>, גרר drag, דהר rush, הלך go, שוב return, שכם start early, שכן settle/lieDown, שלך throw, חזק grab, חזק grasp, חלה weak<be>, חלץ withdraw, טמן hide, טרח burden, יגע weary, ישן smolder, יצא go forth, ירד bring down, כחד conceal, כחד hidden<be>, כסה cover, לאה weary<be>, מהר hurry, מוג melt, מוש depart, מלא filled<are>, נגד display, נמס melt, נשא bear<endure>, נשא carry away, נשא protest, סגר close, סור gone<be>, סור remove, עבד slave, עד witness, עיד testify, עכם shake bangles, עלה go up, עלם conceal, עלם hide, עמק go deep, ענה testify, ערבה desert-plain, ערג long for, עשה make, פרא wild donkey, פתח open, צרר wrap, קול sound, קום arise, קנה purchase, קרא call, ראה show, רשת net, רחק remove far, ריב lawsuit, רמס trample, רקד leap, רתק bind, שום prepare, שפק strikeBargains, תלאה weariness, תפש grasp.

Evaluation -2

אבל mourn, אדם red<be>, אוי woe!, און iniquity, אשם guilty<be>, אשם suffer, אשר reprove, אכל consume, אכל consumed, אלה swearing, אלה wail, אמלל languish, אמלל wither, אמן refuse, אנה mourn, אנח groan, אנקה crying, אסף gather, אסף take away, אפר ashes, באש stench, בגד actTreachersly, בוש ashamed<be>, בחן test, בכה weep, בכי weeping, בלע confuse, בלע swallow up, בער burn, בער consume, ברק gleaming, גאל defile, גבה proud, גבור warrior, גלה revealed, גלה uncover/liftUp, גער rebuke, דבר speak, דחק crowd, דין judge, די need, דם blood, דמעה tears, הרס torn down<are>, זבח sacrifice, זד insolent, זור stranger<be>a>, זמה wicked plan, זנה prostitute, זנה prostitution, זנות prostitution, זנח reject, זעק cry out, זרה spread, זרק sprinkled<are>, זר strange thing, שאג roar, שבי captivity, שבע swearer, שגעון madness, שוב return, שוק overflow, שחד bribe, שחח humbled<be>, שחח humbled<is>, שחט depravity, שחת act corruptly, שחת corrupt, שיב repay, שכח forget, שכר drunk<be>, שלח divorce, שלח put in<send>, שלח send, שלמן reward,

שני scarlet, שפט judge, שפל humbled<be>, שפל humbled<is>, שקוץ detested thing, שקק rush toAnd fro, שקר lie/falsehood, שק sackcloth, שתה bow down/wrshp, שתח worship, חבר unite/join, חול anguish, חזק arrogant<be>, חשב one who plans, חשב plan, חטא sin, חטא sinful, חלחלה anguish, חלף pass on/away, חלק divide, חן charming one, חפר ashamed<be>, חרפה reproach, טחן grind, טמא defile, טפף mince steps, ידד cast lot, יד cast lot, ישב sit, יכח reprove, ילל wail/lament, יסר chastise, יקר dwindle, ירא fear, ירד bring down, ירד tread, כבד weighed down, כזב lie/deceit, כשל causeToStumble, כשל stumble, כשף seduction, כחש lie/deceit, כחש lie/deceive, כלה finished<be>, כתת beat, לא <negative>, לבט thrust down<be>, להב flame/flash, להט set ablaze, לחם fight, לין spend theNight, לעג mocking, לקח take away, מאס spurn/reject, מהל diluted, מוג melt, מוט bar of yoke, מוסר chastise, משל saying/byword, מכר sell, מכר seller, מנהג moan, מנע withheld<are>, מספד wailing, מעט little/few, מעמסה heavy, מערה nakedness, מרה rebel, מרר bitter<be>, מתפפת beating, נאף adulterer, נאף adultery, נאץ reject, נבל make a fool, נבל wither&fall, נגע touch, נדד chased away, נדד draw back, נדד stray, נדה impurity, נדח thrust, נוד grieve, נוע shaken<be>, נטה turn aside, נם sleep, נמש abandon, נערת tinder, נער lad, נפוש scattered<are>, נפח sniffInContmpt, נצב stand, נשא raise/lift up, נשא showPartiality, נשא upheaved, נתך pour forth, נתן trade, נתץ broken down, נתק tear apart, סבא drunkard, סבך entangled, סור take away, סור turn aside, סיג dross, ספד wail, ספד wailing, סרה rebellion, סרר rebel, סרר stubborn<be>, עבר pass away, עבר remove, עבר transgress, עון iniquity, עור arouse, עזב abandon, עמד stand, ענן cloud, ערה naked<be>, ערץ causeToTremble, עשה do, עשה make, עשה work, פארור glow, פוץ dispersed<be>, פזר scatter, פשט strip off, פשע rebel/revolt, פח bird trap, פיק tottering, פרד go apart, פרש dung, פתה foolish, צום fast, צחנה stench, קבץ gather, קדרנית mourners<as>, קש stubble/chaff, קטר offer incense, קלון dishonor, קלל of no account, קנא zealous, קרחה bald spot, קרע rend, ראה spectacle, רגז tremble, רדף pursue, רוע raise a shout, רוע shout an alarm, רשע wicked, רשע wickedness, רשת net, רחק remove far, ריב contender, ריב lawsuit, רמיה lie/deceit, רעה wickedness, רעש quake, רעל shaken<be>, רעל staggering, רעע evildoer, רע evil, רקד jolt, שקר tossSedctvGlnc, תחת instead of, תמהון bewilderment, תנה rcvPrsttutPay, תעה lead astray, תעה led astray<be>, תקע blow, תקע clap.

Evaluation -3

אבד destroyed<is>, אשם guilty<be>, אש fire, אכל consume, אכל devour, אכל eat, אל against, אל against you, אמלל wither, אסף gather, אסף gather against, אף anger, אפה anger, אפלה darkness, ארבה locust B, ארב ambush, ארר cursed, בוז despise, בוקה waste, בזה despised, בז plunder, בלק waste, בער burn, בקק devastate, גאל desecrated, גדל do great thngs, גוב locust E, גויה dead body, גוע perish, גזז sheared off, גזלה plunder, גזל stolen, גלה exile, גמל recompense, גנב stealing, דוי sick, דכא crush, דם bloodshed, דמה destroy, דמם destroy, דקר pierce, הלל act as aMadman, הרג kill, הרס tear down, זעם indignant, זעם indignation, זק fetter, שבבים pieces, שבר breaking, שבר crushed<be>, שגל rape<be>, שדד laid waste, שדד ruined<is>, שד destruction, שוב turn<against>, שחל lion, שחת ruin, שטף flood, שכל bereave, שלך cast away, שלם repay, שמד destroy, שמה waste, שמם desolate<are>, שממה desolation, שסס plunder, שפט judge, שפך shed, חבורה stripe, חזק seize, חשך darkness, חטא punishment, חכה lie in waitFor, חלה severe, חלי sickness, חלל profane, חלל slain ones, חמה wrath, חמס violence, חנק strangle, חצב hew, חרב destroy, חרד terror causer, חרה angry<burn>, חרוץ decision, חרם curse, חרם destruction, חשף strip bark frm, טרי raw wound, טרף tear, יבש dry up, יד from your hand, כי scar, כלה destroy, כלה destruction, כלה finished<be>, כפיר lion, כרת cut down, מבוקה cut off, לבן strip, להט set ablaze, לכד capture, לקח take, כרת cut off, מהפכה devastation, מגפה plague, מדבר wilderness, מהומה panic, מהפכה overthrow, משפט judgment, מכה injury, מכה strike, מכה wound, מלחמה battle, מצור siege, מקק rot, נגף plague, נגף strike, נגש oppressed<be>, נגש oppressor, נוס flee, נורא terrifying, נחם relieved of<be>, נטר maintain, ניצוץ spark, נכה strike, נכה wound, נפל fall, נצר besieged, נקה avenge, נקה deserted, נקם take revenge, נשא lift up, סדם Sodom, סוג displacer, עבש shrivel, עברה anger, עבר pass over, עבר pass through, עורון blindness, עשק oppressed<be>, עשק oppressor, עש moth, עלה carry away, עלה go up, עלה invade, על against, עמרה Gomorrah, ענה oppress, ענן soothsayer, עסס tread down, עקב tracked, ערפל darkness/gloom, ערץ causeToTremble, פגר corpse, פשט raid, פחד dread, פצע bruise, פקד punish, פרץ do violence, פרק plunder, צו worthlessness, קצפה rob, קבץ gather, קבר grave, קדר dark<be>, קדר grow dark, קצפה stump, רגז shake, רהב assail/pester, רשש beaten down<be>, רטש dash in pieces, רמס trample, רעה calamity, רצח murder, רצח murderer, רצץ crushed<be>, רקב rottenness, שנא hate, שפח afflict, שרט injured <be>, שרף burn, תועבה abomination.

Evaluation Noscore

גמל recompense, שמע hear, שמע hearer, חזה see, מכה strike, מקק rot, נבט look, עורון blindness, עלם hide, צפה keep watch, קטר offer incense, ראה see, תקע clap.

3. *English List Of All Activities*

This section lists all words used to indicate activity, according to a basic English translation. Included are the Hebrew root, part of speech, metacategories, categories, and Evaluation numbers. Words are listed more than once if they are coded more than one way (including according to different parts of speech). All activity words are included here, not just those with 'emphasized' categories. The frequency of each word is not included.

Abbreviations for Parts of Speech

AV - adverb; AJ - adjective; CJ - conjunction; DA - demonstrative adjective; DO - direct object marker; IN - interjection; PA - prepositional pronoun; PN - proper name; PP - preposition; PR - pronoun; PT - particle; RP - relative pronoun; SB - nouns and other substantives VB - verb (non-instruction); VI - verbal instructions (roughly equals imperatives).

Metacategory Abbreviations

AN - animals; BN - basic need satisfaction; CO - communication; CP - conditions and processes; DV - divine realm; EL - elements; EM - emotions; ET - ethics; FN - nondescript food; GU - guide, redirection; HU - human beings; IF - Israelite or foreign; IN - institution, society; LO - locations, places; MD - things made by people; MV - movement; OT - other; PS - cognitive (non-emotion); QL - qualifiers; ST - status; VG - plant oriented; WL - weal, good things; WO - woe, bad things.

Category Abbreviations

These can be found in Chapter 5, 'Category and Field Descriptions'.

Hebrew English	p.Spch Metacategories	Context-Dependent Categories	Context-Dependent Evaluation

Hebrew	English	p.Spch Metacategories	Context-Dependent Categories				Context-Dependent Evaluation
לא	\<negative\>	PT QL	NEG				-2
עזב	abandon	VB MV WO	STAY	DEST			-2
נמש	abandon	VB MV WO	STAY	DEST			-2
יכל	able \<be\>	VB CP ST	COND		STRO		+1
תועבה	abomination	SB ET IN		CULT ETHB			-3
לקח	accept	VB IN PS		CULT KEEP			+1
רצה	accept	VB IN PS		CULT KEEP			+1
בגד	actTreachersly	VB ET WO		DEST ETHB			-2
בגד	actTreachersly	VI ET WO		DEST ETHB			-2
הלל	actasaMadman	VB IN PS		MILI NLRT			-3
שחת	actcorruptly	VB ET		ETHB			-2
יסף	addto	VB CP QL	QNTY DO	MSMT			+1
נאף	adulterer	SB ET HU IF BN	HUMN SEX	ETHB			-2
נאף	adultery	SB ET BN		SEX ETHB			-2
נאף	adultery	VB ET BN		SEX ETHB			-2
בצע	advantage	SB WL		PEAC REWD			+2
שפח	afflict	VB WO		PUNI DEST ILL			-3
על	against	PP IN WO		DEST MILI			-3
על	against	PP OT	NSCR				-3
אל	against	PP WO		PUNI			-3
על	against	PP WO		PUNI			-3
אל	againstyou	PA OT	NSCR				-3
כהה	alleviation	SB CP WL	COND	HEAL			+3
נתן	allow	VB GU		ESTB			+1
נתן	allow	VI GU		ESTB			+1
בדד	alone\<be\>	VB QL	QNTY	MSMT			-1
ארב	ambush	SB ET IN WO		CRIM DEAT ETHB DEST			-3
מלאך	angel	SB DV ST	ANGL	SPIR STRO			+3
אף	anger	SB EM WO		PUNI ANGR			-3
עברה	anger	SB EM WO		PUNI ANGR			-3
אפה	anger	SB EM WO		PUNI ANGR			-3
חרה	angry\<burn\>	VB EM WO		PUNI ANGR			-3
חלחלה	anguish	SB EM		FEAR SORR			-2
חול	anguish	VB EM		FEAR SORR			-2
ענה	answer	VB CO		COMS			+1
ראה	appear	VB IN MV	RELO CULT				0

Hebrew English	p.Spch Metacategories	Context-Dependent Categories	Context-Dependent Evaluation
ראה appear	VB MV	RELO	0
שׁית appoint	VB CP GU	COND ESTB	+1
שׂום appoint	VB CP GU	COND ESTB	+1
כון appointed	VB CP GU	COND ESTB	+1
מלך appoint a king	VB GU IN	GOVT ESTB	+1
קרב approach	VB MV	RELO	0
קום arise	VB MV	RELO	0
עור arouse	VB PS	ALRT	-2
ערך arrange	VB GU MV	RELO ASMB	0
חזק arrogant<be>	VB CP EM ET PS ST	COND EXAL PRID RJCT ETHB	-2
חפר ashamed<be>	VB EM ST	DBAS SHAM	-2
בושׁ ashamed<be>	VB EM ST	DBAS SHAM	-2
בושׁ ashamed<be>	VI EM ST	DBAS SHAM	-2
אפר ashes	SB EL WO	MTRL DEST	-2
רהב assail,pester	VB WO	PUNI DEST	-3
קבץ assemble	VI GU MV	RELO ASMB	+1
עצרה assembly	SB GU HU IF IN	HUGP HUMN CULT ASMB	+1
עצרה assembly	VI GU HU IF IN	HUGP HUMN CULT ASMB	+1
שׁלם atpeace	AJ CP WL	COND PEAC	+3
נקה avenge	VB WO	PUNI DEST	-3
קץ awake	VI PS	ALRT	+1
קרחה bald spot	SB EM HU ST WO	HUPT DBAS SHAM ILL DEST	-2
חבשׁ bandage	VB WL	HEAL	+3
מוט bar of yoke	SB IN MD WO	TOOL MILI PUNI	-2
מלחמה battle	SB IN WO	MILI DEST	-3
ילד bear<child>	VB IN	FAML	+2
נשׂא bear<endure>	VB PS	KEEP	-1
נשׂא bear<fruit>	VB CP IN	PROC AGRI	+2
כתת beat	VB CP IN	PROC MILI AGRI	+2
כתת beat	VI CP IN	PROC MILI AGRI	-2
רשׁשׁ beaten down<be	VB WO	DEST ILL	-3
מחפפת beating	VB CO EM	COMS SORR	-2
חמם become hot	VB CP	HEAT	0
היה belong to	VB PS	KEEP	+2
שׁכל bereave	VB IN WO	AGRI PUNI DEST	-3
נצר besieged	SB CP IN WO	COND MILI DEST	-3

Hebrew	English	p.Spch Metacategories	Context-Dependent Categories				Context-Dependent Evaluation
יטב	better than	VB EM ST		EXAL PRID			+2
תמהון	bewilderment	SB PS			NLRT		-2
רתק	bind	VB WO		PUNI			-1
חבש	binderOfWounds	SB HU IF WL	HUMN			HEAL	+3
פח	bird trap	SB BN IN MD	TOOL	HUNT		FOOD	-2
מרר	bitter<be>	VB EM			SORR		-2
ברכה	blessing	SB BN WL		PEAC		FOOD	+3
עורון	blindness	SB CP WO	COND		DEST ILL		-3
דם	blood	SB CP EL	COND COSM				-2
דם	bloodshed	SB ET IN WO		CRIM DEAT ETHB DEST			-3
חקע	blow	VI CO IN		MILI COMS			-2
בשל	boil	VB BN IN CP		CULT HEAT FOOD			-1
קשת	bow	SB IN MD	TOOL	MILI			+1
מזרק	bowl	SB BN ET IN MD	TOOL	CULT ETHG FOOD			+2
שתה	bow down,wrshp	VB DV ET IN		CULT DVOT ETHB			-2
עגה	bread-cake	SB BN IN VG WO	VEGP	AGRI DEST FOOD			+2
שבר	break	VB WL		PEAC			+2
שבר	breaking	SB WO		DEST ILL			-3
בצע	break ranks	VB IN MV	RELO	MILI			-1
שחד	bribe	SB ET IN MD ST	MONY	ECON WLTH ETHB LEGL			-2
בוא	bring	VB IN MV	RELO	SEND CULT			0
בוא	bring	VB MV	RELO	SEND			0
בוא	bring	VI MV	RELO	SEND			+1
ירד	bring down	VB IN MV	RELO	SEND HUNT			-1
ירד	bring down	VB MV	RELO	SEND			-2
נחת	bring down	VI MV	RELO	SEND			0
קרב	bring near	VI IN MV	RELO	CULT SEND			+1
רום	bring up	VB IN MV	RELO	SEND FAML			0
נתץ	broken down	VB WO		DEST			-2
פצע	bruise	SB WO		DEST ILL			-3
בנה	build	VB BN			DWEL		+2
בנה	build up	VB EM ST		EXAL PRID			+2
טרח	burden	SB CP ST	COND		WEAK		-1
בער	burn	VB CP		HEAT			-2
שרף	burn	VB CP		HEAT			-3
בער	burn	VB WO CP		HEAT DEST			-3

Hebrew English	p.Spch Metacategories	Context-Dependent Categories	Context-Dependent Evaluation
רעה calamity	SB WO	PUNI DEST	-3
קרא call	VB CO	COMS	+1
קרא call	VI CO	COMS	+1
אשר call fortunate	VB CO EM WL	COMS JOY PEAC	+2
קרא call upon	VB CO GU	SEEK COMS	+1
שבי captivity	SB CP IN MV WO	COND RELO MILI PUNI	-2
לכד capture	VB CP IN WO	COND MILI DEST	-3
עלה carry away	VB IN MV WO	RELO HUNT PUNI SEND	-3
נשא carry away	VB MV WO	RELO PUNI SEND	-1
שלך cast away	VB MV	RELO SEND	-3
ידד cast lot	VB IN WO	MSTR ECON MILI PUNI	-2
יד cast lot	VB IN	MSTR ECON	-2
כשל causeToStumble	VB ET MV WO	RELO DEST ETHB	-2
ערץ causeToTremble	VB EM	FEAR	-3
שבת cease	VB MV QL	NEG STAY	0
חדל cease	VI MV QL	NEG STAY	0
חג celebrate	VI BN EM IN QL	TIME CULT JOY FOOD	+2
שנה change	VB CP PS	PROC COND REAS	0
מור change	VB CP	PROC COND	0
עבט change course	VB MV	RELO	0
נחם change mind	VB CP PS	PROC COND REAS	+2
חן charming one	SB ET HU IF BN	HUMN SEX ETHB	-2
נדד chased away	VB MV	RELO FLEE	-2
מוסר chastise	VB WO	PUNI	-2
יסר chastise	VB WO	PUNI	-2
ראש chief{of mtns}	SB IN ST	CULT EXAL	+2
בחר choose	VB PS	REAS	0
תלע clad inScarlet	VB BN CP	COND WEAR	0
תקע clap	VB CO EM	COMS SORR	-2
זכה clean yourself	VI CP ET	COND ETHG	+2
עלה climb	VB MV	RELO	0
סגר close	VI IN MV	RELO CULT	-1
לבש clothe	VB BN	WEAR	+1
לבש clothe	VB BN IN	PROP WEAR	+1
ענן cloud	SB EL EM	ELMT FEAR	-2
בוא come	VB MV	RELO	-1

Hebrew English	p.Spch Metacategories	Context-Dependent Categories	Context-Dependent Evaluation
הלך come	VB MV	RELO	+1
בוא come	VI IN MV	RELO CULT	+1
הלך come	VI MV	RELO	0
בוא come	VI MV	RELO	0
בוא come,enter	VB MV	RELO	0
הלך come on!	VI CO	COMS	+1
נחם comforter	SB EM HU WL	HUMN LOVE HEAL	+3
צוה command	VB CO ET IN	LEGL COMS ETHG	+2
צוה command	VB CO IN	LEGL COMS	+1
מצוה commandment	SB CO ET IN	LEGL COMC ETHG	+2
חבר companion	SB GU HU IF	HUMN ASMB	+2
נחם compassion	VB EM	LOVE	+3
נחם compassionate	AJ EM	LOVE	+3
כחד conceal	SB MV	RELO FLEE	-1
עלם conceal	VB MV	RELO FLEE	-1
בלע confuse	VB ET MV PS	RELO NLRT SEND ETHB	-2
קדש consecrate	VI CO GU IN	CULT COMS ASMB	+2
אכל consume	VB WO	DEST	-2
בער consume	VB WO	DEST	-2
אכל consumed	VB WO	DEST	-2
ריב contend	VB CO IN	LEGL COMS	-2
ריב contend	VI CO ET IN	LEGL COMS ETHG	+2
ריב contender	SB CO HU IN PS	HUMN LEGL COMV RJCT	-2
ריב contend for	VI CO ET IN	LEGL COMS ETHG	+2
פגר corpse	SB HU IF WO	HUMN DEAT	-3
שחת corrupt	VB ET WO	DEST ETHB	-2
ברית covenant	SB CO ET GU IN	LEGL COMC ASMB ETHG	+2
כסה cover	VB MV	RELO FLEE	-1
ברא create	VB CP	PROC	+2
דחק crowd	VB IN MV	RELO MILI	-2
דכא crush	VB WO	DEST	-3
שבר crushed<be>	VB WO	DEST	-3
רצץ crushed<be>	VB WO	DEST	-3
אנקה crying	SB CO EM	COMS SORR	-2
זעק cry out	VB CO EM	COMS SORR	-2
נהה cure<mkDepart>	VB WL	HEAL	+3

Hebrew English	p.Spch Metacategories	Context-Dependent Categories					Context-Dependent Evaluation
ארר curse	SB CO ET WO			PUNI	COMC	ETHB	-3
חרם curse	SB CO ET WO			PUNI	COMC	ETHB	-3
ארר curse	VB CO ET WO			PUNI	COMS	ETHB	-3
ארר cursed	AJ CO ET WO			PUNI	COMC	ETHB	-3
כרת cut down	VB WO				DEST		-3
כרת cut off	VB IN WO			AGRI	DEST		-3
כרת cut off	VB WO				DEST	DEAT	-3
כרת cut off	VB WO				DEST		-3
כרת cut off	VI WO				DEST		-3
קדר dark<be>	VB CP EL	ELMT		PROC			-3
אפלה darkness	SB CP EL EM	ELMT	COND	FEAR			-3
חשך darkness	SB CP EL	ELMT	COND				-3
חשך darkness	SB CP EL EM	ELMT	COND	FEAR			-3
ערפל darkness,gloom	SB CP EL EM	ELMT	COND	FEAR			-3
רטש dash in pieces	VB IN WO			FAML	DEST	DEAT	-3
דויד David	PN HU IF IN ST		HUMN	GOVT		STRO	+2
גויה dead body	SB HU IF WO		HUMN	DEAT			-3
יכח decide	VB IN PS			LEGL		REAS	+1
חרוץ decision	SB IN PS			LEGL		REAS	-3
נאם declaration	SB CO				COMS		+1
גנן defend	VB IN WO			MILI	DEST		+3
טמא defile	VB ET IN			CULT		ETHB	-2
גאל defile	VB ET IN			CULT		ETHB	-2
חפץ delight	SB EM			JOY	DESR		+2
חפץ delight	VB EM			JOY	DESR		+2
נצל deliverer	SB HU IN WL		HUMN	MILI	PEAC		+3
מוש depart	VB MV	RELO					0
שחט depravity	SB ET					ETHB	-2
חנה descend	VB MV	RELO					0
גאל desecrate	VB ET IN			CULT		ETHB	-3
גאל desecrated	AJ ET IN			CULT		ETHB	-3
ערבה desert-plain	SB LO	LAND					-1
נקה deserted	VB MV WO	STAY			DEST		-3
חמד desire	VB EM					DESR	+2
שמם desolate<are>	VB CP WO	COND			DEST		-3
שממה desolation	SB CP WO	COND			DEST		-3

Hebrew	English	p.Spch Metacategories	Context-Dependent Categories			Context-Dependent Evaluation	
בוז	despise	VB EM				HATE	-3
בוז	despise	VB EM PS		RJCT		HATE	-3
בזה	despised	VB EM				HATE	-3
שמד	destroy	VB CP WO	COND		DEST		-3
דמה	destroy	VB CP WO	COND		DEST		-3
חרב	destroy	VB CP WO	COND		DEST		-3
כלה	destroy	VB CP WO	COND		DEST		-3
דמם	destroy	VB CP WO	COND		DEST		-3
אבד	destroyed<is>	VB CP WO	COND		DEST		-3
שד	destruction	SB CP WO	COND		DEST		-3
חרם	destruction	SB CP WO	COND		DEST		-3
כלה	destruction	SB CP WO	COND		DEST		-3
יאל	determined<be>	VB PS		KEEP	REAS		+2
שקוץ	detested thing	SB EM				HATE	-2
בקק	devastate	VB WO			DEST		-3
מבוקה	devastation	SB CP WO	COND		DEST		-3
אכל	devour	VB WO			DEST		-3
מהל	diluted	VB CP EM ST	COND	DBAS	SHAM	WEAK	-2
בין	discern	VB PS			REAS		+1
קלון	dishonor	SB EM ST		DBAS	SHAM		-2
פוץ	dispersed<be>	VB MV	RELO		FLEE		-2
סוג	displacer	SB ET HU IN		HUMN	CRIM	ETHB	-3
נגד	display	VB GU			UNCV		-1
ראה	distinguish	VB PS			REAS		+2
חלק	divide	VB CP MV WL	RELO	PROC	PEAC		+2
חלק	divide	VB IN MV WO	RELO	ECON	DEST		-2
שלח	divorce	SB ET IN MV WO		RELO FAML	DEST	ETHB	-2
עשׂה	do	VB CP ET	DO			ETHB	-2
עשׂה	do	VB CP	DO				0
עשׂה	do,act	VB CP	DO				0
יסף	do again	VI CP	DO				0
גדל	do great thngs	VB EM QL ST	QNTY	EXAL	PRID		-3
שפט	do justice for	VI IN		LEGL			+2
פרץ	do violence	VB WO			DEST		-3
גרר	drag	VB GU MV	RELO			ASMB	-1
נדד	draw back	VB MV	RELO		FLEE		-2

Hebrew	English	p.Spch Metacategories	Context-Dependent Categories					Context-Dependent Evaluation
נגש	draw near	VI IN MV	RELO	MILI				0
שאב	draw {water}	VB BN MV	RELO			FOOD		+2
פחד	dread	SB EM		FEAR				-3
חלם	dream	VB CO IN PS		PROP	COMR	KNOW		+1
שתה	drink	VB BN PS			NLRT	FOOD		+1
נטף	drip	VB BN CP	PROC			FOOD		+2
סיג	dross	SB EL EM IN ST	MTRL	DBAS	SHAM	TRAD		-2
שכר	drunk\<be>	VB BN PS			NLRT	FOOD		-2
סבא	drunkard	SB BN HU PS		HUMN	NLRT	FOOD		-2
יבש	dry up	VB CP EL WO	ELMT	PROC	DEST			-3
פרש	dung	SB CP EM ST	COND	DBAS	SHAM			-2
ישב	dwell	VB BN				DWEL		+2
שכן	dwell	VB BN				DWEL		+2
ישב	dwell	VB BN WL				DWEL	PEAC	+2
יקר	dwindle	VB CP	COND	PROC				-2
אכל	eat	VB BN				FOOD		+2
אכל	eat	VB BN WO			DEST	FOOD		-3
אכל	eat	VB WO CP		HEAT	DEST			-3
קצה	end,limit	SB QL	QNTY	MSMT				0
קום	endure	VB GU MV ST	STAY		ESTB	STRO		+1
עמד	endure	VB GU MV ST	STAY		ESTB	STRO		+1
כול	endure	VB GU MV ST	STAY		ESTB	STRO		+1
יכל	endure	VB GU MV ST	STAY		ESTB	STRO		+2
כלכל	endure	VB GU MV ST	STAY		ESTB	STRO		+1
סבך	entangled	VB WO			DEST	ILL		-2
בוא	enter	VB MV	RELO		FLEE			0
בוא	enter	VB MV	RELO					0
בוא	enter	VI IN MV	RELO	MILI				0
בוא	enter	VI MV	RELO					-1
חלה	entreat	VI CO GU		SEEK	COMS			+1
פליטה	escape	SB MV	RELO		FLEE			+2
מלט	escape	VB MV WL	RELO	REWD	FLEE			+2
מלט	escape	VB MV	RELO		FLEE			+2
פליטה	escaper	SB HU IF MV WL	RELO	HUMN	FLEE	LIFE		+2
כון	established\<be	VB CP GU	COND		ESTB			+2
יצב	established\<is	VB CP GU	COND		ESTB			+1

Hebrew	English	p.Spch Metacategories	Context-Dependent Categories					Context-Dependent Evaluation
חשב	esteemed<be>	VB EM ST			EXAL	PRID		+2
רע	evil	AJ CP ET	COND				ETHB	-2
רעע	evil	SB ET					ETHB	-2
רעע	evildoer	SB ET HU IF		HUMN			ETHB	-2
גאון	exaltation	SB EM ST			EXAL	PRID		+2
שגב	exalted<be>	VB CP EM ST	COND		EXAL	PRID		+2
גלה	exile	SB HU IF IN MV WO	RELO	HUMN	MILI	PUNI	SEND	-3
גלה	exile	SB IN MV WO	RELO		MILI	PUNI	SEND	-3
גלה	exile	VB IN MV WO	RELO		MILI	PUNI	SEND	-3
אמן	faithful	AJ CP ET PS		COND	KEEP		ETHG	+2
חסד	faithfulness	SB CP ET PS		COND	KEEP		ETHG	+2
נפל	fall	VB MV	RELO					0
נפל	fall	VB MV PS	RELO			NLRT		-3
נפל	fall	VB MV WO	RELO			DEST		-3
נפל	fall	VB WO	DEAT			DEST		-3
צום	fast	SB BN EM IN QL	TIME	CULT	SORR	FOOD		-2
צום	fast	VI BN EM IN QL	TIME	CULT	SORR	FOOD		-2
אב	father	SB HU IN		HUMN		FAML		+2
אב	father	SB HU IF IN		HUMN		FAML		+2
רצון	favor	SB EM				LOVE		+2
חן	favor	SB EM				LOVE		+2
ירא	fear	SB EM ET PS		FEAR	KEEP		ETHG	+2
ירא	fear	VB EM ET PS		FEAR	KEEP		ETHG	+2
ירא	fear	VI EM		FEAR				-2
נורא	feared	VB EM ET PS		FEAR	KEEP		ETHG	+2
ירא	fearer	SB EM ET HU IF PS	HUMN	FEAR	KEEP		ETHG	+2
אכל	feed	VB BN				FOOD		+2
זק	fetter	SB BN IN MD WO	TOOL		MILI	PUNI	WEAR	-3
לחם	fight	VB IN WO		MILI		DEST		-2
תאנה	fig tree	SB BN IN ST VG	VEGT	AGRI	WEAK	FOOD		+2
מלא	fill,full	VB CP QL	QNTY	COND		MSMT		0
מלא	filled<are>	VB CP QL	QNTY	COND		MSMT		-1
מלא	filled with<be	VB CP QL	QNTY	COND		MSMT		0
מצא	find	VB GU MV	RELO				UNCV	+1
כלה	finished<be>	VB CP QL WO	COND		DEST	MSMT		-2
אש	fire	SB WO CP			HEAT	DEST		-3

Hebrew	English	p.Spch Metacategories	Context-Dependent Categories						Context-Dependent Evaluation
להב flame/flash	SB IN CP			MILI	HEAT			-2
נוס flee	VB MV	RELO			FLEE			-3
שטף flood	SB EL WO	ELMT			DEST			-3
נהר flow	VB CP MV	RELO	PROC					+1
הלך flow	VB CP MV	RELO	PROC					+2
עוף fly	VB MV	RELO			FLEE			+1
טרף food	VI BN FN IN VG	FDND	VEGT	ANHS	HUNT	FOOD	AGRI	+2
פתה foolish	AJ CP EM PS ST	COND		DBAS	SHAM	NLRT		-2
שכח forget	VB PS				NLRT	IGNO		-2
יצר form	VB CP	PROC						+3
יסד found,establsh	VB GU				ESTB			+3
יד from your hand	SB HU IN MV WO	CULT	HUPT	SEND	ILL	RELO		-3
פרי fruit	SB BN IN VG WL	VEGT		AGRI	PEAC	FOOD		+2
שבע full	VB CP EM QL	QNTY	COND	HATE	MSMT			0
מלא full	VB CP QL	QNTY	COND		MSMT			0
אסף gather	VB CP	PROC						-3
קבץ gather	VB EM			FEAR				-2
קבץ gather	VB GU IN MV	RELO		MILI	SEND	ASMB		-2
אסף gather	VB GU IN MV	RELO		MILI	SEND	ASMB		-2
קבץ gather	VB IN MV WO	RELO		MILI	DEST	SEND		-3
אסף gather	VB IN MV WO	RELO		MILI	DEST	SEND		-3
אסף gather	VI GU IN MV	RELO		CULT	SEND	ASMB		+1
קבץ gather	VI GU IN MV	RELO		CULT	SEND	ASMB		+1
קבץ gatherer	SB GU HU MV	RELO	HUMN		SEND	ASMB		+1
אסף gather against	VB GU IN MV WO	RELO		MILI	DEST	ASMB		-3
חגר gird	VI BN IN			CULT		WEAR		+1
חגר girded	VB BN CP IN	COND		CULT		WEAR		+1
נתן give	VB BN EL IN MV	ELMT	AGRI	SEND		FOOD		+2
נתן give	VB MV			SEND				+2
שוב give back	VB MV WL	RELO		SEND	REWD			+1
אזן give ear	VI CO GU			SEEK	COMR			+1
קשב give heed	VI CO PS			COMR	KEEP			+2
ברק gleaming	SB EL CP	ELMT		HEAT				-2
פארור glow	SB EM			FEAR				-2
הלך go	VB MV	RELO						-1
הלך go,walk	VB ET MV	RELO				ETHG		+2

Hebrew	English	p.Spch Metacategories	Context-Dependent Categories					Context-Dependent Evaluation
הלך	go,walk	VB MV	RELO					0
הלך	go,walk	VI MV	RELO					+1
אלהים	God	PN DV ST	GOD			STRO		NS
יצא	going forth	SB MV	RELO					0
עמרה	Gomorrah	PN ET HU IF LO WO	CITY	HUMN HUGP	DEST	ETHB		-3
סור	gone<be>	VB QL	QNTY			MSMT		-1
טוב	good	AJ ET					ETHG	+2
יטב	good	VI ET					ETHG	+2
פרד	go apart	VB ET BN IN MV	RELO		SEX	TRAD	ETHB	-2
הלך	go away	VB MV	RELO					0
עמק	go deep	VB CP QL	QNTY	COND				-1
יצא	go forth	VB CO MV	RELO			COMS		+1
יצא	go forth	VB MV	RELO					+2
יצא	go forth	VI MV	RELO					0
קרב	go near	VB MV	RELO					0
עלה	go up	VB IN MV	RELO	CULT				+1
על	go up	VB IN MV	RELO	CULT				+1
עלה	go up	VB MV WO	RELO			DEST		-3
עלה	go up	VB MV	RELO					-1
עלה	go up	VI IN MV	RELO			MILI		0
עלה	go up	VI IN MV	RELO	MILI				0
עלה	go up	VI MV	RELO					+1
טוב	go well	AJ ET WL		PEAC		ETHG		+2
חזק	grab	VI IN MV		MILI SEND				-1
חנון	gracious	AJ EM				LOVE		+3
מנחה	grain offering	SB BN IN VG	VEGT	AGRI CULT	FOOD			+2
חזק	grasp	VB GU MV	RELO	SEEK SEND				-1
תפש	grasp	VB GU MV	RELO	SEEK SEND				-1
קבר	grave	SB LO WO		LAND DEAT	DEST			-3
גדול	great	AJ QL ST	QNTY	EXAL				+2
רב	great	AJ QL ST	QNTY	EXAL				0
גדל	great	VI QL ST	QNTY	EXAL				+2
נוד	grieve	VB CO EM		COMS SORR				-2
טחן	grind	VB IN WO		AGRI DEST				-2
אנח	groan	VB CO EM		COMS SORR				-2
קדר	grow dark	VB CP EL	ELMT PROC	COND				-3

Hebrew	English	p.Spch Metacategories	Context-Dependent Categories					Context-Dependent Evaluation
פקד guard	VB IN				MILI			+2
נצר guard	VI IN				MILI			+2
אשם guilty<be>	VB EM ET IN				LEGL	SORR	ETHB	-2
אשם guilty<be>	VI ET IN				LEGL		ETHB	-3
קציר harvest	SB BN IN VG		VEGT		AGRI	FOOD		+2
קצר harvest	VB BN IN				AGRI	FOOD		+2
שנא hate	VB EM						HATE	-3
חמל have pity	VB EM				LOVE			+2
רפא heal	VB WL						HEAL	+3
מרפא healing	SB CP WL		COND				HEAL	+3
שמע hear	VB CO GU PS				COMR	SENS	KEEP	+1
שמע hear	VB CO GU				COMR	SENS		+1
שמע hear	VI CO GU				COMR	SENS		+1
שמע hearer	SB CO GU HU			HUMN	COMR	SENS		+1
לבב heart{undrstdg}	SB PS				REAS			+2
מעמסה heavy	SB QL ST WO		QNTY		DEST	MSMT	WEAK	-2
שמר heed	VB ET PS				KEEP	ETHG		+2
שמר heed	VB PS				KEEP			+2
עזרה helper	SB GU HU IF IN			HUMN	MILI		ASMB	+2
חצב hew	VB WO				DEST	ILL		-3
חיה he make usLive	VB WL						LIFE	+3
כחד hidden<be>	VB CP MV		COND				FLEE	-1
עלם hide	VB MV		RELO				FLEE	-1
טמן hide	VI MV		RELO				FLEE	-1
קדש holy	AJ CP ET IN		COND		CULT		ETHG	+2
כבד honor	SB EM PS ST			KEEP	EXAL	PRID		+2
כבד honor	SB EM ST				EXAL	PRID		+2
כבד honor	VB EM PS ST			KEEP	EXAL	PRID		+2
שחח humbled<be>	VB EM ST				DBAS	SHAM		-2
שפל humbled<be>	VB EM ST				DBAS	SHAM		-2
שחח humbled<is>	VB EM ST				DBAS	SHAM		-2
שפל humbled<is>	VB EM ST				DBAS	SHAM		-2
מהר hurry	VB QL		QNTY		MSMT			-1
נדה impurity	SB CP ET		COND				ETHB	-2
פרץ increase	VB IN QL		QNTY		MSMT	FAML		+1
רבב increase	VB QL		QNTY		MSMT			+1

Hebrew English	p.Spch Metacategories	Context-Dependent Categories						Context-Dependent Evaluation
זעם indignant	VB EM WO			PUNI	ANGR			-3
זעם indignation	SB EM WO			PUNI	ANGR			-3
נחל inheritance	SB IF IN LO ST		LAND	ECON	WLTH			+3
און iniquity	SB ET					ETHB		-2
עון iniquity	SB ET					ETHB		-2
שרט injured<be>	VB WO				DEST	ILL		-3
מכה injury	SB WO				DEST	ILL		-3
עולה injustice	SB ET IN			LEGL		ETHB		+2
נקיון innocence	SB CP ET IN		COND	LEGL		ETHG		+2
שאל inquire	VB CO GU				SEEK	COMS		+1
זד insolent	SB ET HU IF PS		HUMN		RJCT	ETHB		-2
תחת instead of	PP QL	NEG						-2
עלה invade	VB IN MV	RELO		MILI				-3
חתת in awe<be>	VB EM ET PS			FEAR	KEEP	ETHG		+2
נגד in front	PP OT	NSCR						NS
קרב in the midst	PP BN	DWEL						+3
רקד jolt	VB IN MV	RELO		MILI				-2
שפט judge	VB IN PS WO			LEGL	REAS	DEST	PUNI	-3
שפט judge	VB IN PS			LEGL	REAS			+1
דין judge	VB IN PS			LEGL	REAS			-2
שפט judge	VB IN PS WO			LEGL	REAS	PUNI		-2
משפט judgment	SB IN PS WO			LEGL	REAS	PUNI		-3
משפט justice	SB ET IN			LEGL		ETHG		+2
משפט justice	VI ET IN			LEGL		ETHG		+2
שמר keep	VB ET PS				KEEP	ETHG		+2
צפה keep watch	VI GU IN			MILI		SENS		+1
הרג kill	VB WO				DEAT	DEST		-3
אור kindle fire	VI IN CP				HEAT	CULT		+1
מלך king	SB DV IN	GOD		GOVT				+1
מלך king	SB IN			GOVT				+1
לוש knead	VB BN					FOOD		+2
ידע know	VB PS				KNOW			+2
ידע know	VI PS				KNOW			+2
דעת knowledge	SB PS				KNOW			+2
נער lad	SB HU IF IN ST		HUMN		FAML	WEAK		-2
שדד laid waste	VB WO				DEST			-3

Hebrew	English	p.Spch	Metacategories	Context-Dependent Metacategories	Categories				Context-Dependent Evaluation
אמלל	languish	VB	EM			SORR			-2
כבס	laundryman	SB	HU IN		HUMN	TRAD			+2
תורה	law,teaching	SB	CO ET IN		LEGL	COMC	ETHG		+2
תורה	law,teaching	VI	CO ET IN		LEGL	COMC	ETHG		+2
ריב	lawsuit	SB	IN PS		LEGL	REAS			-1
ריב	lawsuit	SB	IN		LEGL				-2
תעה	lead astray	VB	ET MV PS	RELO	NLRT	SEND	ETHB		-2
רקד	leap	VB	IN MV	RELO	MILI				-1
למד	learn	VB	PS			KNOW			+1
למד	learn	VI	PS			KNOW			+1
יתר	leave	VB	MV	STAY					+1
עזב	leave	VB	MV WL	STAY		PEAC			+1
שאר	leave	VB	MV	STAY					+1
חמץ	leavened	VB	BN CP	COND			FOOD		+2
נוח	leave alone	VI	MV	STAY					+1
יתר	leave over	VB	MV	STAY					+1
תעה	led astray<be>	VB	ET MV	RELO		SEND	ETHB		-2
עוש	lend aid	VI	IN		MILI				+2
כחש	lie,deceit	SB	CO ET			COMC	ETHB		-2
כזב	lie,deceit	SB	CO ET			COMC	ETHB		-2
רמיה	lie,deceit	SB	CO ET			COMC	ETHB		-2
כחש	lie,deceive	VB	CO ET			COMS	ETHB		-2
שקר	lie,falsehood	SB	CO ET			COMC	ETHB		-2
חכה	lie in waitFor	VB	ET IN MV	STAY	CRIM		ETHB		-3
חיה	life	SB	WL			LIFE			+3
עמס	lift a load	VB	MV ST	RELO		SEND	WEAK		+1
נשא	lift up	VB	IN MV WO	RELO	MILI	SEND	DEST		-3
אור	light	SB	CO ET PS		COMC	KNOW	ETHG		+2
אור	light	SB	EL CP	ELMT		HEAT			+2
כפיר	lion	SB	AN IN WO	ANMW			DEST	WILD	-3
שחל	lion	SB	AN IN WO	ANMW			DEST	WILD	-3
שמע	listen	VB	CO GU PS		SEEK	COMR	KEEP		+1
מעט	little,few	SB	QL	QNTY		MSMT			-2
חיה	live	VB	WL			LIFE			+3
ארבה	locust B	SB	AN IN WO	INSC			DEST	WILD	-3
גוב	locust E	SB	AN IN WO	INSC			DEST	WILD	-3

Hebrew English	p.Spch Metacategories	Context-Dependent Categories					Context-Dependent Evaluation
לון lodge	VB BN MV	STAY				DWEL	+2
ערג long for	VB EM					DESR	-1
נבט look	VB GU					SENS	+1
שחר look early	VB GU PS QL		TIME	SEEK		ALRT	+1
אדון Lord	PN DV	GOD					NS
אסף lose	VB CP MV	RELO		PROC	FLEE		+1
אהב love	SB EM					LOVE	+3
אהב love	VB EM					LOVE	+3
נקה lv unpunished	VB IN WL			LEGL	REWD		+3
שגעון madness	SB PS					NLRT	-2
גדל magnify above	VB EM QL ST	QNTY		EXAL	PRID		+2
נצר maintain	VB GU QL WO	QNTY		PUNI	ESTB	DEST	-3
נתן make	VB CP	DO					0
שום make	VB CP	DO					0
עשה make	VB CP	DO					-1
עשה make	VB CP ET	DO				ETHB	-2
שום make	VB GU				ESTB		0
נבל make a fool	VB EM ST			DBAS	SHAM		-2
ידע make known	VB CO				COMS		+1
רב many	AJ QL	QNTY			MSMT		+1
בעל marry	VB IN				FAML		+2
נמס melt	VB EM WO CP		FEAR	HEAT	DEST		-1
מוג melt	VB WO CP			HEAT	DEST		-2
מלאך messenger	SB CO HU IF		HUMN		COMV		+1
עצמה might	SB CP ST	COND				STRO	+1
עצום mighty	AJ ST					STRO	+1
טפף mince steps	VB ET BN MV	RELO		SEX		ETHB	-2
בלל mix	VB GU					ASMB	-1
חגג mkPilgrimage	VB IN MV QL	RELO	TIME	CULT			+2
מנהג moan	VB CO EM			COMS	SORR		-2
לעג mocking	SB CO EM ST			COMS	SHAM	COMC DBAS	-2
עש moth	SB AN IN WO	INSC			DEST	WILD	-3
אבל mourn	VB CO EM				SORR	COMS	-2
אנה mourn	VB CO EM				SORR	COMS	-2
קדרנית mourners<as>	SB CO EM HU IF		HUMN		SORR	COMS	-2
רב multiplied	AJ QL	QNTY			MSMT		+1

Hebrew	English	p.Spch	Metacategories	Categories (Context-Dependent)						Evaluation (Context-Dependent)
רבה	multiply	VB	QL	QNTY			MSMT			+1
רבב	multiply	VB	QL	QNTY			MSMT			+1
כבד	multiply	VI	QL	QNTY			MSMT			+1
רצח	murder	SB	ET IN WO			CRIM	DEAT	ETHB	DEST	-3
רצח	murder	VB	ET IN WO			CRIM	DEAT	ETHB	DEST	-3
רצח	murderer	SB	ET HU IF IN WO	DEST	HUMN	CRIM	DEAT	ETHB		-3
ערה	naked\<be\>	VB	CP EM ST	COND		DBAS	SHAM			-2
מערה	nakedness	SB	CP EM ST	COND		DBAS	SHAM			-2
שם	name	SB	HU IN		HUPT		FAML			+1
קרב	near	AJ	QL	TIME			MSMT			NS
די	need	SB	CP IN ST	COND		POVT	ECON			-2
רשת	net	SB	IN MD	TOOL		HUNT				-1
נגש	offer,brngNear	VB	IN MV	RELO		CULT	SEND			+2
תרומה	offering	SB	BN IN VG	VEGP		CULT		FOOD		+2
קטר	offer incense	VB	ET IN CP			CULT	HEAT	ETHB		-2
קלל	of no account	VB	EM ST			DBAS	SHAM			-2
חשב	one who plans	SB	HU IF PS		HUMN		REAS	RJCT		-2
פתח	open	VB	GU MV	RELO			SEND	UNCV		+2
ענה	oppress	VB	WO			PUNI	DEST			-3
עשק	oppressed\<be\>	VB	WO			PUNI	DEST			-3
נגש	oppressed\<be\>	VB	WO			PUNI	DEST			-3
עשק	oppressor	SB	ET HU IF ST WO	POVT	HUMN	PUNI	DEST	ETHB		-3
נגש	oppressor	SB	HU IF WO		HUMN	PUNI	DEST			-3
שוק	overflow	VB	QL WO	QNTY			DEST			-2
שוק	overflow	VB	QL WL	QNTY		PEAC				+2
מהפכה	overthrow	VB	IN WO			MILI	DEST			-3
מהומה	panic	SB	EM WO				DEST	FEAR		-3
עבר	pass away	VB	MV WO	RELO			DEST			-2
חלף	pass on/away	VB	MV WO	RELO			DEST			-2
עבר	pass over	VB	MV WO	RELO			DEST			-3
עבר	pass over	VB	MV	RELO						-3
עבר	pass through	VB	MV WO	RELO		DEST				-3
שלם	pay	VB	IN PS			CULT	KEEP			+1
קשב	pay attention	VB	CO PS			COMR	KEEP			+1
שלם	peace	SB	CP WL	COND		PEAC				+3
עשה	perform	VB	CP	DO						0

Hebrew	English	p.Spch	Metacategories	Context-Dependent Categories		Context-Dependent Evaluation
גוע	perish	VB	WO		DEAT DEST	-3
שבבים	pieces	SB	WO		DEST ILL	-3
דקר	pierce	VB	WO		DEAT DEST	-3
חוס	pity	VI	EM		LOVE	+2
מגפה	plague	SB	WO		DEST ILL	-3
נגף	plague	SB	WO		DEST ILL	-3
חשב	plan	VB	ET PS		REAS ETHB	-2
חשב	plan	VB	PS		REAS	-2
טוב	pleasant	AJ	EM WL		PEAC DESR	+3
ערב	pleasing<be>	VB	EM WL		PEAC DESR	+3
את	plowshare	SB	BN IN MD	TOOL	AGRI FOOD	+2
פרק	plunder	SB	IN ST WO		MILI DEST ECON WLTH	-3
גזלה	plunder	SB	IN ST WO		MILI DEST ECON WLTH	-3
שסס	plunder	VB	IN ST WO		MILI DEST ECON WLTH	-3
בזז	plunder	VI	IN ST WO		MILI DEST ECON WLTH	-3
ברכה	pool	SB	BN MD WL	CTPT	DWEL PEAC	+2
ירד	pour down	VB	BN EL IN MV WL	RELO	ELMT SEND AGRI FOOD PEAC	0
נתך	pour forth	VB	MV	RELO	SEND	-2
ריק	pour out	VB	MV	RELO	SEND	+2
שפך	pour out	VB	MV	RELO		+1
שפך	pour out	VB	MV	RELO	SEND	0
הלל	praise	VB	CO EM IN		CULT JOY COMS	+2
תפלה	prayer	SB	CO GU IN		CULT SEEK COMS	+2
עשה	prepare	VB	CP GU	DO	ESTB	0
שום	prepare	VB	GU		ESTB	-1
פנה	prepare	VB	GU		ESTB	0
נגש	present	VB	IN MV	RELO	CULT SEND	+2
נגש	present	VB	IN MV	RELO	SEND CULT	0
שמר	preserve	VI	CO ET PS		KNOW COMS ETHG	+2
זור	press out	VB	WL		HEAL	+3
קרא	proclaim,call	VB	CO		COMS	+1
קרא	proclaim,call	VI	CO		COMS	+1
עשה	produce	VB	CP IN	PROC DO	AGRI	+1
נתן	produce	VB	CP IN	PROC DO	AGRI	+1
חלל	profane	VB	ET IN		CULT ETHB	-3
נבא	prophesy	VB	CO IN		PROP COMS	+1

Hebrew	English	p.Spch Metacategories	Context-Dependent Categories	Context-Dependent Evaluation
נביא	prophet	SB HU IF IN	HUMN PROP	+1
זנה	prostitute	SB ET HU IF BN IN	HUMN SEX TRAD ETHB	-2
זנה	prostitution	SB ET BN IN	SEX TRAD ETHB	-2
זנות	prostitution	SB ET BN IN	SEX TRAD ETHB	-2
זנה	prostitution	VB ET BN IN	SEX TRAD ETHB	-2
נשא	protest	VB CO PS	COMS RJCT	-1
גבה	proud	VB EM ET PS ST	EXAL PRID ETHB KNOW	-2
מזמרה	pruning knife	SB BN IN MD	TOOL AGRI FOOD	+2
פקד	punish	VB IN WO	LEGL DEST PUNI	-3
חטא	punishment	SB IN WO	LEGL DEST PUNI	-3
קנה	purchase	VB IN	ECON MSTR	-1
טהר	purifier	SB CP HU IN	PROC HUMN TRAD	+2
טהר	purify	VB CP ET IN	PROC CULT ETHG	+2
רדף	pursue	VB MV WO	RELO FLEE PUNI	-2
רדף	pursue	VB MV	RELO FLEE	-2
רדף	pursue	VI GU MV PS	RELO SEEK REAS	+2
שום	put,set	VB MV PS	SEND REAS KEEP	0
שלח	put in<send>	VI MV	RELO SEND	-2
רעש	quake	VB CP EL WO	ELMT PROC DEST	-2
כבה	quench	VB WL	HEAL	+3
פשט	raid	VB ET IN WO	CRIM DEST ETHB	-3
מורה	rain	SB BN EL IN WL	ELMT AGRI PEAC FOOD	+2
גשם	rain	SB BN EL IN WL	ELMT AGRI PEAC FOOD	+3
קום	raise	VB MV	RELO SEND	+2
נשא	raise,lift up	VB MV WO	RELO SEND DEST	-2
נשא	raise,lift up	VB MV	RELO SEND	-2
נשא	raise,lift up	VI EM MV ST	RELO EXAL PRID	+1
רוע	raise a shout	VI CO IN	MILI COMS	-2
גדל	raise {a child}	VB IN	FAML	+2
פדה	ransom	VB MV	FLEE	+2
פדה	ransomed<be>	VB CP MV	COND FLEE	+2
שגל	rape<be>	VB ET BN WO	SEX DEST ETHB	-3
שרי	raw wound	AJ WO	DEST ILL	-3
תנה	rcvPrsttutPay	VB ET IN BN ST	TRAD SEX WLTH ETHB ECON	-2
נגע	reach	VB MV	RELO	0
יכח	reason	VI CO PS	COMS REAS COMR	+1

Hebrew	English	p.Spch Metacategories	Context-Dependent Categories						Context-Dependent Evaluation
סרר	rebel	SB ET HU IF PS		HUMN		RJCT	ETHB		-2
מרה	rebel	VB ET PS				RJCT	ETHB		-2
פשע	rebel,revolt	VB ET PS				RJCT	ETHB		-2
סרה	rebellion	SB ET PS				RJCT	ETHB		-2
גער	rebuke	VB CO WO			PUNI	COMS			-2
גער	rebuke	VB CO WO			PUNI	COMS	DEST		-2
גמל	recompense	SB WO			PUNI	DEST			-3
גמל	recompense	VB WO			PUNI	DEST			-3
אדם	red	AJ CP IN	COND	MILI					0
אדם	red<be>	VB CP EM ET IN ST	COND		CULT	SHAM	ETHB	DBAS	-2
זקק	refine	VB CP IN	PROC		TRAD	HEAT			+2
צרף	refiner,smeltr	SB HU IN CP		HUMN	TRAD	HEAT			+2
מחסה	refuge	SB BN LO MV WL	PEAC	LAND	LIFE	FLEE	DWEL		+2
מעוז	refuge	SB BN LO MV WL	PEAC	LAND	LIFE	FLEE	DWEL		+2
מעוז	refuge	SB BN LO MV WL		LAND	LIFE	FLEE	DWEL		+2
חסה	refuge seeker	SB BN GU HU MV	RELO	HUMN	SEEK	FLEE	DWEL		+1
אמן	refuse	VB ET PS				RJCT	ETHB		-2
נשא	regard	VB CO PS			COMR	REAS			+1
פנה	regard	VB PS			KEEP	REAS			+1
חשב	regard	VB PS				REAS			+1
נשא	regard	VB PS				REAS			+1
זנח	reject	VB ET PS				RJCT	ETHB		-2
נאץ	reject	VB ET PS				RJCT	ETHB		-2
שמח	rejoice	VB CO EM			COMS	JOY			+2
גיל	rejoice	VI CO EM			COMS	JOY			+2
שמח	rejoice	VI CO EM			COMS	JOY			+2
ששון	rejoicing	SB CO EM			COMS	JOY			+2
נחם	relieved of<be	VB CP WO	COND		PUNI	DEST			-3
ישב	remain	VB BN GU MV	STAY			ESTB	DWEL		+1
יתר	remain	VB BN MV	STAY				DWEL		+1
שאר	remain	VB GU MV	STAY			ESTB			+1
זכר	remember	VB PS				KNOW	ALRT		+1
זכר	remember	VI PS			KEEP	KNOW	ALRT		+1
סור	remove	VB MV	RELO		SEND				-1
עבר	remove	VB MV WO	RELO		SEND	DEST			-2
סור	remove	VI MV	RELO		SEND				+2

Hebrew	English	p.Spch	Metacategories	Context-Dependent Categories					Context-Dependent Evaluation
רחק	remove far	VB	IF MV	RELO	SEND	FLEE			-2
קרע	rend	VI	BN EM IN		CULT	SORR	WEAR		-2
שלם	repay	VB	EM WO		PUNI	DEST	HATE		-3
שיב	repay	VB	EM WO		PUNI	DEST	HATE		-2
שלם	repay	VB	WL			REWD			+2
שוב	repent	VB	ET GU PS		SEEK	KEEP	ETHG		+2
שוב	repent<make>	VB	ET GU PS		SEEK	KEEP	ETHG		+2
שמע	report	SB	CO		COMV				+2
חרפה	reproach	SB	CO EM ST		COMC	SHAM	DBAS		-2
אשר	reprove	VI	CO WO		PUNI	COMS			-2
יכח	reprove	VI	CO WO		PUNI	COMS			-2
בקש	require	VB	IN PS		LEGL	KEEP			+1
שוב	restore	VB	GU WL		PEAC	ESTB			+1
שוב	return	VB	ET GU MV	RELO		SEEK	ETHG		+2
שוב	return	VB	GU PS		SEEK		KEEP		+2
שוב	return	VB	MV	RELO					0
שוב	return	VB	MV WO	RELO	PUNI				-2
פנה	return	VB	MV	STAY					+1
שוב	return	VI	ET GU MV	RELO		SEEK	ETHG		+2
גלה	revealed	VB	GU				UNCV		-2
ירא	revere,fear	VB	EM ET PS		FEAR	KEEP	ETHG		+2
שלמן	reward	SB	ET IN MD ST WL	MONY	REWD	WLTH	ETHB	ECON	-2
צדק	righteous	SB	ET HU IF	HUMN			ETHG		+2
צדק	righteousness	SB	ET				ETHG		+2
צדקה	righteousness	SB	ET				ETHG		+2
בשל	ripen	VB	CP IN	COND	PROC	AGRI			+2
ראם	rise	VB	MV	RELO					+1
זרח	rise	VB	MV	RELO					+1
שאג	roar	VB	CO			COMS			-2
קבע	rob	VB	ET IN WO		CRIM	DEST	ETHB		-3
מקק	rot	VB	WO			DEST	ILL		-3
רקב	rottenness	SB	CP IN WO	COND	AGRI	DEST	ILL		-3
עור	rouse	VI	MV PS	RELO			ALRT		+1
עור	rouse oneself	VB	PS				ALR T		+1
עור	rouse oneself	VI	IN PS			MILI	AL RT		+1
עור	rouse oneself	VI	PS				A LRT		+1

Hebrew	English	p.Spch Metacategories				Context-Dependent Categories				Context-Dependent Evaluation
שחת	ruin	VB WO						DEST		-3
שדד	ruined\<is\>	VB CP WO			COND			DEST		-3
משל	rule	VB IN						GOVT		+1
קצין	ruler	SB HU IF IN				HUMN GOVT				+1
רוץ	run	VB IN MV			RELO		MILI			0
שקק	run	VB IN MV			RELO		MILI			0
דהר	rush	VB IN MV			RELO		MILI			-1
שקק	rush toAnd fro	VB IN MV			RELO		MILI			-2
שק	sackcloth	SB BN EM MD ST			CLTH POVT	DBAS	SORR	WEAR		-2
זבח	sacrifice	SB AN IN			ANMD		ANHS	CULT		+2
זבח	sacrifice	VB ET IN					ANHS	CULT	ETHB	-2
זבח	sacrifice	VB IN					ANHS	CULT		+2
זבח	sacrificer	SB HU IF IN				HUMN CULT				+2
קדש	sanctify	VI ET IN					MILI	CULT	ETHG	+2
שבע	satisfied,full	VB BN CP QL WL			COND		PEAC	MSMT	FOOD	+2
שבע	satisfied,full	VB CP QL WL			COND		PEAC	MSMT		+2
ישע	save,deliver	VB IN WL					MILI	PEAC		+3
אמר	say	VB CO						COMS		+1
אמר	say	VI CO						COMS		+1
משל	saying,byword	SB CO EM					COMC SHAM			-2
כי	scar	SB WO						DEST	ILL	-3
שני	scarlet	SB BN CP EM MD ST			CLTH COND	DBAS	SHAM	WEAR		-2
זרע	scatter	VB CO MV						COMS	SEND	+1
פזר	scatter	VB IN MV WO			RELO		MILI	PUNI	SEND	-2
נפוש	scattered\<are\>	VB IN MV			RELO		MILI	FLEE	SEND	-2
בטח	security	SB CP WL			COND		PEAC			+2
כשף	seduction	SB CO ET BN					SEX	COMC	ETHB	-2
ראה	see	VB CO GU IN					PROP	COMR	SENS	+1
חזה	see	VB CO GU IN					PROP	COMR	SENS	+1
ראה	see	VB GU							SENS	+1
בקש	seek	VB GU					SEEK			+1
דרש	seek	VI GU					SEEK			+1
בקש	seek	VI GU					SEEK			+1
חזק	seize	VB MV WO			RELO		SEND	DEST	ILL	-3
מכר	sell	VB IN				MSTR ECON				-2
מכר	seller	SB HU IF IN ST			MSTR HUMN ECON	WLTH				-2

Hebrew	English	p.Spch Metacategories	Context-Dependent Categories	Context-Dependent Evaluation
שלח	send	VB IN MV WL	RELO AGRI SEND PEAC	+2
שלח	send	VB MV	RELO SEND	0
עבד	serve	VB ET PS	KEEP ETHG	+2
נתן	set	VB EL MV WO CP	COSM HEAT SEND DEST	+2
שכן	settle/lieDown	VB MV PS	STAY NLRT	-1
להט	set ablaze	VB WO CP	HEAT DEST	-3
כון	set up	VB GU MV	STAY ESTB	+1
חלה	severe	VB QL WO	QNTY DEST	-3
רגז	shake	VB CP EL WO	ELMT PROC DEST	-3
נוע	shaken\<be\>	VB WO	DEST	-2
רעל	shaken\<be\>	VB WO	DEST	-2
עכס	shake bangles	VB CO ET BN	SEX COMS ETHB	-1
גזז	sheared off	VB WO	DEST	-3
שפך	shed	VB ET IN WO	CRIM DEAT DEST ETHB DEST	-3
רוע	shout an alarm	VI CO IN	MILI COMS	-2
ראה	show	VB GU	UNCV	-1
נשא	showPartiality	VB ET IN	LEGL ETHB	-2
חנן	show favor	VB EM	LOVE	+2
עבש	shrivel	VB CP IN WO	AGRI DEST PROC	-3
דוי	sick	AJ CP WO	COND DEST ILL	-3
חלי	sickness	SB CP WO	COND DEST ILL	-3
מצור	siege	SB IN WO	MILI DEST	-3
חטא	sin	SB ET	ETHB	-2
חטא	sin	VB ET	ETHB	-2
חטא	sinful	AJ CP ET	COND ETHB	-2
ישב	sit	VB MV	STAY	0
ישב	situated	VB LO QL	LAND MSMT	+1
חלל	slain ones	SB HU IF WO	HUMN DEAT	-3
עבד	slave	SB HU IF IN	HUMN MSTR	-1
נם	sleep	VB PS	NLRT	-2
צרף	smelt	VB CP IN	PROC HEAT TRAD	+1
ישן	smolder	VB PS CP	HEAT NLRT	-1
נפח	sniffInContmpt	VB EM IN	CULT HATE	-2
סדם	Sodom	PN ET HU IF LO WO	CITY HUMN HUGP DEST ETHB	-3
רכך	softened	VB CP WL	COND HEAL	+3
ענן	soothsayer	SB DV ET HU IF IN	HUMN CULT DVOT ETHB	-3

Hebrew	English	p.Spch Metacategories	Context-Dependent Categories				Context-Dependent Evaluation
קול sound		SB CO			COMV		+1
מתם soundness		SB CP WL	COND			HEAL	+3
זרע sow		VB IN		AGRI			+2
חמל spare,havePity		VB EM WL		PEAC	LOVE		+2
ניצוץ spark		SB WO CP		HEAT	DEST		-3
דבר speak		VB CO PS			COMS	RJCT	-2
דבר speak		VB CO			COMS		+1
ראה spectacle		SB CP EM ST	COND		DBAS	SHAM	-2
לין spend theNight		VI EM IN QL	TIME	CULT		SORR	-2
רוח Spirit		SB DV	GOD			SPIR	+3
בקע split<be>		VB MV WO	RELO			DEST	-1
זרה spread		VB MV WO	RELO		SEND	DEST	-2
פרש spread out		VB CO IN		CULT		COMS	+1
פרש spread out		VB MV	RELO		SEND		0
מקור spring		SB BN ET LO	LAND		ETHG	FOOD	+2
פוש spring about		VB EM MV	RELO		JOY		+2
זרק sprinkled<are>		VB CP WO	COND			DEST	-2
דשא sprout		VB CP IN	PROC		AGRI		+2
מאס spurn,reject		VB PS			RJCT		-2
רעל staggering		SB MV PS	RELO			NLRT	-2
עמד stand		VB IN MV	STAY	LEGL			-2
נצב stand		VB MV	STAY				-2
עמד stand		VB MV	STAY				0
שכם start early		VB MV PS QL	RELO TIME			ALRT	-1
גנב stealing		SB ET IN			CRIM	ETHB	-3
באש stench		SB CP WO	COND		DEST		-2
צחנה stench		SB CP WO	COND		DEST		-2
עור stir up <fire>		VB CP			HEAT		0
גזל stolen		SB AN ET IN	ANMD		CRIM ANHS	ETHB	-3
אבן stone		SB EL ST	MTRL		STRO		-1
עמד stop		VI MV	STAY				0
זור stranger<be a>		VB CP IF PS	COND			RJCT	-2
זר strange thing		SB IF PS			RJCT		-2
חנק strangle		VB WO			DEAT	DEST	-3
נדד stray		VB ET MV PS	RELO		RJCT	ETHB	-2
כח strength		SB CP ST	COND			STRO	+2

Hebrew	English	p.Spch Metacategories	Context-Dependent Categories		Context-Dependent Evaluation		
חיל	strength	SB CP ST	COND			STRO	+2
חזק	strengthen	VB ST				STRO	+2
חזק	strengthen	VI ST				STRO	+2
משך	stretch out	VB MV	RELO	SEND			0
נטה	stretch out	VB MV	RELO	SEND			0
נגף	strike	VB WO			DEST	ILL	-3
נכה	strike	VB WO			DEST	ILL	-3
מכה	strike	VB WO			DEST	ILL	-3
נכה	strike	VI WO			DEST	ILL	-3
שפק	strikeBargains	VB CO GU IN		ECON	COMS	ASMB	-1
לבן	strip	VB IN WO		AGRI	DEST		-3
חבורה	stripe	SB WO			DEST	ILL	-3
חשף	strip bark frm	VB IN WO		AGRI	DEST		-3
פשט	strip off	VB WO			DEST		-2
אמץ	strong\<be\>	VB CP ST	COND			STRO	+2
אמץ	strong\<be\>	VI CP ST	COND			STRO	+2
קש	stubble,chaff	SB IN VG WO	VEGT	AGRI	DEST		-2
סרר	stubborn\<be\>	VB ET PS			RJCT	ETHB	-2
כשל	stumble	VB MV PS ST WO	RELO	NLRT	DEST	WEAK	-2
קצפה	stump	SB IN VG	VEGT	AGRI			-3
אשם	suffer	VB EM			SORR		-2
חנן	supplication	SB CO GU		SEEK	COMC		+1
כון	sure\<be\>	VB CP GU	COND		ESTB		0
סבב	surround	VB QL			MSMT		0
סבב	surrounding	PP LO QL	LAND		MSMT		+1
שריד	survivor	SB HU IF MV WL	HUMN		FLEE	LIFE	+2
בלע	swallow up	VB BN WO			DEST	FOOD	-2
שבע	swear	VI CO			COMS		+1
שבע	swearer	SB CO ET HU IF IN	HUMN	CULT	COMV	ETHB	-2
אלה	swearing	SB CO ET			COMC	ETHB	-2
לקח	take	VB ET IN MV	RELO	SEND	CRIM	ETHB	-3
לקח	take	VB MV	RELO	SEND			0
סור	take away	VB MV	RELO	SEND			-2
אסף	take away	VB MV	RELO	SEND			-2
לקח	take away	VB PS			NLRT		-2
אסף	take away	VI MV	RELO	SEND			+2

Hebrew	English	p.Spch	Context-Dependent Metacategories	Context-Dependent Categories	Evaluation
רצה	take delight	VB	EM	DESR	+3
שמר	take heed	VI	PS	KEEP	+1
נקם	take revenge	VB	EM WO	PUNI DEST HATE	-3
ירה	teach	VB	CO PS	REAS COMS	+2
טרף	tear	VB	WO	DEST ILL	-3
דמעה	tears	SB	CO EM	COMS SORR	-2
נתק	tear apart	VB	WO	DEST	-2
הרס	tear down	VB	WO	DEST	-3
נגד	tell	VB	CO	COMS	+1
ספר	tell	VI	CO	COMS	+1
רעה	tend	VB	IN WL	ANHS PEAC	+2
נורא	terrifying	AJ	EM	FEAR	-3
חרד	terror causer	SB	EM HU IF WO	HUMN FEAR DEST	-3
בחן	test	VB	ET GU PS	SEEK REAS ETHB	-2
בחן	test	VB	GU IN PS	SEEK REAS TRAD	+1
בחן	test	VI	GU PS	SEEK REAS	+1
ענה	testify	VB	CO IN	LEGL COMS	-1
עיד	testify	VB	CO IN	LEGL COMS	-1
אין	there is not	PT	CP QL WO	NEG PROC DEST	NS
אין	there is not	PT	QL	NEG	NS
אמר	think	VB	PS	REAS	+1
חשב	thinkers	SB	HU IF PS	HUMN REAS	+1
שלך	throw	VB	MV	RELO SEND	-1
שלך	throw	VB	MV WO	RELO SEND DEST	-1
נדח	thrust	VB	IN MV	RELO MILI SEND	-2
לבט	thrust down<be	VB	WO	DEST	-2
נערת	tinder	SB	IN VG WO CP	VEGT AGRI HEAT DEST	-2
מעשר	tithe	SB	BN IN VG	VEGP AGRI CULT FOOD	+2
מעשר	tithe	VI	BN IN VG	VEGP AGRI CULT FOOD	+2
אל	to	PP	OT	NSCR	NS
הרס	torn down<are>	VB	WO	DEST	-2
שקר	tossSedctvGlnc	VB	CO ET BN	SEX COMS ETHB	-2
פיק	tottering	VB	EM PS ST WO	FEAR NLRT DEST WEAK	-2
נגע	touch	VB	MV	SEND	-2
היה	to be	VB	BN EL	ELMT FOOD	NS
היה	to be	VB	CO	COMC	NS

Hebrew English	p.Spch Metacategories	Context-Dependent Categories	Context-Dependent Evaluation
היה to be	VB CO	COMS	NS
היה to be	VB IN	GOVT	NS
היה to be	VB OT	NSCR	NS
עקב tracked	VB CP ET IN WO	COND CRIM DEAT ETHB	-3
נתן trade	VB IN	MSTR ECON	-2
כנען trader	SB HU IF IN	HUMN TRAD ECON	+1
יסר train	VB CO PS	KNOW COMS	+2
רמס trample	VB IN MV	RELO CULT	-1
רמס trample	VI IN MV	RELO MILI	-3
עבר transgress	VB ET	ETHB	-2
ירד tread	VI IN MV WO	RELO MILI DEST	-2
עסס tread down	VB MV WO	RELO DEST	-3
רגז tremble	VI EM	FEAR	-2
אמת truth	SB ET PS	KNOW ETHG	+2
שוב turn	VB EM ET MV	RELO LOVE ETHG	+2
שוב turn	VB GU PS	SEEK REAS	0
שוב turn\<against\>	VB MV WO	RELO PUNI DEST	-3
סור turn aside	VB ET MV PS	RELO RJCT ETHB	-2
נטה turn aside	VB ET MV WO	RELO DEST ETHB	-2
סור turn aside	VB MV WO	RELO DEST	-2
הפך turn over	VB BN	FOOD	+1
שוב turn unto	VI ET GU PS	SEEK KNOW ETHG	+2
שוב turn unto	VI ET GU PS	SEEK ETHG KNOW	+2
גלה uncover,liftUp	VB EM GU MV ST	RELO SHAM SEND UNCV DBAS	-2
חבר unite,join	VB ET GU	ETHB ASMB	-2
נשא upheaved	VB CP EL WO	ELMT PROC DEST	-2
מישור uprightness	SB ET	ETHG	+2
נתן utter	VB CO	COMS	+2
חמס violence	SB ET WO	DEST ETHB	-3
חזן vision	SB CO IN PS	PROP COMV KNOW	+1
נדר vow	SB CO IN	CULT COMS	+1
נדר vow	VB CO ET IN	CULT COMS ETHG	+2
ספד wail	VB CO EM	COMS SORR	-2
ספד wail	VI CO EM	COMS SORR	-2
אלה wail	VI CO EM	COMS SORR	-2
ילל wail,lament	VB CO EM	COMS SORR	-2

Hebrew	English	p.Spch Metacategories	Context-Dependent Categories	Context-Dependent Evaluation	
ילל	wail,lament	VI CO EM	COMS	SORR	-2
ספד	wailing	SB CO EM	COMS	SORR	-2
מספד	wailing	VI CO EM	COMS	SORR	-2
הלך	walk	VB ET MV PS	RELO ETHG	KEEP	+2
הלך	walk	VB MV	RELO		0
בוך	wander	VB GU MV PS ST	RELO SEEK NLRT	WEAK	-1
גבור	warrior	SB HU IF IN ST WO	HUMN MILI DEST	STRO	-2
רחץ	wash off	VI ET IN	CULT	ETHG	+2
בלק	waste	SB WO		DEST	-3
שמה	waste	SB WO		DEST	-3
בוקה	waste	SB WO		DEST	-3
שמר	watch,beCarefl	VI PS		KEEP	+1
מים	water	SB BN EL	ELMT	FOOD	+2
שקה	water	VB BN EL	ELMT	FOOD	+2
ירה	water	VB BN EL	ELMT	FOOD	+2
חלה	weak<be>	VB CP PS ST	COND NLRT	WEAK	-1
תלאה	weariness	SB CP EM ST	COND HATE	WEAK	-1
יגע	weary	VB CP ST	COND	WEAK	-1
לאה	weary<be>	VB CP ST	COND	WEAK	-1
בכה	weep	VI CO EM	COMS	SORR	-2
בכי	weeping	SB CO EM	COMS	SORR	-2
כבד	weighed down	VB CP ST	COND	WEAK	-2
לבן	white<be>	VB CP EM ET IN ST	COND CULT PRID ETHG	EXAL	+2
רשע	wicked	AJ ET		ETHB	-2
רשע	wicked	SB ET HU IF	HUMN	ETHB	-2
רשע	wickedness	SB ET		ETHB	-2
רעה	wickedness	SB ET		ETHB	-2
רעה	wickedness	VI ET		ETHB	-2
זמה	wicked plan	SB ET PS		ETHB KNOW	-2
מדבר	wilderness	SB LO	LAND		-3
פרא	wild donkey	SB AN IN	ANMW	WILD	-1
אבה	willing<be>	VB PS		KEEP	+2
חלץ	withdraw	VB MV PS	RELO	RJCT	-1
אמלל	wither	VB CP WO	PROC	DEST	-3
נבל	wither&fall	VB CP WO	PROC	DEST	-2
מנע	withheld<are>	VB CP WO	COND	DEST	-2

Hebrew	English	p.Spch Metacategories	Context-Dependent Categories			Context-Dependent Evaluation
עד	witness	SB CO DV IN WO	GOD		LEGL PUNI COMV	-1
אוי	woe!	IN EM			SORR	-2
אשה	woman	SB HU IN ST		HUMN	FAML WEAK	+2
פלא	wondrously act	VB WL		PEAC		+3
צמר	wool	SB AN BN ET IN MD	ANMP CLTH ANHS		ETHG WEAR	+2
דבר	word	SB CO			COMC	+1
דבר	word	SB CO ET			COMC ETHG	+2
עשה	work	SB CP DV ET IN	DO		CULT DVOT TRAD ETHB	-2
שחה	worship	VB CO IN			CULT COMS	+2
שחה	worship	VB DV ET IN			CULT DVOT ETHB	-2
וצ	worthlessness	SB ET			ETHB	-3
מכה	wound	SB WO			DEST ILL	-3
נכה	wound	SB WO			DEST ILL	-3
צרר	wrap	VB CP		PROC		-1
חמה	wrath	SB WO			PUNI DEST	-3
כתב	write	VB CO			COMS	+1
ל	you have	PA OT	NSCR			+1
קנא	zealous	VB EM			DESR	-2

4. Hebrew List Of All Activities

This section lists all words used to indicate activity, according to the Hebrew root. Included are a basic English translation, part of speech, metacategories, categories, and Evaluation numbers. Words are listed more than once if they are coded more than one way (including according to different parts of speech). All activity words are included here, not just those with 'emphasized' categories. The frequency of each word is not included.

Abbreviations For Parts Of Speech

AV - adverb; AJ - adjective; CJ - conjunction; DA - demonstrative adjective; DO - direct object marker; IN - interjection; PA - prepositional pronoun; PN - proper name; PP - preposition; PR - pronoun; PT - particle; RP - relative pronoun; SB - nouns and other substantives VB - verb (non-instruction); VI - verbal instructions (roughly equals imperatives).

Metacategory Abbreviations

AN - animals; BN - basic need satisfaction; CO - communication; CP - conditions and processes; DV - divine realm; EL - elements; EM - emotions; ET - ethics; FN - nondescript food; GU - guide, redirection; HU - human beings; IF - Israelite or foreign; IN - institution, society; LO - locations, places; MD - things made by people; MV - movement; OT - other; PS - cognitive (non-emotion); QL - qualifiers; ST - status; VG - plant oriented; WL - weal, good things; WO - woe, bad things.

Category Abbreviations

Category abbreviations can be found in Chapter 5, 'Category and Field Descriptions'.

Hebrew	English	p.Spch	Metacategories	Context-Dependent Categories		Context-Dependent Evaluation
אב	father	SB	HU IF IN	HUMN	FAML	+2
אב	father	SB	HU IN	HUMN	FAML	+2
אבד	destroyed<is>	VB	CP WO	COND	DEST	-3
אבה	willing<be>	VB	PS		KEEP	+2
אבל	mourn	VB	CO EM		SORR COMS	-2
אבן	stone	SB	EL ST	MTRL	STRO	-1
אדון	Lord	PN	DV	GOD		NS
אדם	red	AJ	CP IN	COND	MILI	0
אדם	red<be>	VB	CP EM ET IN ST	COND	CULT SHAM ETHB DBAS	-2
אהב	love	SB	EM		LOVE	+3
אהב	love	VB	EM		LOVE	+3
אוי	woe!	IN	EM		SORR	-2
און	iniquity	SB	ET		ETHB	-2
אור	kindle fire	VI	IN CP		HEAT CULT	+1
אור	light	SB	CO ET PS		COMC KNOW ETHG	+2
אור	light	SB	EL CP	ELMT	HEAT	+2
אזן	given ear	VI	CO GU		SEEK COMR	+1
אין	there is not	PT	CP QL WO	NEG	PROC DEST	NS
אין	there is not	PT	QL	NEG		NS
אכל	consume	VB	WO		DEST	-2
אכל	consumed	VB	WO		DEST	-2

Hebrew	English	p.Spch Metacategories	Context-Dependent Categories		Context-Dependent Evaluation
אכל	devour	VB WO		DEST	-3
אכל	eat	VB BN		FOOD	+2
אכל	eat	VB BN WO		DEST FOOD	-3
אכל	eat	VB WO CP		HEAT DEST	-3
אכל	feed	VB BN		FOOD	+2
אל	against	PP WO		PUNI	-3
אל	against you	PA OT	NSCR		-3
אל	to	PP OT	NSCR		NS
אלה	swearing	SB CO ET		COMC ETHB	-2
אלה	wail	VI CO EM		COMS SORR	-2
אלהים	God	PN DV ST	GOD	STRO	NS
אמלל	languish	VB EM		SORR	-2
אמלל	wither	VB CP WO	PROC	DEST	-3
אמן	faithful	AJ CP ET PS	COND	KEEP ETHG	+2
אמן	refuse	VB ET PS		RJCT ETHB	-2
אמץ	strong<be>	VB CP ST	COND	STRO	+2
אמץ	strong<be>	VI CP ST	COND	STRO	+2
אמר	say	VB CO		COMS	+1
אמר	say	VI CO		COMS	+1
אמר	think	VB PS		REAS	+1
אמת	truth	SB ET PS		KNOW ETHG	+2
אנה	mourn	VB CO EM		SORR COMS	-2
אנח	groan	VB CO EM		COMS SORR	-2
אנקה	crying	SB CO EM		COMS SORR	-2
אסף	gather	VB CP	PROC		-3
אסף	gather	VB GU IN MV	RELO	MILI SEND ASMB	-2
אסף	gather	VB IN MV WO	RELO	MILI DEST SEND	-3
אסף	gather	VI GU IN MV	RELO	CULT SEND ASMB	+1
אסף	gather against	VB GU IN MV WO	RELO	MILI DEST ASMB	-3
אסף	lose	VB CP MV	RELO	PROC FLEE	+1
אסף	take away	VB MV	RELO	SEND	-2
אסף	take away	VI MV	RELO	SEND	+2
אף	anger	SB EM WO		PUNI ANGR	-3
אפה	anger	SB EM WO		PUNI ANGR	-3
אפלה	darkness	SB CP EL EM	ELMT COND	FEAR	-3
אפר	ashes	SB EL WO	MTRL	DEST	-2

Hebrew	English	p.Spch Metacategories	Context-Dependent Categories						Context-Dependent Evaluation
ארב	ambush	SB ET IN WO			CRIM	DEAT	ETHB	DEST	-3
ארבה	locust B	SB AN IN WO	INSC				DEST	WILD	-3
ארר	curse	SB CO ET WO			PUNI	COMC	ETHB		-3
ארר	curse	VB CO ET WO			PUNI	COMS	ETHB		-3
ארר	cursed	AJ CO ET WO			PUNI	COMC	ETHB		-3
אש	fire	SB WO CP			HEAT	DEST			-3
אשה	woman	SB HU IN ST		HUMN			FAML	WEAK	+2
אשם	guilty<be>	VB EM ET IN			LEGL	SORR	ETHB		-2
אשם	guilty<be>	VI ET IN			LEGL		ETHB		-3
אשם	suffer	VB EM				SORR			-2
אשר	call fortunate	VB CO EM WL			COMS	JOY	PEAC		+2
אשר	reprove	VI CO WO			PUNI	COMS			-2
את	plowshare	SB BN IN MD	TOOL		AGRI			FOOD	+2
באש	stench	SB CP WO	COND				DEST		-2
בגד	actTreachersly	VB ET WO				DEST	ETHB		-2
בגד	actTreachersly	VI ET WO				DEST	ETHB		-2
בדד	alone<be>	VB QL	QNTY			MSMT			-1
בוא	bring	VB IN MV	RELO		SEND	CULT			0
בוא	bring	VB MV	RELO		SEND				0
בוא	bring	VI MV	RELO		SEND				+1
בוא	come	VB MV	RELO						-1
בוא	come	VI IN MV	RELO		CULT				+1
בוא	come	VI MV	RELO						0
בוא	come,enter	VB MV	RELO						0
בוא	enter	VB MV	RELO			FLEE			0
בוא	enter	VB MV	RELO						0
בוא	enter	VI IN MV	RELO		MILI				0
בוא	enter	VI MV	RELO						-1
בוז	despise	VB EM					HATE		-3
בוז	despise	VB EM PS			RJCT		HATE		-3
בוך	wander	VB GU MV PS ST	RELO		SEEK	NLRT	WEAK		-1
בוקה	waste	SB WO				DEST			-3
בוש	ashamed<be>	VB EM ST			DBAS	SHAM			-2
בוש	ashamed<be>	VI EM ST			DBAS	SHAM			-2
בזה	despised	VB EM					HATE		-3
בזז	plunder	VI IN ST WO			MILI	DEST	ECON	WLTH	-3

Hebrew	English	p.Spch Metacategories	Context-Dependent Categories				Context-Dependent Evaluation
בחן	test	VB ET GU PS		SEEK REAS ETHB			-2
בחן	test	VB GU IN PS		SEEK REAS TRAD			+1
בחן	test	VI GU PS		SEEK REAS			+1
בחר	choose	VB PS		REAS			0
בטח	security	SB CP WL	COND	PEAC			+2
בין	di scern	VB PS		REAS			+1
בכה	weep	VI CO EM		COMS SORR			-2
בכי	weeping	SB CO EM		COMS SORR			-2
בלל	mix	VB GU				ASMB	-1
בלע	confuse	VB ET MV PS	RELO	NLRT SEND ETHB			-2
בלע	swallow up	VB BN WO		DEST FOOD			-2
בלק	waste	SB WO		DEST			-3
בנה	build	VB BN				DWEL	+2
בנה	build up	VB EM ST		EXAL PRID			+2
בעל	marry	VB IN		FAML			+2
בער	burn	VB CP		HEAT			-2
בער	burn	VB WO CP		HEAT DEST			-3
בער	consume	VB WO		DEST			-2
בצע	advantage	SB WL		PEAC REWD			+2
בצע	break ranks	VB IN MV	RELO	MILI			-1
בקע	split<be>	VB MV WO	RELO	DEST			-1
בקק	devastate	VB WO		DEST			-3
בקש	require	VB IN PS		LEGL KEEP			+1
בקש	seek	VB GU		SEEK			+1
בקש	seek	VI GU		SEEK			+1
ברא	create	VB CP		PROC			+2
ברית	covenant	SB CO ET GU IN		LEGL COMC ASMB ETHG			+2
ברכה	blessing	SB BN WL		PEAC FOOD			+3
ברכה	pool	SB BN MD WL	CTPT	DWEL PEAC			+2
ברק	gleaming	SB EL CP	ELMT	HEAT			-2
בשל	boil	VB BN IN CP		CULT HEAT FOOD			-1
בשל	ripen	VB CP IN	COND PROC	AGRI			+2
גאון	exaltation	SB EM ST		EXAL PRID			+2
גאל	defile	VB ET IN		CULT ETHB			-2
גאל	desecrate	VB ET IN		CULT ETHB			-3
גאל	desecrated	AJ ET IN		CULT ETHB			-3

Hebrew English	p.Spch Metacategories	Context-Dependent Categories						Context-Dependent Evaluation
נבה proud	VB EM ET PS ST			EXAL	PRID	ETHB	KNOW	-2
גבור warrior	SB HU IF IN ST WO		HUMN	MILI	DEST	STRO		-2
גדול great	AJ QL ST	QNTY		EXAL				+2
גדל do great thngs	VB EM QL ST	QNTY		EXAL	PRID			-3
גדל great	VI QL ST	QNTY		EXAL				+2
גדל magnify above	VB EM QL ST	QNTY		EXAL	PRID			+2
גדל raise {a child}	VB IN				FAML			+2
נהה cure<mkDepart>	VB WL					HEAL		+3
גוב locust E	SB AN IN WO	INSC			DEST		WILD	-3
גויה dead body	SB HU IF WO		HUMN	DEAT				-3
גוע perish	VB WO			DEAT	DEST			-3
גזז sheared off	VB WO				DEST			-3
גזל stolen	SB AN ET IN	ANMD		CRIM	ANHS	ETHB		-3
גזלה plunder	SB IN ST WO			MILI	DEST	ECON	WLTH	-3
גיל rejoice	VI CO EM			COMS	JOY			+2
גלה exile	SB HU IF IN MV WO	RELO	HUMN	MILI	PUNI	SEND		-3
גלה exile	SB IN MV WO	RELO		MILI	PUNI	SEND		-3
גלה exile	VB IN MV WO	RELO		MILI	PUNI	SEND		-3
גלה revealed	VB GU					UNCV		-2
גלה uncover,liftUp	VB EM GU MV ST	RELO		SHAM	SEND	UNCV	DBAS	-2
גמל recompense	SB WO			PUNI	DEST			-3
גמל recompense	VB WO			PUNI	DEST			-3
גנב stealing	SB ET IN			CRIM		ETHB		-3
גנן defend	VB IN WO			MILI	DEST			+3
גער rebuke	VB CO WO			PUNI	COMS	DEST		-2
גער rebuke	VB CO WO			PUNI	COMS			-2
גרר drag	VB GU MV	RELO				ASMB		-1
גשם rain	SB BN EL IN WL	ELMT		AGRI	PEAC	FOOD		+3
דבר speak	VB CO PS			COMS	RJCT			-2
דבר speak	VB CO			COMS				+1
דבר word	SB CO ET			COMC	ETHG			+2
דבר word	SB CO			COMC				+1
דהר rush	VB IN MV	RELO		MILI				-1
דוי sick	AJ CP WO	COND			DEST	ILL		-3
דויד David	PN HU IF IN ST		HUMN	GOVT		STRO		+2
דחק crowd	VB IN MV	RELO		MILI				-2

Hebrew	English	p.Spch Metacategories	Context-Dependent Categories					Context-Dependent Evaluation
דִי	need	SB CP IN ST	COND	POVT		ECON		-2
דִין	judge	VB IN PS		LEGL	REAS			-2
דכא	crush	VB WO			DEST			-3
דם	blood	SB CP EL	COND COSM					-2
דם	bloodshed	SB ET IN WO		CRIM	DEAT	ETHB	DEST	-3
דמה	destroy	VB CP WO	COND		DEST			-3
דמם	destroy	VB CP WO	COND		DEST			-3
דמעה	tears	SB CO EM			COMS	SORR		-2
דעת	knowledge	SB PS			KNOW			+2
דקר	pierce	VB WO		DEAT	DEST			-3
דרש	seek	VI GU		SEEK				+1
דשא	sprout	VB CP IN	PROC	AGRI				+2
היה	belong to	VB PS			KEEP			+2
היה	to be	VB BN EL	ELMT	FOOD				NS
היה	to be	VB CO			COMC			NS
היה	to be	VB CO			COMS			NS
היה	to be	VB IN	GOVT					NS
היה	to be	VB OT	NSCR					NS
הלך	come	VB MV	RELO					+1
הלך	come	VI MV	RELO					0
הלך	come on!	VI CO			COMS			+1
הלך	flow	VB CP MV	RELO	PROC				+2
הלך	go	VB MV	RELO					-1
הלך	go away	VB MV	RELO					0
הלך	go,walk	VB ET MV	RELO			ETHG		+2
הלך	go,walk	VB MV	RELO					0
הלך	go,walk	VI MV	RELO					+1
הלך	walk	VB ET MV PS	RELO			ETHG	KEEP	+2
הלך	walk	VB MV	RELO					0
הלל	act as aMadman	VB IN PS		MILI	NLRT			-3
הלל	praise	VB CO EM IN		CULT	JOY	COMS		+2
הפך	turn over	VB BN				FOOD		+1
הרג	kill	VB WO		DEAT	DEST			-3
הרס	tear down	VB WO			DEST			-3
הרס	torn down<are>	VB WO			DEST			-2
זבח	sacrifice	VB ET IN		ANHS	CULT	ETHB		-2

Hebrew	English	p.Spch Metacategories	Context-Dependent Categories	Context-Dependent Evaluation
זבח	sacrificer	SB HU IF IN	HUMN CULT	+2
זבח	sacrifice	VB IN	ANHS CULT	+2
זבח	sacrifice	SB AN IN	ANMD ANHS CULT	+2
זד	insolent	SB ET HU IF PS	HUMN RJCT ETHB	-2
זור	press out	VB WL	HEAL	+3
זור	stranger<be a>	VB CP IF PS	COND RJCT	-2
זכה	clean yourself	VI CP ET	COND ETHG	+2
זכר	remember	VB PS	KNOW ALRT	+1
זכר	remember	VI PS	KEEP KNOW ALRT	+1
זמה	wicked plan	SB ET PS	ETHB KNOW	-2
זנה	prostitute	SB ET HU IF BN IN	HUMN SEX TRAD ETHB	-2
זנה	prostitution	VB ET BN IN	SEX TRAD ETHB	-2
זנה	prostitution	SB ET BN IN	SEX TRAD ETHB	-2
זנות	prostitution	SB ET BN IN	SEX TRAD ETHB	-2
זנח	reject	VB ET PS	RJCT ETHB	-2
זעם	indignation	SB EM WO	PUNI ANGR	-3
זעם	indignant	VB EM WO	PUNI ANGR	-3
זעק	cry out	VB CO EM	COMS SORR	-2
זק	fetter	SB BN IN MD WO	TOOL MILI PUNI WEAR	-3
זקק	refine	VB CP IN	PROC TRAD HEAT	+2
זר	strange thing	SB IF PS	RJCT	-2
זרה	spread	VB MV WO	RELO SEND DEST	-2
זרח	rise	VB MV	RELO	+1
זרע	scatter	VB CO MV	COMS SEND	+1
זרע	sow	VB IN	AGRI	+2
זרק	sprinkled<are>	VB CP WO	COND DEST	-2
חבורה	stripe	SB WO	DEST ILL	-3
חבר	companion	SB GU HU IF	HUMN ASMB	+2
חבר	unite,join	VB ET GU	ETHB ASMB	-2
חבש	bandage	VB WL	HEAL	+3
חבש	binderOfWounds	SB HU IF WL	HUMN HEAL	+3
חג	celebrate	VI BN EM IN QL	TIME CULT JOY FOOD	+2
חגג	mkPilgrimage	VB IN MV QL	RELO TIME CULT	+2
חגר	gird	VI BN IN	CULT WEAR	+1
חגר	girded	VB BN CP IN	COND CULT WEAR	+1
חדל	cease	VI MV QL	NEG STAY	0

Hebrew	English	p.Spch Metacategories	Context-Dependent	Categories	Context-Dependent Evaluation
חול	anguish	VB EM		FEAR SORR	-2
חוס	pity	VI EM		LOVE	+2
חזה	see	VB CO GU IN		PROP COMR SENS	+1
חזון	vision	SB CO IN PS		PROP COMV KNOW	+1
חזק	arrogant<be>	VB CP EM ET PS ST	COND	EXAL PRID RJCT ETHB	-2
חזק	grab	VI IN MV		MILI SEND	-1
חזק	grasp	VB GU MV	RELO	SEEK SEND	-1
חזק	seize	VB MV WO	RELO	SEND DEST ILL	-3
חזק	strengthen	VB ST		STRO	+2
חזק	strengthen	VI ST		STRO	+2
חטא	punishment	SB IN WO		LEGL DEST PUNI	-3
חטא	sin	VB ET		ETHB	-2
חטא	sin	SB ET		ETHB	-2
חטא	sinful	AJ CP ET	COND	ETHB	-2
חיה	he make usLive	VB WL		LIFE	+3
חיה	life	SB WL		LIFE	+3
חיה	live	VB WL		LIFE	+3
חיל	strength	SB CP ST	COND	STRO	+2
חכה	lie in waitFor	VB ET IN MV	STAY	CRIM ETHB	-3
חלה	entreat	VI CO GU		SEEK COMS	+1
חלה	severe	VB QL WO	QNTY	DEST	-3
חלה	weak<be>	VB CP PS ST	COND	NLRT WEAK	-1
חלחלה	anguish	SB EM		FEAR SORR	-2
חלי	sickness	SB CP WO	COND	DEST ILL	-3
חלל	profane	VB ET IN		CULT ETHB	-3
חלל	slain ones	SB HU IF WO		HUMN DEAT	-3
חלם	dream	VB CO IN PS		PROP COMR KNOW	+1
חלף	pass on/away	VB MV WO	RELO	DEST	-2
חלץ	withdraw	VB MV PS	RELO	RJCT	-1
חלק	divide	VB IN MV WO	RELO	ECON DEST	-2
חלק	divide	VB CP MV WL	RELO	PROC PEAC	+2
חמד	desire	VB EM		DESR	+2
חמה	wrath	SB WO		PUNI DEST	-3
חמל	have pity	VB EM		LOVE	+2
חמל	spare,havePity	VB EM WL		PEAC LOVE	+2
חמם	become hot	VB CP		HEAT	0

Hebrew	English	p.Spch Metacategories	Context-Dependent Categories				Context-Dependent Evaluation	
חמס	violence	SB ET WO				DEST	ETHB	-3
חמץ	leavened	VB BN CP	COND				FOOD	+2
חן	charming one	SB ET HU IF BN		HUMN	SEX		ETHB	-2
חן	favor	SB EM					LOVE	+2
חנה	descend	VB MV	RELO					0
חנון	gracious	AJ EM					LOVE	+3
חנן	show favor	VB EM					LOVE	+2
חנן	supplication	SB CO GU			SEEK	COMC		+1
חנק	strangle	VB WO			DEAT	DEST		-3
חסד	faithfulness	SB CP ET PS	COND			KEEP	ETHG	+2
חסה	refuge seeker	SB BN GU HU MV	RELO	HUMN	SEEK	FLEE	DWEL	+1
חפץ	delight	SB EM				JOY	DESR	+2
חפץ	delight	VB EM				JOY	DESR	+2
חפר	ashamed\<be>	VB EM ST			DBAS	SHAM		-2
חצב	hew	VB WO				DEST	ILL	-3
חרב	destroy	VB CP WO	COND			DEST		-3
חרד	terror causer	SB EM HU IF WO		HUMN	FEAR	DEST		-3
חרה	angry\<burn>	VB EM WO			PUNI	ANGR		-3
חרון	decision	SB IN PS			LEGL		REAS	-3
חרם	curse	SB CO ET WO			PUNI	COMC	ETHB	-3
חרם	destruction	SB CP WO	COND			DEST		-3
חרפה	reproach	SB CO EM ST			COMC	SHAM	DBAS	-2
חשׂף	strip bark frm	VB IN WO			AGRI	DEST		-3
חשׁב	esteemed\<be>	VB EM ST			EXAL	PRID		+2
חשׁב	one who plans	SB HU IF PS		HUMN		REAS	RJCT	-2
חשׁב	plan	VB ET PS				REAS	ETHB	-2
חשׁב	plan	VB PS				REAS		-2
חשׁב	regard	VB PS				REAS		+1
חשׁב	thinkers	SB HU IF PS		HUMN		REAS		+1
חשׁך	darkness	SB CP EL EM	ELMT	COND	FEAR			-3
חשׁך	darkness	SB CP EL	ELMT	COND				-3
חתת	in awe\<be>	VB EM ET PS			FEAR	KEEP	ETHG	+2
טהר	purifier	SB CP HU IN	PROC	HUMN	TRAD			+2
טהר	purify	VB CP ET IN	PROC		CULT		ETHG	+2
טוב	good	AJ ET					ETHG	+2
טוב	go well	AJ ET WL			PEAC		ETHG	+2

Hebrew	English	p.Spch Metacategories	Context-Dependent Categories						Context-Dependent Evaluation
טוב	pleasant	AJ EM WL			PEAC		DESR		+3
טחן	grind	VB IN WO			AGRI	DEST			-2
טמא	defile	VB ET IN			CULT		ETHB		-2
טמן	hide	VI MV		RELO		FLEE			-1
טפף	mince steps	VB ET BN MV		RELO	SEX		ETHB		-2
טרח	burden	SB CP ST		COND			WEAK		-1
טרי	raw wound	AJ WO			DEST	ILL			-3
טרף	food	VI BN FN IN VG	FDND	VEGT	ANHS	HUNT	FOOD	AGRI	+2
טרף	tear	VB WO			DEST	ILL			-3
יאל	determined<be>	VB PS			KEEP	REAS			+2
יבש	dry up	VB CP EL WO		ELMT	PROC	DEST			-3
יגע	weary	VB CP ST		COND			WEAK		-1
יד	cast lot	VB IN		MSTR	ECON				-2
יד	from your hand	SB HU IN MV WO	CULT	HUPT	SEND	ILL	RELO		-3
ידד	cast lot	VB IN WO		MSTR	ECON	MILI	PUNI		-2
ידע	know	VI PS				KNOW			+2
ידע	know	VB PS				KNOW			+2
ידע	make known	VB CO				COMS			+1
יטב	better than	VB EM ST			EXAL	PRID			+2
יטב	good	VI ET					ETHG		+2
יכח	decide	VB IN PS			LEGL		REAS		+1
יכח	reason	VI CO PS			COMS	REAS	COMR		+1
יכח	reprove	VI CO WO			PUNI	COMS			-2
יכל	able<be>	VB CP ST		COND			STRO		+1
יכל	endure	VB GU MV ST		STAY		ESTB	STRO		+2
ילד	bear<child>	VB IN				FAML			+2
ילל	wail,lament	VB CO EM			COMS	SORR			-2
ילל	wail,lament	VI CO EM			COMS	SORR			-2
יסד	found,establsh	VB GU				ESTB			+3
יסף	add to	VB CP QL		QNTY DO		MSMT			+1
יסף	do again	VI CP		DO					0
יסר	chastise	VB WO			PUNI				-2
יסר	train	VB CO PS			KNOW	COMS			+2
יצא	going forth	SB MV		RELO					0
יצא	go forth	VI MV		RELO					0
יצא	go forth	VB MV		RELO					+2

Hebrew	English	p.Spch Metacategories	Context-Dependent Categories	Context-Dependent Evaluation
יצא	go forth	VB CO MV	RELO · COMS	+1
יצר	form	VB CP	PROC	+3
יקר	dwindle	VB CP	COND PROC	-2
ירא	fear	VI EM	FEAR	-2
ירא	fe ar	SB EM ET PS	FEAR KEEP ETHG	+2
ירא	fear	VB EM ET PS	FEAR KEEP ETHG	+2
ירא	fearer	SB EM ET HU IF PS	HUMN FEAR KEEP ETHG	+2
ירא	revere,fear	VB EM ET PS	FEAR KEEP ETHG	+2
ירד	bring down	VB IN MV	RELO SEND HUNT	-1
ירד	bring down	VB MV	RELO SEND	-2
ירד	pour down	VB BN EL IN MV WL	RELO ELMT SEND AGRI FOOD PEAC	0
ירד	tread	VI IN MV WO	RELO MILI DEST	-2
ירה	teach	VB CO PS	REAS COMS	+2
ירה	water	VB BN EL	ELMT FOOD	+2
ישב	dwell	VB BN WL	DWEL PEAC	+2
ישב	dwell	VB BN	DWEL	+2
ישב	remain	VB BN GU MV	STAY ESTB DWEL	+1
ישב	sit	VB MV	STAY	0
ישב	situated	VB LO QL	LAND MSMT	+1
ישן	smolder	VB PS CP	HEAT NLRT	-1
ישע	save,deliver	VB IN WL	MILI PEAC	+3
יתר	leave	VB MV	STAY	+1
יתר	leave over	VB MV	STAY	+1
יתר	remain	VB BN MV	STAY DWEL	+1
כבד	honor	SB EM ST	EXAL PRID	+2
כבד	honor	VB EM PS ST	KEEP EXAL PRID	+2
כבד	honor	SB EM PS ST	KEEP EXAL PRID	+2
כבד	multiply	VI QL	QNTY MSMT	+1
כבד	weighed down	VB CP ST	COND WEAK	-2
כבה	quench	VB WL	HEAL	+3
כבס	laundryman	SB HU IN	HUMN TRAD	+2
כהה	alleviation	SB CP WL	COND HEAL	+3
כול	endure	VB GU MV ST	STAY ESTB STRO	+1
כון	appointed	VB CP GU	COND ESTB	+1
כון	established<be	VB CP GU	COND ESTB	+2
כון	set up	VB GU MV	STAY ESTB	+1

Hebrew	English	p.Spch Metacategories	Context-Dependent Categories					Context-Dependent Evaluation
כון	sure\<be>	VB CP GU	COND		ESTB			0
כזב	lie,deceit	SB CO ET			COMC	ETHB		-2
כח	strength	SB CP ST	COND				STRO	+2
כחד	conceal	SB MV	RELO		FLEE			-1
כחד	hidden\<be>	VB CP MV	COND		FLEE			-1
כחש	lie,deceit	SB CO ET			COMC	ETHB		-2
כחש	lie,deceive	VB CO ET			COMS	ETHB		-2
כי	scar	SB WO			DEST	ILL		-3
כלה	destroy	VB CP WO	COND		DEST			-3
כלה	destruction	SB CP WO	COND		DEST			-3
כלה	finished\<be>	VB CP QL WO	COND		DEST	MSMT		-2
כלכל	endure	VB GU MV ST	STAY		ESTB		STRO	+1
כנען	trader	SB HU IF IN		HUMN	TRAD	ECON		+1
כסה	cover	VB MV	RELO		FLEE			-1
כפיר	lion	SB AN IN WO	ANMW		DEST		WILD	-3
כרת	cut down	VB WO			DEST			-3
כרת	cut off	VB IN WO		AGRI	DEST			-3
כרת	cut off	VB WO			DEST	DEAT		-3
כרת	cut off	VB WO			DEST			-3
כרת	cut off	VI WO			DEST			-3
כשל	causeToStumble	VB ET MV WO	RELO		DEST	ETHB		-2
כשל	stumble	VB MV PS ST WO	RELO	NLRT	DEST		WEAK	-2
כשף	seduction	SB CO ET BN		SEX	COMC	ETHB		-2
כתב	write	VB CO			COMS			+1
כתת	beat	VI CP IN	PROC	MILI	AGRI			-2
כתת	beat	VB CP IN	PROC	MILI	AGRI			+2
ל	you have	PA OT	NSCR					+1
לא	\<negative>	PT QL	NEG					-2
לאה	weary\<be>	VB CP ST	COND				WEAK	-1
לבב	heart{undrstdg	SB PS			REAS			+2
לבט	thrust down\<be	VB WO			DEST			-2
לבן	strip	VB IN WO		AGRI	DEST			-3
לבן	white\<be>	VB CP EM ET IN ST	COND	CULT	PRID	ETHG	EXAL	+2
לבש	clothe	VB BN					WEAR	+1
לבש	clothe	VB BN IN		PROP			WEAR	+1
להב	flame/flash	SB IN CP		MILI		HEAT		-2

Hebrew	English	p.Spch Metacategories	Context-Dependent Categories						Context-Dependent Evaluation
להט	set ablaze	VB WO CP			HEAT	DEST			-3
לון	lodge	VB BN MV	STAY				DWEL		+2
לוש	knead	VB BN					FOOD		+2
לחם	fight	VB IN WO			MILI	DEST			-2
לין	spend theNight	VI EM IN QL		TIME	CULT	SORR			-2
לכד	capture	VB CP IN WO	COND		MILI	DEST			-3
למד	learn	VB PS				KNOW			+1
למד	learn	VI PS				KNOW			+1
לעג	mocking	SB CO EM ST			COMS	SHAM	COMC	DBAS	-2
לקח	accept	VB IN PS			CULT	KEEP			+1
לקח	take	VB ET IN MV	RELO		SEND	CRIM	ETHB		-3
לקח	take	VB MV	RELO		SEND				0
לקח	take away	VB PS				NLRT			-2
מאס	spurn,reject	VB PS				RJCT			-2
מבוקה	devastation	SB CP WO	COND			DEST			-3
מגפה	plague	SB WO				DEST	ILL		-3
מדבר	wilderness	SB LO	LAND						-3
מהומה	panic	SB EM WO				DEST	FEAR		-3
מהל	diluted	VB CP EM ST	COND		DBAS	SHAM	WEAK		-2
מהפכה	overthrow	VB IN WO			MILI	DEST			-3
מהר	hurry	VB QL	QNTY			MSMT			-1
מוג	melt	VB WO CP			HEAT	DEST			-2
מוט	bar of yoke	SB IN MD WO	TOOL		MILI	PUNI			-2
מוסר	chastise	VB WO			PUNI				-2
מור	change	VB CP	PROC	COND					0
מורה	rain	SB BN EL IN WL	ELMT		AGRI	PEAC	FOOD		+2
מוש	depart	VB MV	RELO						0
מזמרה	pruning knife	SB BN IN MD	TOOL		AGRI		FOOD		+2
מזרק	bowl	SB BN ET IN MD	TOOL		CULT	ETHG	FOOD		+2
מחסה	refuge	SB BN LO MV WL	PEAC	LAND	LIFE	FLEE	DWEL		+2
מים	water	SB BN EL	ELMT				FOOD		+2
מישור	uprightness	SB ET					ETHG		+2
מכה	injury	SB WO				DEST	ILL		-3
מכה	strike	VB WO				DEST	ILL		-3
מכה	wound	SB WO				DEST	ILL		-3
מכר	sell	VB IN		MSTR	ECON				-2

Hebrew	English	p.Spch	Metacategories	Context-Dependent Categories	Context-Dependent Evaluation
מכר	seller	SB	HU IF IN ST	MSTR HUMN ECON WLTH	-2
מלא	fill,full	VB	CP QL	QNTY COND MSMT	0
מלא	filled<are>	VB	CP QL	QNTY COND MSMT	-1
מלא	filled with<be	VB	CP QL	QNTY COND MSMT	0
מלא	full	VB	CP QL	QNTY COND MSMT	0
מלאך	angel	SB	DV ST	ANGL SPIR STRO	+3
מלאך	messenger	SB	CO HU IF	HUMN COMV	+1
מלחמה	battle	SB	IN WO	MILI DEST	-3
מלט	escape	VB	MV	RELO FLEE	+2
מלט	escape	VB	MV WL	RELO REWD FLEE	+2
מלך	appoint a king	VB	GU IN	GOVT ESTB	+1
מלך	king	SB	DV IN	GOD GOVT	+1
מלך	king	SB	IN	GOVT	+1
מנהג	moan	VB	CO EM	COMS SORR	-2
מנחה	grain offering	SB	BN IN VG	VEGT AGRI CULT FOOD	+2
מנע	withheld<are>	VB	CP WO	COND DEST	-2
מספד	wailing	VI	CO EM	COMS SORR	-2
מעוז	refuge	SB	BN LO MV WL	PEAC LAND LIFE FLEE DWEL	+2
מעוז	refuge	SB	BN LO MV WL	LAND LIFE FLEE DWEL	+2
מעט	little, few	SB	QL	QNTY MSMT	-2
מעמסה	heavy	SB	QL ST WO	QNTY DEST MSMT WEAK	-2
מערה	nakedness	SB	CP EM ST	COND DBAS SHAM	-2
מעשׂר	tithe	SB	BN IN VG	VEGP AGRI CULT FOOD	+2
מעשׂר	tithe	VI	BN IN VG	VEGP AGRI CULT FOOD	+2
מפרא	healing	SB	CP WL	COND HEAL	+3
מצא	find	VB	GU MV	RELO UNCV	+1
מצוה	commandment	SB	CO ET IN	LEGL COMC ETHG	+2
מצור	siege	SB	IN WO	MILI DEST	-3
מקור	spring	SB	BN ET LO	LAND ETHG FOOD	+2
מקק	rot	VB	WO	DEST ILL	-3
מרה	rebel	VB	ET PS	RJCT ETHB	-2
מרר	bitter<be>	VB	EM	SORR	-2
משׁך	stretch out	VB	MV	RELO SEND	0
משׁל	rule	VB	IN	GOVT	+1
משׁל	saying,byword	SB	CO EM	COMC SHAM	-2
משׁפט	judgment	SB	IN PS WO	LEGL REAS PUNI	-3

Hebrew	English	p.Spch Metacategories	Context-Dependent Categories				Context-Dependent Evaluation
משפט	justice	VI ET IN		LEGL		ETHG	+2
משפט	justice	SB ET IN		LEGL		ETHG	+2
מתם	soundness	SB CP WL	COND			HEAL	+3
מתפפת	beating	VB CO EM			COMS	SORR	-2
נאם	declaration	SB CO			COMS		+1
נאף	adultery	VB ET BN		SEX		ETHB	-2
נאף	adultery	SB ET BN		SEX		ETHB	-2
נאף	adulterer	SB ET HU IF BN		HUMN SEX		ETHB	-2
נאץ	reject	VB ET PS			RJCT	ETHB	-2
נבא	prophesy	VB CO IN		PROP	COMS		+1
נבט	look	VB GU				SENS	+1
נביא	prophet	SB HU IF IN		HUMN PROP			+1
נבל	make a fool	VB EM ST		DBAS	SHAM		-2
נבל	wither&fall	VB CP WO	PROC	DEST			-2
נגד	display	VB GU				UNCV	-1
נגד	in front	PP OT	NSCR				NS
נגד	tell	VB CO			COMS		+1
נגע	reach	VB MV	RELO				0
נגע	touch	VB MV		SEND			-2
נגף	plague	SB WO		DEST		ILL	-3
נגף	strike	VB WO		DEST		ILL	-3
נגש	oppressed<be>	VB WO		PUNI DEST			-3
נגש	oppressor	SB HU IF WO		HUMN PUNI DEST			-3
נגש	draw near	VI IN MV	RELO	MILI			0
נגש	offer,brngNear	VB IN MV	RELO	CULT SEND			+2
נגש	present	VB IN MV	RELO	SEND		CULT	0
נגש	present	VB IN MV	RELO	CULT SEND			+2
נדד	chased away	VB MV	RELO		FLEE		-2
נדד	draw back	VB MV	RELO		FLEE		-2
נדד	stray	VB ET MV PS	RELO		RJCT	ETHB	-2
נדה	impurity	SB CP ET	COND			ETHB	-2
נדח	thrust	VB IN MV	RELO	MILI SEND			-2
נדר	vow	SB CO IN		CULT	COMS		+1
נדר	vow	VB CO ET IN		CULT	COMS	ETHG	+2
נהר	flow	VB CP MV	RELO	PROC			+1
נוד	grieve	VB CO EM			COMS	SORR	-2

Hebrew	English	p.Spch Metacategories	Context-Dependent Categories				Context-Dependent Evaluation
נוח	leave alone	VI MV	STAY				+1
נוס	flee	VB MV	RELO		FLEE		-3
נוע	shaken<be>	VB WO			DEST		-2
נורא	feared	VB EM ET PS		FEAR	KEEP	ETHG	+2
נורא	terrifying	AJ EM		FEAR			-3
נחל	inheritance	SB IF IN LO ST		LAND	ECON	WLTH	+3
נחם	change mind	VB CP PS	PROC	COND	REAS		+2
נחם	comforter	SB EM HU WL		HUMN	LOVE	HEAL	+3
נחם	compassion	VB EM			LOVE		+3
נחם	compassionnate	AJ EM			LOVE		+3
נחם	relieved of<be	VB CP WO	COND		PUNI	DEST	-3
נחת	bringdown	VI MV	RELO	SEND			0
נטה	stretch out	VB MV	RELO	SEND			0
נטה	turn aside	VB ET MV WO	RELO		DEST	ETHB	-2
נטף	drip	VB BN CP	PROC			FOOD	+2
נטר	maintain	VB GU QL WO	QNTY	PUNI	ESTB	DEST	-3
ניצוץ	spark	SB WO CP		HEAT	DEST		-3
נכה	strike	VI WO			DEST	ILL	-3
נכה	strike	VB WO			DEST	ILL	-3
נכה	wound	SB WO			DEST	ILL	-3
נם	sleep	VB PS			NLRT		-2
נמס	melt	VB EM WO CP		FEAR	HEAT	DEST	-1
נמש	abandon	VB MV WO	STAY		DEST		-2
נער	lad	SB HU IF IN ST		HUMN	FAML	WEAK	-2
נערת	tinder	SB IN VG WO CP	VEGT	AGRI	HEAT	DEST	-2
נפוש	scattered<are>	VB IN MV	RELO	MILI	FLEE	SEND	-2
נפח	sniffInContmpt	VB EM IN		CULT		HATE	-2
נפל	fall	VB MV WO	RELO		DEST		-3
נפל	fall	VB WO		DEAT	DEST		-3
נפל	fall	VB MV PS	RELO		NLRT		-3
נפל	fall	VB MV	RELO				0
נצב	established<is	VB CP GU	COND		ESTB		+1
נצב	stand	VB MV	STAY				-2
נצל	deliverer	SB HU IN WL		HUMN	MILI	PEAC	+3
נצר	besieged	SB CP IN WO	COND	MILI	DEST		-3
נצר	guard	VI IN		MILI			+2

Hebrew	English	p.Spch	Metacategories	Context-Dependent Categories				Context-Dependent Evaluation
נקה	avenge	VB WO			PUNI	DEST		-3
נקה	deserted	VB MV WO	STAY			DEST		-3
נקה	lv unpunished	VB IN WL			LEGL	REWD		+3
נקיון	innocence	SB CP ET IN		COND	LEGL		ETHG	+2
נקם	take revenge	VB EM WO			PUNI	DEST	HATE	-3
נשא	bear<endure>	VB PS				KEEP		-1
נשא	bear<fruit>	VB CP IN	PROC		AGRI			+2
נשא	carry away	VB MV WO	RELO			PUNI	SEND	-1
נשא	lift up	VB IN MV WO	RELO		MILI	SEND	DEST	-3
נשא	protest	VB CO PS			COMS	RJCT		-1
נשא	raise,lift up	VI EM MV ST	RELO		EXAL	PRID		+1
נשא	raise,lift up	VB MV WO	RELO		SEND		DEST	-2
נשא	raise,lift up	VB MV	RELO		SEND			-2
נשא	regard	VB PS				REAS		+1
נשא	regard	VB CO PS			COMR	REAS		+1
נשא	showPartiality	VB ET IN			LEGL		ETHB	-2
נשא	upheaved	VB CP EL WO	ELMT		PROC	DEST		-2
נתך	pour forth	VB MV	RELO		SEND			-2
נתן	allow	VI GU				ESTB		+1
נתן	allow	VB GU				ESTB		+1
נתן	give	VB MV			SEND			+2
נתן	give	VB BN EL IN MV	ELMT	AGRI	SEND		FOOD	+2
נתן	make	VB CP	DO					0
נתן	produce	VB CP IN	PROC	DO	AGRI			+1
נתן	set	VB EL MV WO CP	COSM	HEAT	SEND	DEST		+2
נתן	trade	VB IN		MSTR	ECON			-2
נתן	utter	VB CO				COMS		+2
נתץ	broken down	VB WO				DEST		-2
נתק	tear apart	VB WO				DEST		-2
סבא	drunkard	SB BN HU PS		HUMN		NLRT	FOOD	-2
סבב	surrounding	PP LO QL		LAND		MSMT		+1
סבב	surround	VB QL				MSMT		0
סבך	entangled	VB WO				DEST	ILL	-2
סגר	close	VI IN MV	RELO		CULT			-1
סדם	Sodom	PN ET HU IF LO WO	CITY	HUMN	HUGP	DEST	ETHB	-3
סוג	displacer	SB ET HU IN		HUMN	CRIM		ETHB	-3

Hebrew English	p.Spch Metacategories	Context-Dependent Categories				Context-Dependent Evaluation
סור gone\<be>	VB QL	QNTY		MSMT		-1
סור remove	VI MV	RELO	SEND			+2
סור remove	VB MV	RELO	SEND			-1
סור take away	VB MV	RELO	SEND			-2
סור turn aside	VB MV WO	RELO		DEST		-2
סור turn aside	VB ET MV PS	RELO		RJCT	ETHB	-2
סיג dross	SB EL EM IN ST	MTRL	DBAS	SHAM	TRAD	-2
ספד wail	VI CO EM		COMS	SORR		-2
ספד wail	VB CO EM		COMS	SORR		-2
ספד wailing	SB CO EM		COMS	SORR		-2
ספר tell	VI CO		COMS			+1
סרה rebellion	SB ET PS			RJCT	ETHB	-2
סרר rebel	SB ET HU IF PS		HUMN	RJCT	ETHB	-2
סרר stubborn\<be>	VB ET PS			RJCT	ETHB	-2
עבד serve	VB ET PS			KEEP	ETHG	+2
עבד slave	SB HU IF IN		HUMN	MSTR		-1
עבט change course	VB MV	RELO				0
עבר pass away	VB MV WO	RELO		DEST		-2
עבר pass over	VB MV WO	RELO		DEST		-3
עבר pass over	VB MV	RELO				-3
עבר pass through	VB MV WO	RELO	DEST			-3
עבר remove	VB MV WO	RELO	SEND	DEST		-2
עבר transgress	VB ET				ETHB	-2
עברה anger	SB EM WO		PUNI	ANGR		-3
עבש shrivel	VB CP IN WO		AGRI	DEST	PROC	-3
עגה bread-cake	SB BN IN VG WO	VEGP	AGRI	DEST	FOOD	+2
עד witness	SB CO DV IN WO	GOD		LEGL PUNI	COMV	-1
עולה injustice	SB ET IN		LEGL		ETHB	+2
עון iniquity	SB ET				ETHB	-2
עוף fly	VB MV	RELO		FLEE		+1
עור arouse	VB PS			ALRT		-2
עור rouse	VI MV PS	RELO		ALRT		+1
עור rouse oneself	VB PS			ALRT		+1
עור rouse oneself	VI PS			ALRT		+1
עור rouse oneself	VI IN PS		MILI	ALRT		+1
עור stir up\<fire>	VB CP		HEAT			0

Hebrew	English	p.Spch Metacategories	Context-Dependent Categories					Context-Dependent Evaluation
עורון	blindness	SB CP WO	COND			DEST	ILL	-3
עוש	lend aid	VI IN			MILI			+2
עזב	abandon	VB MV WO	STAY			DEST		-2
עזב	leave	VB MV WL	STAY			PEAC		+1
עזרה	helper	SB GU HU IF IN		HUMN	MILI		ASMB	+2
עיד	testify	VB CO IN			LEGL	COMS		-1
עכס	shake bangles	VB CO ET BN			SEX	COMS	ETHB	-1
על	against	PP WO			PUNI			-3
על	against	PP IN WO				DEST	MILI	-3
על	against	PP OT	NSCR					-3
על	go up	VB IN MV	RELO		CULT			+1
עלה	carry away	VB IN MV WO	RELO		HUNT	PUNI	SEND	-3
עלה	climb	VB MV	RELO					0
עלה	go up	VI IN MV	RELO			MILI		0
עלה	go up	VI MV	RELO					+1
עלה	go up	VB MV	RELO					-1
עלה	go up	VI IN MV	RELO		MILI			0
עלה	go up	VB IN MV	RELO		CULT			+1
עלה	go up	VB MV WO	RELO			DEST		-3
עלה	invade	VB IN MV	RELO		MILI			-3
עלם	conceal	VB MV	RELO			FLEE		-1
עלם	hide	VB MV	RELO			FLEE		-1
עמד	endure	VB GU MV ST	STAY			ESTB	STRO	+1
עמד	stand	VB IN MV	STAY		LEGL			-2
עמד	stand	VB MV	STAY					0
עמד	stop	VI MV	STAY					0
עמס	lift a load	VB MV ST	RELO			SEND	WEAK	+1
עמק	go deep	VB CP QL	QNTY	COND				-1
עמרה	Gomorrah	PN ET HU IF LO WO	CITY	HUMN	HUGP	DEST	ETHB	-3
ענה	answer	VB CO				COMS		+1
ענה	oppress	VB WO			PUNI	DEST		-3
ענה	testify	VB CO IN			LEGL	COMS		-1
ענן	cloud	SB EL EM	ELMT		FEAR			-2
ענן	soothsayer	SB DV ET HU IF IN		HUMN	CULT	DVOT	ETHB	-3
עסס	tread down	VB MV WO			RELO	DEST		-3
עצום	mighty	AJ ST					STRO	+1

Hebrew	English	p.Spch Metacategories	Context-Dependent Categories	Context-Dependent Evaluation
עצמה	might	SB CP ST	COND	STRO +1
עצרה	assembly	SB GU HU IF IN	HUGP HUMN CULT	ASMB +1
עצרה	assembly	VI GU HU IF IN	HUGP HUMN CULT	ASMB +1
עקב	tracked	VB CP ET IN WO	COND CRIM DEAT	ETHB -3
ערב	ple asing\<be>	VB EM WL	PEAC	DESR +3
ערבה	dese rt-plain	SB LO	LAND	-1
ערג	long f or	VB EM		DESR -1
ערה	naked\<be>	VB CP EM ST	COND DBAS SHAM	-2
ערך	arrange	VB GU MV	RELO	ASMB 0
ערפל	darkness,gloom	SB CP EL EM	ELMT COND FEAR	-3
ערץ	causeToTremble	VB EM	FEAR	-3
עשה	do	VB CP	DO	0
עשה	do	VB CP ET	DO	ETHB -2
עשה	do,act	VB CP	DO	0
עשה	make	VB CP	DO	-1
עשה	make	VB CP ET	DO	ETHB -2
עשה	perform	VB CP	DO	0
עשה	prepare	VB CP GU	DO	ESTB 0
עשה	produce	VB CP IN	PROC DO AGRI	+1
עשה	work	SB CP DV ET IN	DO CULT DVOT TRAD	ETHB -2
עש	moth	SB AN IN WO	INSC DEST	WILD -3
עשק	oppressed\<be>	VB WO	PUNI DEST	-3
עשק	oppressor	SB ET HU IF ST WO	POVT HUMN PUNI DEST	ETHB -3
פארור	glow	SB EM	FEAR	-2
פגר	corpse	SB HU IF WO	HUMN DEAT	-3
פדה	ransom	VB MV	FLEE	+2
פדה	ransomed\<be>	VB CP MV	COND FLEE	+2
פוץ	dispersed\<be>	VB MV	RELO FLEE	-2
פוש	spring about	VB EM MV	RELO JOY	+2
פזר	scatter	VB IN MV WO	RELO MILI PUNI SEND	-2
פח	bird trap	SB BN IN MD	TOOL HUNT FOOD	-2
פחד	dread	SB EM	FEAR	-3
פיק	tottering	VB EM PS ST WO	FEAR NLRT DEST	WEAK -2
פלא	wondrously act	VB WL	PEAC	+3
פליטה	escape	SB MV	RELO FLEE	+2
פליטה	escaper	SB HU IF MV WL	RELO HUMN FLEE	LIFE +2

Hebrew English	p.Spch Metacategories	Context-Dependent Categories		Context-Dependent Evaluation
פנה prepare	VB GU		ESTB	0
פנה regard	VB PS		KEEP REAS	+1
פנה return	VB MV	STAY		+1
פצע bruise	SB WO		DEST ILL	-3
פקד punish	VB IN WO		LEGL DEST PUNI	-3
פקח guard	VB IN		MILI	+2
פרא wild donkey	SB AN IN	ANMW		WILD -1
פרד go apart	VB ET BN IN MV	RELO	SEX TRAD ETHB	-2
פרי fruit	SB BN IN VG WL	VEGT	AGRI PEAC FOOD	+2
פרץ do violence	VB WO		DEST	-3
פרץ increase	VB IN QL	QNTY	MSMT FAML	+1
פרק plunder	SB IN ST WO		MILI DEST ECON WLTH	-3
פרש spread out	VB CO IN		CULT COMS	+1
פרש spread out	VB MV	RELO	SEND	0
פרש dung	SB CP EM ST	COND	DBAS SHAM	-2
פשט raid	VB ET IN WO		CRIM DEST ETHB	-3
פשט strip off	VB WO		DEST	-2
פשע rebel,revolt	VB ET PS		RJCT ETHB	-2
פתה foolish	AJ CP EM PS ST	COND	DBAS SHAM NLRT	-2
פתח open	VB GU MV	RELO	SEND UNCV	+2
צדק righteous	SB ET HU IF	HUMN	ETHG	+2
צדק righteousness	SB ET		ETHG	+2
צו worthlessness	SB ET		ETHB	-3
צוה command	VB CO IN		LEGL COMS	+1
צוה command	VB CO ET IN		LEGL COMS ETHG	+2
צום fast	SB BN EM IN QL		TIME CULT SORR FOOD	-2
צום fast	VI BN EM IN QL		TIME CULT SORR FOOD	-2
צחנה stench	SB CP WO	COND	DEST	-2
צמר wool	SB AN BN ET IN MD	ANMP CLTH ANHS ETHG WEAR		+2
צפה keep watch	VI GU IN		MILI SENS	+1
צרף refiner,smeltr	SB HU IN CP	HUMN TRAD HEAT		+2
צרף smelt	VB CP IN	PROC	HEAT TRAD	+1
צדקה righteousness	SB ET		ETHG	+2
צרר wrap	VB CP		PROC	-1
קבע rob	VB ET IN WO		CRIM DEST ETHB	-3
קבץ assemble	VI GU MV	RELO	ASMB	+1

Hebrew	English	p.Spch Metacategories	Context-Dependent Categories				Context-Dependent Evaluation
קבץ	gather	VI GU IN MV	RELO	CULT	SEND	ASMB	+1
קבץ	gather	VB IN MV WO	RELO	MILI	DEST	SEND	-3
קבץ	gather	VB GU IN MV	RELO	MILI	SEND	ASMB	-2
קבץ	gatherer	SB GU HU MV	RELO HUMN		SEND	ASMB	+1
קבץ	gather	VB EM		FEAR			-2
קבר	grave	SB LO WO	LAND	DEAT	DEST		-3
קדר	dark<be>	VB CP EL	ELMT	PROC			-3
קדר	grow dark	VB CP EL	ELMT	PROC	COND		-3
קדרנית	mourners<as>	SB CO EM HU IF		HUMN	SORR	COMS	-2
קדש	consecrate	VI CO GU IN		CULT	COMS	ASMB	+2
קדש	holy	AJ CP ET IN	COND	CULT		ETHG	+2
קדש	sanctify	VI ET IN		MILI	CULT	ETHG	+2
קול	sound	SB CO			COMV		+1
קום	arise	VB MV	RELO				0
קום	endure	VB GU MV ST	STAY		ESTB	STRO	+1
קום	raise	VB MV	RELO	SEND			+2
קטר	offer incense	VB ET IN CP		CULT	HEAT	ETHB	-2
קיץ	awake	VI PS			ALRT		+1
קלון	dishonor	SB EM ST		DBAS	SHAM		-2
קלל	of no account	VB EM ST		DBAS	SHAM		-2
קנא	zealous	VB EM				DESR	-2
קנה	purchase	VB IN		ECON	MSTR		-1
קצה	end,limit	SB QL	QNTY		MSMT		0
קצין	ruler	SB HU IF IN		HUMN GOVT			+1
קציר	harvest	SB BN IN VG	VEGT	AGRI		FOOD	+2
קצפה	stump	SB IN VG	VEGT	AGRI			-3
קצר	harvest	VB BN IN		AGRI		FOOD	+2
קרא	call	VB CO			COMS		+1
קרא	call	VI CO			COMS		+1
קרא	call upon	VB CO GU		SEEK	COMS		+1
קרא	proclaim,call	VI CO			COMS		+1
קרא	proclaim,call	VB CO			COMS		+1
קרב	approach	VB MV	RELO				0
קרב	bring near	VI IN MV	RELO	CULT	SEND		+1
קרב	go near	VB MV	RELO				0
קרב	in the midst	PP BN	DWEL				+3

Hebrew English	p.Spch Metacategories	Context-Dependent Categories	Context-Dependent Evaluation
קרב near	AJ QL TIME	MSMT	NS
קרחה bald spot	SB EM HU ST WO	HUPT DBAS SHAM ILL DEST	-2
קרע rend	VI BN EM IN	CULT SORR WEAR	-2
קש stubble,chaff	SB IN VG WO VEGT	AGRI DEST	-2
קשב give heed	VI CO PS	COMR KEEP	+2
קשב pay attention	VB CO PS	COMR KEEP	+1
קשת bow	SB IN MD TOOL	MILI	+1
ראה appear	VB IN MV RELO	CULT	0
ראה appear	VB MV RELO		0
ראה distinguish	VB PS	REAS	+2
ראה see	VB GU	SENS	+1
ראה see	VB CO GU IN	PROP COMR SENS	+1
ראה show	VB GU	UNCV	-1
ראה spectacle	SB CP EM ST COND	DBAS SHAM	-2
ראם rise	VB MV RELO		+1
ראש chief{ofmtns}	SB IN ST	CULT EXAL	+2
רב great	AJ QL ST QNTY	EXAL	0
רב many	AJ QL QNTY	MSMT	+1
רב multiplied	AJ QL QNTY	MSMT	+1
רבב increase	VB QL QNTY	MSMT	+1
רבב multiply	VB QL QNTY	MSMT	+1
רבה multiply	VB QL QNTY	MSMT	+1
רגז shake	VB CP EL WO ELMT	PROC DEST	-3
רגז tremble	VI EM	FEAR	-2
רדף pursue	VI GU MV PS RELO	SEEK REAS	+2
רדף pursue	VB MV WO RELO	FLEE PUNI	-2
רדף pursue	VB MV RELO	FLEE	-2
רהב assail,pester	VB WO	PUNI DEST	-3
רוח Spirit	SB DV GOD	SPIR	+3
רום bring up	VB IN MV RELO	SEND FAML	0
רוע raise a shout	VI CO IN	MILI COMS	-2
רוע shout an alarm	VI CO IN	MILI COMS	-2
רוץ run	VB IN MV RELO	MILI	0
רחץ wash off	VI ET IN	CULT ETHG	+2
רחק remove far	VB IF MV RELO	SEND FLEE	-2
רטש dash in pieces	VB IN WO	FAML DEST DEAT	-3

Hebrew	English	p.Spch Metacategories	Context-Dependent Categories						Context-Dependent Evaluation
ריב	contender	SB CO HU IN PS		HUMN	LEGL	COMV	RJCT		-2
ריב	contend	VB CO IN			LEGL	COMS			-2
ריב	contend	VI CO ET IN			LEGL	COMS	ETHG		+2
ריב	contend for	VI CO ET IN			LEGL	COMS	ETHG		+2
ריב	lawsuit	SB IN PS			LEGL	REAS			-1
ריב	lawsuit	SB IN			LEGL				-2
ריק	pour out	VB MV	RELO		SEND				+2
רכך	softened	VB CP WL	COND				HEAL		+3
רמיה	lie,deceit	SB CO ET				COMC	ETHB		-2
רמס	trample	VI IN MV	RELO		MILI				-3
רמס	trample	VB IN MV	RELO		CULT				-1
רע	evil	AJ CP ET	COND				ETHB		-2
רעה	calamity	SB WO			PUNI	DEST			-3
רעה	tend	VB IN WL			ANHS	PEAC			+2
רעה	wickedness	VI ET					ETHB		-2
רעה	wickedness	SB ET					ETHB		-2
רעל	shaken<be>	VB WO				DEST			-2
רעל	staggering	SB MV PS	RELO			NLRT			-2
רעע	evil	SB ET					ETHB		-2
רעע	evildoer	SB ET HU IF		HUMN			ETHB		-2
רעש	quake	VB CP EL WO	ELMT		PROC	DEST			-2
רפא	heal	VB WL					HEAL		+3
רצה	accept	VB IN PS			CULT	KEEP			+1
רצה	take delight	VB EM					DESR		+3
רצון	favor	SB EM				LOVE			+2
רצח	murder	VB ET IN WO			CRIM	DEAT	ETHB	DEST	-3
רצח	murder	SB ET IN WO			CRIM	DEAT	ETHB	DEST	-3
רצח	murderer	SB ET HU IF IN WO	DEST	HUMN	CRIM	DEAT	ETHB		-3
רצץ	crushed<be>	VB WO				DEST			-3
רקב	rottenness	SB CP IN WO	COND		AGRI	DEST	ILL		-3
רקד	jolt	VB IN MV	RELO		MILI				-2
רקד	leap	VB IN MV	RELO		MILI				-1
רשע	wicked	AJ ET					ETHB		-2
רשע	wickedness	SB ET					ETHB		-2
רשע	wicked	SB ET HU IF		HUMN			ETHB		-2
רשש	beaten down<be	VB WO				DEST	ILL		-3

Hebrew English		p.Spch Metacategories	Context-Dependent Categories					Context-Dependent Evaluation
רשת	net	SB IN MD	TOOL		HUNT			-1
רתק	bind	VB WO			PUNI			-1
שבע	full	VB CP EM QL	QNTY	COND	HATE	MSMT		0
שבע	satisfied,full	VB BN CP QL WL	COND		PEAC	MSMT	FOOD	+2
שבע	satisfied,full	VB CP QL WL	COND		PEAC	MSMT		+2
שׂגב	exalted<be>	VB CP EM ST	COND		EXAL	PRID		+2
שום	appoint	VB CP GU	COND			ESTB		+1
שום	make	VB CP	DO					0
שום	make	VB GU				ESTB		0
שום	prepare	VB GU				ESTB		-1
שום	put,set	VB MV PS			SEND	REAS	KEEP	0
שמח	rejoice	VB CO EM			COMS	JOY		+2
שמח	rejoice	VI CO EM			COMS	JOY		+2
שנא	hate	VB EM					HATE	-3
שפח	afflict	VB WO			PUNI	DEST	ILL	-3
שפק	strikeBargains	VB CO GU IN		ECON	COMS		ASMB	-1
שקר	tossSedctvGlnc	VB CO ET BN			SEX	COMS	ETHB	-2
שרט	injured<be>	VB WO				DEST	ILL	-3
שרף	burn	VB CP			HEAT			-3
שאב	draw {water}	VB BN MV	RELO				FOOD	+2
שאג	roar	VB CO				COMS		-2
שאל	inquire	VB CO GU			SEEK	COMS		+1
שאר	leave	VB MV	STAY					+1
שאר	remain	VB GU MV	STAY			ESTB		+1
שבבים	pieces	SB WO				DEST	ILL	-3
שבי	captivity	SB CP IN MV WO	COND	RELO	MILI	PUNI		-2
שבע	swear	VI CO				COMS		+1
שבע	swearer	SB CO ET HU IF IN		HUMN	CULT	COMV	ETHB	-2
שבר	break	VB WL				PEAC		+2
שבר	breaking	SB WO				DEST	ILL	-3
שבר	crushed<be>	VB WO				DEST		-3
שבת	cease	VB MV QL	NEG	STAY				0
שגל	rape<be>	VB ET BN WO			SEX	DEST	ETHB	-3
שגעון	madness	SB PS				NLRT		-2
שד	destruction	SB CP WO	COND			DEST		-3
שדד	laid waste	VB WO				DEST		-3

Hebrew	English	p.Spch Metacategories	Context-Dependent Categories				Context-Dependent Evaluation
שדד	ruined<is>	VB CP WO	COND	DEST			-3
שוב	give back	VB MV　　WL	RELO	SEND	REWD		+1
שוב	repent	VB ET GU PS		SEEK	KEEP	ETHG	+2
שוב	repent<make>	VB ET GU PS		SEEK	KEEP	ETHG	+2
שוב	restore	VB GU WL		PEAC	ESTB		+1
שוב	return	VB MV	RELO				0
שוב	return	VB ET GU MV	RELO		SEEK	ETHG	+2
שוב	return	VB GU PS		SEEK		KEEP	+2
שוב	return	VI ET GU MV	RELO		SEEK	ETHG	+2
שוב	return	VB MV WO	RELO	PUNI			-2
שוב	turn	VB EM ET MV	RELO		LOVE	ETHG	+2
שוב	turn	VB GU PS		SEEK	REAS		0
שוב	turn<against>	VB MV WO	RELO	PUNI	DEST		-3
שוב	turn unto	VI ET GU PS		SEEK	KNOW	ETHG	+2
שוב	turn unto	VI ET GU PS		SEEK		ETHG KNOW	+2
שוק	overflow	VB QL WL	QNTY	PEAC			+2
שוק	overflow	VB QL WO	QNTY		DEST		-2
שחד	bribe	SB ET IN　　MD ST	MONY	ECON WLTH ETHB LEGL			-2
שחח	humbled<is>	VB EM ST		DBAS SHAM			-2
שחח	humbled<be>	VB EM ST		DBAS SHAM			-2
שחט	depravity	SB ET			ETHB		-2
שחל	lion	SB AN IN WO	ANMW		DEST	WILD	-3
שחר	look early	VB GU PS QL	TIME SEEK		ALRT		+1
שחת	act corruptly	VB ET			ETHB		-2
שחת	corrupt	VB ET WO		DEST	ETHB		-2
שחת	ruin	VB WO		DEST			-3
שטף	flood	SB EL WO	ELMT	DEST			-3
שיב	repay	VB EM WO		PUNI	DEST	HATE	-2
שית	appoint	VB CP GU	COND	ESTB			+1
שכח	forget	VB PS		NLRT	IGNO		-2
שכל	bereave	VB IN WO		AGRI PUNI		DEST	-3
שכם	start early	VB MV PS QL	RELO TIME		ALRT		-1
שכן	dwell	VB BN			DWEL		+2
שכן	settle/lieDown	VB MV PS	STAY	NLRT			-1
שכר	drunk<be>	VB BN PS		NLRT	FOOD		-2
שלח	divorce	SB ET IN MV WO	RELO FAML DEST ETHB				-2

Hebrew English	p.Spch Metacategories	Context-Dependent Categories	Context-Dependent Evaluation
שלח put in<send>	VI MV	RELO SEND	-2
שלח send	VB IN MV WL	RELO AGRI SEND PEAC	+2
שלח send	VB MV	RELO SEND	0
שלך cast away	VB MV	RELO SEND	-3
שלך throw	VB MV WO	RELO SEND DEST	-1
שלך throw	VB MV	RELO SEND	-1
שלם at peace	AJ CP WL	COND PEAC	+3
שלם pay	VB IN PS	CULT KEEP	+1
שלם peace	SB CP WL	COND PEAC	+3
שלם repay	VB EM WO	PUNI DEST HATE	-3
שלם repay	VB WL	REWD	+2
שלמן reward	SB ET IN MD ST WL	MONY REWD WLTH ETHB ECON	-2
שם name	SB HU IN	HUPT FAML	+1
שמד destroy	VB CP WO	COND DEST	-3
שמה waste	SB WO	DEST	-3
שמם desolate<are>	VB CP WO	COND DEST	-3
שממה desolation	SB CP WO	COND DEST	-3
שמע hear	VB CO GU PS	COMR SENS KEEP	+1
שמע hear	VI CO GU	COMR SENS	+1
שמע hear	VB CO GU	COMR SENS	+1
שמע hearer	SB CO GU HU	HUMN COMR SENS	+1
שמע listen	VB CO GU PS	SEEK COMR KEEP	+1
שמע report	SB CO	COMV	+2
שמר heed	VB PS	KEEP	+2
שמר heed	VB ET PS	KEEP ETHG	+2
שמר keep	VB ET PS	KEEP ETHG	+2
שמר preserve	VI CO ET PS	KNOW COMS ETHG	+2
שמר take heed	VI PS	KEEP	+1
שמר watch,beCarefl	VI PS	KEEP	+1
שנה change	VB CP PS	PROC COND REAS	0
שני scarlet	SB BN CP EM MD ST	CLTH COND DBAS SHAM WEAR	-2
שסס plunder	VB IN ST WO	MILI DEST ECON WLTH	-3
שפט do justice for	VI IN	LEGL	+2
שפט judge	VB IN PS WO	LEGL REAS PUNI	-2
שפט judge	VB IN PS WO	LEGL REAS DEST PUNI	-3
שפט judge	VB IN PS	LEGL REAS	+1

Hebrew	English	p.Spch Metacategories	Context-Dependent Categories						Context-Dependent Evaluation
שפך	pour out	VB MV	RELO		SEND				0
שפך	pour out	VB MV	RELO						+1
שפך	shed	VB ET IN WO		CRIM	DEAT	DEST	ETHB	DEST	-3
שפל	humbled\<is\>	VB EM ST			DBAS	SHAM			-2
שפל	humbled\<be\>	VB EM ST			DBAS	SHAM			-2
שק	sackcloth	SB BN EM MD ST	CLTH	POVT	DBAS	SORR	WEAR		-2
שקה	water	VB BN EL	ELMT				FOOD		+2
שקוץ	detested thing	SB EM					HATE		-2
שקק	run	VB IN MV	RELO		MILI				0
שקק	rush toAnd fro	VB IN MV	RELO		MILI				-2
שקר	lie,falsehood	SB CO ET			COMC	ETHB			-2
שריד	survivor	SB HU IF MV WL		HUMN		FLEE	LIFE		+2
ששון	rejoicing	SB CO EM			COMS	JOY			+2
שתה	bow down,wrshp	VB DV ET IN			CULT	DVOT	ETHB		-2
שתה	drink	VB BN PS				NLRT	FOOD		+1
שתח	worship	VB DV ET IN			CULT	DVOT	ETHB		-2
שתח	worship	VB CO IN			CULT	COMS			+2
תאנה	fig tree	SB BN IN ST VG	VEGT		AGRI	WEAK	FOOD		+2
תועבה	abomination	SB ET IN			CULT		ETHB		-3
תורה	law,teaching	VI CO ET IN			LEGL	COMC	ETHG		+2
תורה	law,teaching	SB CO ET IN			LEGL	COMC	ETHG		+2
תחת	instead of	PP QL	NEG						-2
תלאה	weariness	SB CP EM ST	COND			HATE	WEAK		-1
תלע	clad inScarlet	VB BN CP	COND				WEAR		0
תמהון	bewilderment	SB PS				NLRT			-2
תנה	rcvPrsttutPay	VB ET IN BN ST		TRAD	SEX	WLTH	ETHB	ECON	-2
תעה	lead astray	VB ET MV PS	RELO		NLRT	SEND	ETHB		-2
תעה	led astray\<be\>	VB ET MV	RELO			SEND	ETHB		-2
תפלה	prayer	SB CO GU IN			CULT	SEEK	COMS		+2
תפש	grasp	VB GU MV	RELO		SEEK	SEND			-1
תקע	blow	VI CO IN			MILI	COMS			-2
תקע	clap	VB CO EM			COMS	SORR			-2
תרומה	offering	SB BN IN VG	VEGP		CULT		FOOD		+2

BIBLIOGRAPHY

Ahlström, G.W., *Joel and the Temple Cult of Jerusalem* (Leiden: Brill, 1971).

Allen, L.C., *The Books of Joel, Obadiah, Jonah, and Micah* (Grand Rapids: Eerdmans, 1976).

Baab, O.J., *The Theology of the Old Testament* (New York: Abingdon Press, 1949).

Baird, J.A., *Audience Criticism and the Historical Jesus* (Philadelphia: Westminster Press, 1969).

—'Content Analysis and the Computer: A Case-Study in the Application of the Scientific Method to Biblical Research', *JBL* 95 (1976), pp. 255-76.

Balentine, S.E., *The Hidden God: The Hiding of the Face of God in the Old Testament* (Oxford: Oxford University Press, 1983).

Barr, J., *The Semantics of Biblical Language* (London: Oxford University Press, 1961).

Barstad, H.M., *The Religious Polemics of Amos* (Leiden: Brill, 1984).

Berelson, B. and P.F. Lazarsfeld, *The Analysis of Communication Content* (preliminary draft; University of Chicago and Columbia University, 1948).

Bewer, J.A., *The Book of the Twelve Prophets* (2 vols.; New York: Harper & Brothers, 1949).

Braddac, J.J. (ed.), *Message Effects in Communication Science* (Newbury Park: Sage Publications, 1989).

Brueggemann, W., 'Presence of God, Cultic', *IDBSup*, p. 682.

Burrows, M., *An Outline of Biblical Theology* (Philadelphia: Westminster Press, 1946).

Buss, M.J., *The Prophetic Word of Hosea: A Morphological Study* (BZAW, III; Berlin: Töpelmann, 1969).

—*Encounter with the Text: Form and History in the Hebrew Bible* (Philadelphia: Fortress Press; Missoula: Scholars Press, 1979).

Carroll, R.P., 'Eschatological Delay in the Prophetic Tradition (Isa 11.25; 59; Hab 2.3; Joel 2.1; Hag 1)', *ZAW* 94 (1982), pp. 47-58.

Cerny, L., *The Day of Yahweh and Some Relevant Problems* (V Praze: Nakladem Filosoficke Fakulty University Karlovy, 1948).

Cherbonnier, E., 'The Logic of Biblical Anthropomorphism', *HTR* 55 (1962), pp. 187-209.

Childs, B.S., *Biblical Theology of the Old and New Testaments* (Minneapolis: Fortress Press, 1992).

Clines, D., 'The Image of God in Man', *TynBul* 19 (1968), pp. 53-104.

Craigie, P.C., *Twelve Prophets* (Philadelphia: Westminster Press, 1984).

Cross, F.M., *Canaanite Myth and Hebrew Epic* (Cambridge, MA: Harvard University Press, 1973).

Driver, S.R., *The Books of Joel and Amos* (Cambridge: Cambridge University Press, 1907).

Eichrodt, W., *Theology of the Old Testament* (2 vols.; Philadelphia: Westminster Press, 1961, 1967).

Eslinger, L.M., *Into the Hands of the Living God* (Sheffield: Almond Press, 1989).

Everson, A. J., 'Days of Yahweh', *JBL* 93 (1974), pp. 329-37.

Fan, D., *Predictions of Public Opinion from the Mass Media: Computer Content Analysis and Mathematical Modeling* (New York: Greenwood Press, 1988).

Fretheim, T.E., *The Suffering of God: An Old Testament Perspective* (Philadelphia: Fortress Press, 1984).

Garrett, D., 'The Structure of Joel', *JETS* 28 (1985), pp. 289-97.

Gerbner, G., O.R. Holsti, K. Krippendorff, W.J. Paisley and P.J. Stone (eds.), *The Analysis of Communication Content:: Developments in Scientific Theories and Computer Techniques* (New York: John Wiley & Sons, 1969).

Gilkey, L., 'Cosmology, Ontology, and the Travail of Biblical Language', *JR* 41.3 (1961), pp. 194-205.

Gordon, G.N., *The Languages of Communication: A Logical and Psychological Examination* (New York: Hastings House, 1969).

Gray, J., 'The Day of Yahweh in Cultic Experience and Eschatological Prospect', *SEÅ* 39 (1974), pp. 5-37.

Hall, C.S., and R. Van de Castle, *The Content Analysis of Dreams* (New York: Appleton-Century-Crofts, 1966).

Hasel, G.F., *Old Testament Theology: Basic Issues in the Current Debate* (Grand Rapids: Eerdmans, 4th edn, 1991).

Heschel, A.J., *The Prophets* (2 vols.; New York: Harper & Row, 1962).

Hoffmann, Y., 'The Day of the Lord as a Concept and a Term in the Prophetic Literature', *ZAW* 93 (1981), pp. 37-50.

Holsti, O.R., *Content Analysis for the Social Sciences and Humanities* (Reading: Addison-Wesley, 1969).

Hurowitz, V., 'Joel's Locust Plague in light of Sargon II's Hymn to Nanaya', *JBL* 112 (1993), pp. 597-603.

Jacob, E., *Theology of the Old Testament* (London: Hodder & Stoughton, 1958).

Jervell, J., *Imago Dei* (Göttingen: Vandenhoeck & Ruprecht, 1960).

Jones, D.R., *Isaiah 56-66 and Joel* (London: SCM Press, 1964).

Kapelrud, A.S., *Joel Studies* (Uppsala: Lundeqvist, 1948).

Kaufman, G., 'On the Meaning of "Act of God"', in *idem, God the Problem* (Cambridge, MA: Harvard University Press, 1972).

Krippendorff, K., *Content Analysis: An Introduction to its Methodology* (Beverly Hills: Sage Publications, 1980).

Laffal, J., *A Concept Dictionary of English* (Essex: Gallery Press, 1973).

—*A Concept Dictionary of English with Computer Programs for Content Analysis* (Essex: Gallery Press, 1990).

Loretz, O., *Regenritual und Jahwetag im Joelbuch* (Altenberge: CIS-Verlag, 1986).

Miller, J.M., 'In the "Image" and "Likeness" of God', *JBL* 91 (1972), pp. 289-304.

Miller, P.D., *Sin and Judgment in the Prophets* (Chico, CA: Scholars Press, 1982).

Moore, R. (ed.), *Stereotypes, Distortions, and Omissions in US History Textbooks: A Content Analysis Instrument for Detecting Racism and Sexism* (New York: Council on Interracial Books for Children Inc., 1977).

Morton, A., 'A Computer Challenges the Church', *Observer* (November 1963).

Mowinckel, S., *He That Cometh* (Nashville: Abingdon Press, 1965).

Nicholson, E.W., *God and His People* (Oxford: Clarendon Press, 1986).

North, R.C., O. Holsti, M. Zaninovich and D. Zinnes, *Content Analysis: A Handbook with Applications for the Study of International Crisis* (Evanston, IL: Northwestern University Press, 1963).

Ogunyemi, E.S., *A Content Analysis of Selected Documents dealing with some Relationships between Christians and Romans during the First Three Centuries* (dissertation; Emory University, 1976).

Osgood, C.E., 'The Representational Model and Relevant Research Methods', in I. Pool (ed.), *Trends in Content Analysis,* pp. 33-88.

—*Focus on Meaning* (The Hague: Mouton, 1976).

Osgood, C.E., G. Suci, and P. Tannenbaum, *The Measurement of Meaning* (Urbana: University of Illinois Press, 1967).

Osgood, C.E., W. May, and M. Miron, *Cross-Cultural Universals of Affective Meaning* (Urbana: University of Illinois Press, 1975).

Patrick, D., *The Rendering of God in the Old Testament* (Philadelphia: Fortress Press, 1981).

Pelikan, J.J., *Christianity and Classical Culture* (New Haven: Yale University Press, 1993).

Pettinari, C.J., *Task, Talk, and Text in the Operating Room: A Study in Medical Discourse* (Norwood: Ablex, 1988).

Polanyi, L., *Telling the American Story: A Structural and Cultural Analysis of Conversational Storytelling* (Cambridge, MA: MIT Press, 1989).

Pool, I., *The Prestige Press: A Comparative Study of Political Symbols* (Cambridge, MA: MIT Press, 1970).

Pool, I. (ed.), *Trends in Content Analysis* (Urbana: University of Illinois Press, 1959).

Preuss, H.D., *Theologie des Alten Testaments*, Band I (Stuttgart: Verlag W. Kohlhammer, 1991).

Prinsloo, W.S., *The Theology of the Book of Joel* (Berlin: de Gruyter, 1985).

Rad, G. von, 'The Origin of the Concept of the Day of Yahweh', *JSS* 4 (1959), pp. 97-108 (repeated in *Old Testament Theology* [Edinburgh: Oliver & Boyd, 1965], II, pp. 119-25).

—*Old Testament Theology* (New York: Harper & Row, 1965).

Scullion, J., 'God', *Anchor Bible Dictionary.*

Simkins, R., *Yahweh's Activity in History and Nature in the Book of Joel* (Lewiston, NY: Edwin Mellen Press, 1991).

Stone, P., D. Dunphy, M. Smith, and D. Ogilvie, *The General Inquirer: A Computer Approach to Content Analysis* (Cambridge, MA: MIT Press, 1966).

Stuart, D.K., *Hosea-Jonah* (Waco, TX: Word Books, 1987).

Toolin, C., 'American Civil Religion from 1789 to 1981: A Content Analysis of Presidential Inaugural Addresses', *Review of Religious Research* 25 (1983), pp. 39-48.

Weber, R.P., *Basic Content Analysis* (Beverly Hills: Sage Publications, 1985).

Westermann, C., *Elements of Old Testament Theology* (Atlanta: John Knox, 1978).

—*Genesis 1–11* (Minneapolis: Augsburg, 1984).

Wolff, H.W., *Joel and Amos* (Philadelphia: Fortress Press, 1977).

Wright, G.E., *The Old Testament and Theology* (New York: Harper & Row, 1969).

Zimmerli, W., *Old Testament Theology in Outline* (Atlanta: John Knox, 1978).

INDEX OF AUTHORS